NIETZSCHE:
Disciple of Dionysus

NIETZSCHE:
Disciple of Dionysus

Rose Pfeffer

Lewisburg
BUCKNELL UNIVERSITY PRESS

© 1972 by Associated University Presses, Inc.

Associated University Presses, Inc.
Cranbury, New Jersey 08512

Library of Congress Cataloging in Publication Data

Pfeffer, Rose, date
    Nietzsche: Disciple of Dionysus.

    Bibliography: p.
    1. Nietzsche, Friedrich Wilhelm, 1844–1900.
2. Dionysus. I. Title.
B3317.P43   193   76-178041
ISBN 0-8387-1069-7

Printed in the United States of America

To my daughters,
Doris and Barbara

CONTENTS

FOREWORD

Dr. Rose Pfeffer's interpretation of Nietzsche's work is an important contribution to the understanding of this ever-challenging philosopher. Her book takes due account of recent scholarship, but her own contribution is based on a careful reappraisal of Nietzsche's own writings. Recognizing the significance of Nietzsche's repudiation of conventional philosophic system building, she rejects the often asserted criticism that his work is incoherent. She does this by following his own lead in emphasizing the essential element which characterizes his thought from first to last, the profoundly tragic sense of life in terms of which Dr. Pfeffer identifies Nietzsche as Disciple of Dionysus.

This tragic world view, never to be confused with pessimism despite the acknowledged influence of Schopenhauer on Nietzsche's philosophic education, is carefully analyzed in Dr. Pfeffer's introductory chapters and then serves as the guideline through the intricacies of the Nietzschean doctrine of Eternal Recurrence. It is one of Mrs. Pfeffer's notable achievements that, without oversimplification or any attempt to popularize this central theme, she traces the development of Nietzsche's doctrine avoiding the obfuscations which sometimes make the summaries of commentators more difficult than the original.

In attaining a high degree of clarification, Dr. Pfeffer places herself in the tradition represented by Walter Kaufmann in his authoritative studies of Nietzsche. Though Mrs. Pfeffer does not hesitate to differ with Kaufmann and with other interpreters, European and American, she builds on the foundations established by many scholars. Among German authors she is most clearly indebted to Jaspers, Loewith, and Heidegger. But she differentiates her agreement with the latter's insistence on the organic nature of Nietzsche's thought by avoiding Heidegger's subjectivism and holding firmly to Nietzsche's own exposition.

Her constant reliance on the primary texts makes Mrs. Pfeffer's work valuable for students, but also gives assurance that her book can be read as an introduction to Nietzsche's thought. Best of all, it should serve the purpose of any introduction and guide the reader to the original texts. Those who follow Dr. Pfeffer's lead in this way will approach a writer whose significance, as she demonstrates, is enhanced by contemporary developments in Western culture which he himself anticipated.

It is primarily as a philosopher of culture that Nietzsche remains preeminent. Dr. Pfeffer rightly stresses his vision of "tragic culture" as the culmination of his essentially aesthetic outlook, just as she previously emphasized the cultural intent of the doctrine of eternal recurrence. In doing this she walks in the footsteps of one of the earliest serious contributors to the study of Nietzsche in America, William M. Salter, whose *Nietzsche, the Thinker* is too often neglected. Another contemporary scholar, Arthur Danto, recognizes Salter's importance, though Danto's recent book on Nietzsche contrasts markedly with Dr. Pfeffer's study.

Indeed, it is noteworthy that Nietzsche has stimulated a wide variety of legitimate interpretations. This is not only evidence of his status as a literary artist—all great poets justify numerous well-considered interpretations—but places him among the philosophical poets and poet-philosophers whom he hailed as free spirits. The names of Goethe and Schiller occur again and again in the pages that follow, and their voices, as well as those of such poet-Nietzscheans as Kafka and Camus, Sartre and Auden, echo in Dr. Pfeffer's chapters.

Among philosophers, Nietzsche stands in that great tradition extending from Plato to John Dewey which views art as a key to the understanding of human experience. In a succinct expression of this view, quoted below, Albert Hofstadter has written: "In art a certain absoluteness of existence is in fact arrived at by man." This conviction characterizes the works of Friedrich Nietzsche. It is a principal merit of Dr. Pfeffer's book that this characteristic of the Disciple of Dionysus is never a secondary or incidental consideration, but that his tragic outlook is seen to be the clue to his entire philosophy.

Columbia University   James Gutmann

PREFACE

That the long logic of a quite determinate philosophical sensibility is involved here, and not a confusion of a hundred indiscriminate paradoxes: of that, I believe, nothing has dawned even on my most benevolent readers.[1]

The above quotation is from a letter written by Nietzsche to Georg Brandes, one of the first scholars to lecture on Nietzsche. Since then, many decades have passed, many "benevolent readers" have been added, and many more books and articles about Nietzsche have been written. But Nietzsche's words, as expressed to Brandes, remain true. Not only do the not-so-benevolent readers deny the presence of unity and consistency in his thought, but this is also true of many scholars who do acknowledge his major philosophical contributions. The former see in Nietzsche's writings a disconnected collection of more or less brilliant insights that possess human pathos and dramatic qualities rather than philosophical significance; the latter, while recognizing him as a serious thinker and philosopher, nevertheless point to irreconcilable contradictions among his central concepts.

No matter how much the interpretations and evaluations

of Nietzsche's writings diverge, they often have one characteristic in common, namely, the failure to view his thought as a coherent and unified whole. Although some very recent studies have begun to acknowledge Nietzsche as a systematic philosopher, they have not stressed this point. Nor have they attempted to demonstrate the prevalent theme that runs through his thought in order to exhibit its coherent structure, its external form notwithstanding. One important exception is Martin Heidegger's brilliant analysis, which emphasizes the systematic unity and interrelation of the major concepts in Nietzsche's philosophy.* But Heidegger's penetrating interpretation is largely subjective, and can be understood only in terms of his own philosophical views, as I will try to show in Part II of this book.

It is the central aim of this study to show that Nietzsche's philosophy represents a unified world view in which the various seemingly disconnected and contradictory concepts share one common underlying principle. This unifying principle is indeed not easily discernible through Nietzsche's dramatic and aphoristic style, but it is nonetheless always present in his thought, and provides the fundamental basis for his metaphysical, ethical, and religious views.

The unification of Nietzsche's thought is here attempted in the awareness of the dangers of oversystematization and oversimplification, the danger of presenting Nietzsche with an order that is not his own. Nietzsche is a philosopher of life and existence whose ideas grow out of passionate personal experience. He cannot be understood by means of logical formulas and closed systems. His mode of thinking is dialectical, and intrinsically opposed to dogmatic finality and static completeness. Thus, if I speak of unity, it must

---

* Martin Heidegger, *Nietzsche*, 2 vols. (Pfullingen: Neske, 1961).

be understood as a unity that grows out of multiplicity, change, and complexity: a unity that remains open-ended and problematic, and achieves a balance and form that include diversity and polarity.

Many interpreters of Nietzsche have claimed that not only is his work unsystematic, but deliberately anti-systematic. They rightfully point to many passages where he attacks traditional philosophical systems as lacking intellectual integrity. But what must be understood is that it is only certain kinds of systems that he rejects, systems which "hold a thought complex to be truer when it can be inscribed in previously designed schemes or tables of categories. There are countless self-deceptions in this field; almost all great systems belong here."[2] These systems, he claims, are based on the unquestioned acceptance of *a priori* presuppositions and empty, meaningless deductions. Their perpetrators are, in his opinion, intellectually dishonest, motivated by a craving for security rather than a desire for truth. But Nietzsche nowhere denies the desirability of a systematic unity that is achieved honestly and unintentionally, one arrived at chiefly in retrospect and not in advance of investigation; a unity which he compares to a living organism that grows and develops with inner necessity and inevitability. The following quotation from *The Genealogy of Morals* stresses this point:

We philosophers have no right to be fragmentary in any respect: we may neither err piecemeal, nor piecemeal strike the truth. On the contrary, our thoughts, our values, our yeas and nays and ifs and whethers grow out of us with the inevitability with which a tree bears fruit—all together related and corresponding with one another, and presenting evidence of one will, one health, one soil, one sun.[3]

Likewise, letters written to his friends Erwin Rohde and Peter Gast have the same emphasis.

> Without my intention, but precisely on that account to my delight, all my writings are taking a quite definite direction; they all point like telegraph poles toward a goal in my studies which I shall soon have finally in view.[4]

> Very curious! I have understood my own writings for four weeks . . . . I now have the absolute conviction that everything is well done from the beginning . . . everything is one and means one.[5]

Thus, as above claimed, Nietzsche's systematic unity differs significantly from those that he attacks. Because his system, like a living organism, grows and changes, it implies the quality of incompleteness; because it evolves out of personal experience, it contains—like all existential knowledge—unresolved complexities and riddles. His philosophical system remains a constant task whose ideas grow with the "inevitability with which a tree bears fruit," all interconnected and related, and based upon one central, ever-present, consuming idea that possesses "one will, one health, one soil, one sun."

Although there are many acceptable and valuable ways of studying Nietzsche's philosophy, I believe that interpreting and organizing the various aspects of his thought by relating them to one single, immanent, central concept can contribute significantly to a clearer and deeper understanding. It can order the complexity of Nietzsche's ideas—the whole maze of aphorisms, remarks, and notes, and his many loosely constructed books—into a compelling pattern, and help remove many of the contradictions that have been attributed to him. The ideas which at first appear isolated and disconnected will, I believe, begin to fit together and become *Gestalten* of one central, basic perspective.

The basic concept that I have taken to be the unifying, organizing principle for the various aspects of Nietzsche's philosophy is the "tragic world view," the meaning of which will be explored throughout this study. My choice is, in some sense, an arbitrary one. Since, in my opinion, a systematic interconnectedness exists between Nietzsche's basic ideas, any other of these ideas—such as the will to power, the eternal recurrence, or the overman—could have served as a basis for demonstrating the coherent structure of his thought. All these central concepts form a unity and express Nietzsche's fundamental world view. But I have preferred this concept over any other with the expectation that it will additionally serve to demonstrate the importance of Nietzsche's philosophy for our own age. This fact was not recognized in the English-speaking world so early as in continental Europe. However, it becomes everywhere clearer how much of contemporary thought reveals the heritage of Nietzsche, how much his writings help to illuminate the tendencies of thought in the science, psychology, and philosophy of the last half century. Indeed, Nietzsche is closer to the temper of our age than he was to that of his own. He suffered our present predicaments and ills more than half a century in advance. Problems that are today experienced by many and are at the center of contemporary existential thought, Nietzsche also suffered, but alone and misunderstood. His writings are documents of our times more than of his own; the sickness of his soul is the sickness of this present generation.

Like us, he heard Zarathustra's message of the "death of God," and deeply experienced the sense of loss, anxiety, and despair that resulted from this death through the collapse of traditional Judaeo-Christian values. With us, he felt the absurdity of the human condition wherein nothing exists to which we can sincerely commit ourselves and dedicate our lives. Like many today, he rebelled against those who, while no longer believing in the old traditions, nevertheless are too hypocritical to acknowledge their fall, and too complacent to undertake a meaningful revaluation of values. He rebelled against a civilization that is increasingly dehumanizing man and depreciating the value of the individual.

But, like contemporary existentialist thought of which he is a precursor, Nietzsche's philosophy is not a philosophy of defeatism and negativity. His importance does not lie only in the fact that he dares to question relentlessly in order to unmask the hypocrisies and illusions of outworn value systems. His real importance is that he can come to terms with a world that is deprived of the values long thought to be its central living purpose, a world that seems absurd and senseless. He offers a vision of life that is significant for twentieth-century man precisely because it is based not upon comfortable illusions and transcendent hopes, but upon the experience of despair, suffering, and the reality of evil.

Nietzsche's world view is not comforting and does not offer easy solutions, but it presents a task that makes the highest demands upon the strength, courage, and integrity of man. In so doing, it expresses a profound trust in man and in life. Nietzsche's rebellion, like that of Camus, "cannot exist without a strange form of love." Like our contemporary artists and writers, Nietzsche speaks in anger and despair; but, like theirs, his anger is full of hope and longing. Like Beckett, Genet, and Camus, he is an atheist whose heart is filled with the sacred. Like the great painters of our age, he sees beauty in the seemingly ugly, and uncovers meaning where others see only confusion. His reverence for life speaks through his anger, his rebellion, through his shrill and tortured language. It is a reverence for life in all its forms, and a belief that—after a long night of doubt "in which all the gods are dead"—there will arise a culture capable of satisfying the true needs of man, a culture that is tragic in the Nietzschean sense.

Nietzsche's vision of this "tragic culture," which represents his hope for the future of mankind, is based on his "tragic world view," whose meaning should become progressively clear as the various parts of this study develop. The various chapters of the book are interdependent. They are structured in such a way as to develop the central concept gradually, introducing it in an expository manner in the first chapter and letting it grow in complexity and depth as the book progresses.

Part I introduces the various aspects of the tragic as viewed under the symbol of Dionysus. Its major aims are: a general explication of Nietzsche's concept of the tragic and its derivation from Greek tragedy; an analysis of Nietzsche's conception of nihilism and its essential connection with the tragic; and an examination of the meaning of truth within Nietzsche's tragic view.

Part II deals with Nietzsche's teaching of the "Eternal Recurrence" in its scientific, metaphysical, and ethical meanings. This teaching has been subject to boundless dispute among Nietzsche scholars, for it is here that they locate most of the contradictions and ambiguities which they attribute to Nietzsche's thought. Since this study denies the existence of such alleged contradictions and stresses the consistency in Nietzsche's views, the concept of eternal recurrence assumes a special significance. Using the tragic view as a basis for interpretation, I intend to show why no conflicts exist in this Nietzschean teaching.

Part III discusses Nietzsche's concept of the "Innocence of Becoming," which again is of special importance and interest for this study, since it is here that the various aspects of Nietzsche's philosophy are integrated in a conception of the universe that is essentially aesthetic. In the "Innocence of Becoming" the traditional philosophical distinctions are abolished and Nietzsche's metaphysics, ethics, and aesthetics merge within a unified world view that Nietzsche calls tragic or Dionysian.

In documenting this study, I have drawn heavily from Nietzsche's posthumously published notes, the so-called *Nachlass*, as published in the *Grossoktav-Ausgabe*. The *Nachlass* has become a subject of controversy among Nietzsche scholars. Some, among them Martin Heidegger and Karl Loewith, consider the posthumous publications indispensable for understanding Nietzsche's major philosophical concepts. Heidegger goes as far as to call everything that Nietzsche himself published the foreground for his essential philosophy, as contained in the opus posthumum. For Loewith, the *Nachlass* is Nietzsche's unfinished magnum opus. The heterogeneous mass of fragments and notes represents to him the unmistakable structure of a major philosophical work. Others, among them Karl Schlechta, reject the *Nachlass* and deny its importance. Schlechta, in his book *Der Fall Nietzsche,* calls the *Nachlass* a "Machwerk" of its editors, a falsification of Nietzsche's thought, as compiled primarily by his sister, Elizabeth Foerster-Nietzsche, the self-appointed executrix of her brother's literary estate. Furthermore, Schlechta claims, the *Nachlass* contains nothing significantly new; it gives no new insights that are not already contained in Nietzsche's own publications.

Unfortunately, the question whether Schlechta is justified in his severe criticism of the *Nachlass* can hardly be solved

by the Nietzsche student and reader who has no direct access
to the original material in the Nietzsche archives. The fact
remains that the material, as contained in the *Grossoktav-
Ausgabe*, is of extraordinary richness and wealth, and is by
no means unoriginal or unimportant. In addition, it must be
recognized that any ordering of this vast, scattered, fragmentary material, no matter by whom, must inevitably be
problematic and subjective. But however sceptical we may
remain, the elimination of the *Nachlass* in a publication of
Nietzsche's works would deprive the reader and Nietzsche
scholar of an unquestionably rich reference source. The fact
is that the great majority of Nietzsche scholars have used
the material contained in the *Nachlass* extensively as a means
to elucidate and develop the major concepts of Nietzsche's
philosophy.

The translations of the Nietzsche quotations cited in this
study are my own, although I have benefited greatly from
the excellent translations of Marianne Cowan, Francis
Golffing, and Walter Kaufmann. My own translations are
used for two reasons: many of the quotations from the
Nachlass have not yet been translated and those from Nietzsche's own publications have not been translated by one
person. Thus, in order to be able to use all the material from
the *Nachlass* and, further, in order to attain a stylistic unity,
I have used my own translations.

ACKNOWLEDGMENTS

I would like to express my deep appreciation to Lynne Belaief, Justus Buchler, Arthur Danto, Gail Belaief-Foote, Albert Hofstadter, and Richard Kuhns for their help and advice, and for many exciting hours of conversation on Nietzsche. I am especially grateful to James Gutmann, whose never-failing encouragement and intellectual example have been of major importance in my philosophical development.

Further, I am greatly indebted to Dowling College for a leave of absence that enabled me to complete this book, and to Lynne Belaief for reading the manuscript and making many valuable suggestions for its improvement. My thanks are also due to Virginia Sperl for helping with the Index and proofreading.

I wish to acknowledge my appreciation to the following publishers for their permission to reprint passages from their publications:

Alfred A. Knopf, Inc., New York, for excerpts from *The Myth of Sisyphus and Other Essays* by Albert Camus, translated by Justin O'Brien, © 1961, and from *No Exit* (bound with) *The Flies* by Jean Paul Sartre, translated by Stuart Gilbert, © 1947.

The Personalist, for excerpts from "The Problem of Truth

in Nietzsche's Philosophy" by Rose Pfeffer (Winter 1967).

The Review of Metaphysics, for excerpts from "Eternal Recurrence in Nietzsche's Philosophy" by Rose Pfeffer (December 1965).

Yale University Press, New Haven, for excerpts from *The Courage to Be* by Paul Tillich, © 1952.

NIETZSCHE:
Disciple of Dionysus

PART I

Dionysus

Herewith I . . . stand on the soil out of which my will, my ability grows—I the last disciple of the philosopher Dionysus.

Saying yes to life even in its strangest and hardest problems, the will to life, rejoicing over its own inexhaustibility even in the sacrifice of its highest types—that is what I call Dionysian.
                    Nietzsche, Twilight of the Idols *(VIII, 173)*.

THE TRAGIC WORLD VIEW

There is only one hope and one guarantee for the future of that which is human; it lies in this, that the tragic disposition shall not perish.[1]

—Nietzsche

I

Nietzsche's philosophy is based on the conviction that the greatness of man and the development of culture can be realized only within a spirit that he calls tragic. I contend that it is the central aim and purpose of his philosophical writings to clarify the meaning of the "tragic disposition" and to help initiate the coming of a tragic age, which he sees as the only hope for the future of mankind. In order to understand Nietzsche's thought—his metaphysical, epistemological, and ethical views, it is necessary to clarify and comprehend his central thesis, its roots and characteristics. The following pages will analyze the meaning of Nietzsche's concept of the tragic, tracing it through the various aspects of his philosophy in order to show that, on the basis of this central concept, his thought assumes a consistent and meaningful pattern in which all his ideas become variations of one underlying, fundamental theme.

Nietzsche presents his tragic world view under the symbol of Dionysus and calls himself the "disciple of Dionysus."[2] Dionysus is the god of chaos and destruction, but he is also the god of fertility and productivity. He is the old nature god of Greek mythology, connected with vegetation and fruitfulness, who comes to life in the spring and brings all men together in joyful intoxication and abandonment. Dionysian worship had its origin in Thrace and Phrygia, where it was associated with orgiastic rites and drunken frenzy. But when introduced into Greece and received by the priesthood of Apollo, the old Thracian god was united with the native gods of Olympus and the non-Hellenic orgiastic elements of Dionysian excess merged with the measured sublimity and form-giving force of Apollo. Because of these dual characteristics, Dionysus was at once the patron deity of Greek tragic festivals at the height of Greek culture while, simultaneously, he also represented the most primitive and archaic spirit of Greek history. Thus he became the symbol of the most sublime achievements of Greek culture while, at the same time, he represented the realm of primitive instincts and urges.

In choosing Dionysus as the patron of his own tragic world view, Nietzsche stresses the god's dual character, which contains the elements of destruction and chaos as well as those of productivity, power, and form, "the psychology of the orgiastic as an overflowing feeling of life and strength where even pain has the effect of a stimulus."[3] Without the full recognition that Dionysus, to Nietzsche, is a synthesis of the negative and the positive, a fusion of opposing forces, the most essential aspects of his conception of the tragic, which underlie his whole philosophical thought, cannot be understood.

However, in his early works this synthesis is not yet accomplished, and the two opposing principles are presented separately under the banner of two deities. Thus, in *The Birth of Tragedy*, Apollo, the god of light, beauty, and harmony is in opposition to Dionysian drunkenness and chaos. Yet, even here in this early work, written in 1871–72, Nietzsche did not glorify one principle in favor of the other, but stressed the fact that they mutually require one another. Even here he claimed that only the interaction between the Apollonian and Dionysian, each opposing and yet enhancing the other, can achieve the artistic ideal and the highest culture, which he designated as tragic: "The difficult relation between the Apollonian and Dionysian in tragedy may be symbolized by a fraternal union of the two deities; Dionysus speaks the language of Apollo, but Apollo finally speaks the language of Dionysus; thereby the highest goal of tragedy is reached."[4] In his later philosophy, the two deities are no longer separated and the concept of Dionysus represents a synthesis in which negation and affirmation, suffering and joy, are reconciled in terms of a Dionysian faith that includes both gods and achieves true tragic greatness. However, this synthesis must never be understood as a static and finalistic one, in which the contest between the opposing forces is abolished and the dialectical elements are destroyed. Dionysus remains, as Nietzsche calls him, "the great ambivalent one," forever changing, forever struggling, and yet forever giving structure and form.

The fraternal union of Apollo and Dionysus that forms the basis of Nietzsche's tragic view is, according to him, symbolized in art, and specifically in Greek tragedy. Here a deep structural unity is accomplished and the salient features of both gods are exhibited: Apollonian clarity and visual beauty, as expressed in dialogue and image, and Dionysian intensity and depth of feeling, as contained in the music of the chorus. While Greek tragedy was an off-spring of a Dionysian cult, it reached its greatness and height when it succeeded in counterbalancing the orgiastic forces of Dionysus with the formative powers of Apollo. For Nietzsche, the highest goal of tragedy is achieved in this interpenetration of the Dionysian and Apollonian, in the harmony between two radically distinct realms of art, between the principles that govern Apollonian plastic arts and epic poetry and those that govern the Dionysian art of music. In this union, Apollonian art is no longer limited to mere surfaces but, with the aid of music, reaches a higher intensity and greater depth. At the same time, Dionysian musical excitement and intensity is released in Apollonian images, thereby gaining clarity and concreteness.

The problems of art and tragedy are not examined by Nietzsche in terms of conventional aesthetics; under the influence of Schopenhauer, the aesthetic interpretation is widened into a metaphysical one. Thus, he says in *The Birth of Tragedy*, referring to the duality of the Apollonian and Dionysian:

> After recognizing this immense antithesis, I felt a deep need to explore the nature of Greek tragedy which is the profound-est manifestation of the Hellenic genius; only now did I seem to possess the key to probe deeply into the essential problems of tragedy that were no longer derived from conventional aesthetics.[5]

Art is interpreted as a dialectical process that symbolizes the productive activity of nature. The two art-sponsoring deities become symbols of the metaphysical principles of life and being; the two interacting artistic impulses, in their continuous evolution of Apollonian and Dionysian duality and their continuous reconciliation, are likened to the very forces of nature, which contain both decay and generation, both passing away and coming into being. Both art and nature work according to the same pattern, a pattern that Nietzsche calls tragic, consisting of two opposing yet complementary activities that inevitably belong together, eternally destroying and perishing and eternally creating and giving birth.

As noted before, to understand Nietzsche's tragic concept fully, we have to look primarily to his later, mature works and also to the posthumously published notes, the *Nachlass*. To overlook the development in Nietzsche's thought, to ignore his many modifications and even rejections of earlier ideas, and to accept his early works as his final position is to misinterpret his philosophy. This is particularly the case in regard to *The Birth of Tragedy*, which has become Nietzsche's most read, most celebrated, and also his most overrated book. Some interpreters continue to regard this early work as the expression of Nietzsche's full and complete views on tragedy and art, and ignore his later revisions and his own criticism of this work. They point to passages such as these: "Tragic perception requires, in order to be endured, the refuge and remedy of art. . . . Art, that sorceress expert in healing . . . she alone can turn nausea and disgust with the horrors and absurdities of life into imaginations with which it is possible to live."[6] On the basis of these and similar pronouncements from *The Birth of Tragedy*, they interpret Nietzsche's position on art in this manner: Art is a mechanism of escape which throws a veil of illusion over the chaos and suffering of life in order to make it bearable. Expressed respectively in "vision and the orgiastic" Apol-

Ionian and Dionysian art is likened to states that we experience in dreams and in intoxication, states which transform the pain and struggle of existence into a world of beautiful images and fair illusions. Artistic activity does not aim at truth, but at an escape from it. Art is not a metaphysical activity, reproducing the dialectical processes of nature; rather, it creates a deceptive world alongside the real one in order to transcend the terrors and contradictions of life.

But Nietzsche himself, in a preface to *The Birth of Tragedy*, added in 1886 and entitled "An Attempt at Self-criticism," calls his early work (1871–72), "impossible, embarrassingly confused . . . containing every possible fault of adolescence," adding that it was a book that "obscured and spoiled Dionysian hints with formulas borrowed from Schopenhauer." He refers to the aesthetic views expressed in this book as "an aesthetic metaphysics to be rejected out of hand as so much prattle or rant."[7] Yet, it would be utterly false and misleading if we dismissed *The Birth of Tragedy* as so much "prattle or rant" and failed to recognize its deep and fascinating insights and "Dionysian hints." Again Nietzsche himself points to this in his belated preface, and says in defense of his early work: "Yet in its essential traits it already prefigured that spirit of deep distrust and defiance which Schopenhauer spent all his life fulminating against."[8]

While recognizing the novel and original contributions of this early work, we must remain aware that it does not represent Nietzsche's final views on tragedy and art. As he himself admits, *The Birth of Tragedy* was written under the influence of his "educator" Schopenhauer, and his conception of art as a mechanism of escape was "borrowed from Schopenhauer." There is no doubt that Schopenhauer's thought had a great, and even lasting, influence upon Nietzsche, but this influence never stifled or curtailed Nietzsche's own originality and development. Just as Nietzsche goes beyond Schopenhauer's philosophical ideas in the development of his own metaphysics, as shown below, he later also rejects the Schopenhauerian interpretation of the aesthetic experience, calling it a turning away from life, a false deliverance from the ever-struggling and ever-suffering will to live.

Nietzsche's later thought and interpretation of art, while already contained in "Dionysian hints" in his early work, still "stands as veiled and obscured as possible in *The Birth of Tragedy*."[9] Only in his later writings do his views on art become clear. There, art is no longer seen as a mode of escape from life, but as containing the very elements of life itself. Like life and being, it is a continuous struggle and a continuous oscillation between opposite poles. The creative act can no more abolish its dialectical elements of struggle and opposition than can nature and life produce and give birth without also destroying. The aesthetic experience enters into the depth of being, into the chaos and terrors of existence, but not to turn away toward the solace of fair images and illusions. Instead, it reaches its highest fulfillment and joy in the formative activity of art, which contains both suffering and exultation, both creation and destruction. In order to reach a comprehensive conception of Nietzsche's interpretation of art, a full analysis of his tragic view must first be attempted. I will return to the discussion of art in a later chapter.

II

Dionysus, the spirit of tragedy, whose essence is expressed in the continuous struggle of opposing powers, their mutual enhancement and final reconciliation, assumes many forms and masks in Nietzsche's philosophical works. Their meanings will be discussed throughout this study. Dionysus is Prometheus, Faust, Zarathustra; he is sceptic, critic, destroyer, and he is builder and creator. He is the "Ur-Eine," primal oneness and the ground of being, ever contradictory and ever suffering; he is Heraclitean flux and becoming; he is Schopenhauer's eternally striving will. But he is also the will to power, the will to overcome, to affirm, and to create. Dionysus, the old Thraco-Phrygian deity, becomes, above all, the symbol of modern man who has lost all traditional values and beliefs and faces nihilism and despair. But he also represents the heroic individual who overcomes nihilism and finds a new meaning of life, one that Nietzsche designates as Dionysian and tragic.

Nietzsche's tragic, Dionysian world view does not represent a negative, but a positive attitude that leads to the highest affirmation of life. He calls himself "the first tragic philosopher . . . that is the most extreme opposite and antipode of a pessimistic philosopher."[10] But this "Yes" to life is arrived at through the most uncompromising nihilistic position, in full realization of the negative elements of life. An affirmation of life that would fail to recognize its inescapable conflicts and contradictions would, for Nietzsche, be hollow and false, lacking that very spirit which he admired above all: the spirit of the heroic individual who has the strength and courage to accept life as meaningful and joyful in spite of its inevitable tensions, pain, and evil. This Nietzschean view is of particular importance to our own age of anxiety precisely because it faces existence as it really is, without optimistic illusions and mechanisms of escape; precisely because it achieves an affirmation of life by first recognizing its nihilistic foundation. Our dilemmas and anxieties cannot be eliminated by a return to the optimism and confidence of former ages, whose claims we deny and whose beliefs we no longer share. They can, however, I believe, be "overcome" by a spirit that Nietzsche calls tragic—a spirit that is affirmative, yet not optimistic.

The tragic spirit is defined by Nietzsche as "pessimism and its overcoming." This is the central theme that pervades all of Nietzsche's works, early and late; and it is this theme that draws him to the study of Greek culture and art. In the *Nachlass* we find the following note: "This contrariety of the Apollonian and Dionysian within the Greek soul is one of the greatest riddles by which I felt myself attracted in the presence of Greek culture. At bottom I strove to do nothing but divine precisely why the Greek Apollonism had to grow out of Dionysian soil."[11] In *Ecce Homo*, looking back at his earlier work, *The Birth of Tragedy*, he says: " 'Hellenism and Pessimism,' this would have been an unambiguous title for the first statement of the Greek teaching of the overcoming of pessimism. Tragedy as the proof that the Greeks were not pessimists."[12]

The Hellenic spirit exhibits for Nietzsche those characteristics which are fundamental for his conception of the tragic, for it achieves its greatness and superiority by an "overcoming of pessimism." The whole existence of the ancient Greeks rested, Nietzsche claims, upon a base of suffering and pain, of extreme tension and violent emotion. Their Apollonian consciousness, and its whole Olympian magic mountain, had their roots and foundation in Dionysian soil. Their serenity and harmony were not conditions of undisturbed complacency, but arose out of an awareness of the horrors and contradictions inherent in life. The Dionysian elements of barbarism and titanism were as fundamental in Greek culture as were Apollonian elements of sublimity and measure.

Only both together, both Dionysus and Apollo, can, in Nietzsche's view, explain the achievements of the Greek genius—its beauty, its serenity, its gaiety, and optimism. "Wherever [we have] Apollonian culture, we must first triumph over titans and kill monsters."[13]

Nietzsche's interpretation of Greek culture is in sharp conflict with that of the great classicists of the eighteenth century. In the classic view, it is not Dionysus, or the union of Dionysus and Apollo, but Apollo alone who is the central phenomenon of the Greek genius. His greatness consists in a peaceful serenity and sublimity, and in a clarity and harmony that are free of doubt and Dionysian discord. Nietzsche challenged these familiar conceptions of the Greek genius, as held by Goethe, Schiller, and Winckelmann, among others. They "did not succeed in forcing the enchanted gate that leads to the magic mountain of Hellenism,"[14] but failed at a crucial point to penetrate its secrets. The ideal of "noble simplicity and quiet grandeur" that Winckelmann sees realized in Greek culture and art does not constitute greatness, according to Nietzsche, because it lacks the depth of tension and the strength of orgiastic power. The ideal of the classicists, based upon "Apollonian consciousness [, is] but a thin veil hiding the Dionysian realm. . . . In order to comprehend this, we must take down the elaborate structure of Apollonian culture stone by stone until we discover its foundation."[15] And, indeed, Nietzsche demolishes Winckelmann's structure stone by stone. Into the classic Olympus, where only Apollo, the "lucid one" reigned, Nietzsche leads Dionysus, whose bands of drunken bacchants and satyrs shatter the quiet serenity of the Olympian realm.

The union of Apollo and Dionysus expresses the essence of Nietzsche's tragic view which, as noted above, is also defined as "pessimism and its overcoming." However, in defining it thus, we have to bear in mind that the concepts of "tragedy," "pessimism," and "overcoming" are not used by Nietzsche in a familiar or traditional sense. The tragic view, although growing out of a pessimistic foundation, is nonetheless positive, leading to the affirmation of the totality of life and being, where even the negative and destructive aspects are seen as necessary and ultimately productive. Pessimism, when neither weak nor sentimental, is not a negative attitude that should be annihilated; its fundamental elements of struggle, pain, and opposition are metaphysically grounded, derived from life and being. They cannot be eliminated without destroying life itself. However, they can be made to function as stimulants in the development of the human personality and culture by a process that Nietzsche calls "overcoming." This process does not aim at the total abolishment of the pessimistic foundation of life; rather, it is based on the awareness of its inevitability and its creative force, and on the recognition that annihilation and origination, good and evil, abyss and height, belong together and form an inseparable unity in the creative activity of nature and man.

"Overcoming" is a process that is perhaps best understood through reference to Hegel's use of the concept of "aufheben." The German verb *aufheben,* one of Hegel's characteristic key words, signifies three distinct meanings and functions: to annul, to preserve, and to lift up. It is an essential part of Hegel's system to show that everything in the development of the life of the world, what he calls "the dialectic of history," exhibits a rhythmic pattern and destiny moving endlessly in a triadic development from thesis to antithesis to synthesis. Reality is a continuous dynamic process, a perpetual transition of everything that is into its opposite, and finally into a synthesis wherein the elements of the prior phases are at once canceled, preserved, and elevated; that is, they are *aufgehoben*. This dialectical process has no termination, since every effective synthesis becomes in turn the thesis of a new opposition representing a more integrated, although also only partial, view of reality.

Nietzsche's tragic view, described as "pessimism and its overcoming," is in its triadic development analogous to the Hegelian dialectical movement. The overcoming of the pessimistic premise is manifested in a threefold function and activity: to cancel those elements of pessimism which are false and decadent and are contained in what Nietzsche calls "weak pessimism"; to preserve those elements which, despite their nihilistic aspects, are found to be constructive and creative; and to elevate them into a synthesis which represents a deeper and more honest understanding of the meaning of life. Thus, in Nietzsche's "overcoming of pessimism" we have the Hegelian process of *aufheben*: canceling, preserving, and lifting up all at once, moving from a pessimism that Nietzsche calls weak to one that he designates as classic and strong.

III

Nietzsche's tragic culture is radically opposed to all optimistic views, which, he maintains, are at bottom nothing but symptoms of declining strength that arise typically in periods of dissolution and weakness. These views, he claims, are not the result of an honest search for truth but are motivated by fear of uncertainties and contradictions, revealing man's poverty of courage in facing reality as it truly is. What is involved here is "the psychology of the herd man," who fears struggle and pain and invents deceptions and illusions in order to satisfy his longing for a passive, comfortable existence, for a "green pasture happiness."

Nietzsche calls the spirit from which optimism arises "the spirit of gravity . . . that draws downward toward the abyss . . . dripping lead into my ears, leaden thoughts into my brain."[16] This spirit is symbolized in the figure of the dwarf who accompanies the wanderer, Zarathustra, on his mountain climb, but jumps off Zarathustra's shoulder when he cannot bear the dizzy heights of the mountain cliffs and the dangers and loneliness of its icy ridges and peaks, where there are no mists and veils but only stark and piercing clarity. The dwarf is one of many figures that Nietzsche uses to symbolize the unheroic, nontragic attitude of the "herd man," the spirit of mediocrity and lazy optimism. We meet the dwarf again in many guises. He is the jester whom Zarathustra encounters among the multitude of the marketplace after his descent from the mountains; the jester who mocks the tightrope dancer and "his dangerous vocation" and, jumping over him, causes his death.[17] He is the shepherd into whose mouth the serpent crawls and with it "all that is heaviest and blackest."[18] But, more importantly, he is also a part of every individual and even of Zarathustra, the mountain climber whose pet animals are the serpent and the eagle, the one drawing him up to the mountain cliffs, the other pulling him down into the abyss.

Nietzsche's opposition to all forms of optimism was influenced by the teaching of Schopenhauer and the latter's voluntaristic, pessimistic metaphysics. His first reading of *The World as Will and Idea*, picked up accidentally in a book store in Leipzig, made him an immediate disciple. He "belonged to those readers of Schopenhauer who knew perfectly well after they had turned the first page that they will read all his works and listen to every word he has spoken."[19]

What attracted and influenced Nietzsche was Schopenhauer's voluntarism and pessimism, both of which broke
with the fundamental presuppositions of a harmony of existence, a notion upon which Western philosophical tradition had long been based. The innermost essence of the
world, which underlies all things, is described by Schopenhauer as a blind impulse toward existence, an irrational,
ceaselessly striving and suffering will. Happiness and harmony can never be achieved, for the will can never attain
its wants; it merely alternates between pain and boredom.
Thus suffering is seen as essential to all life, and will be further increased by every increase of knowledge. In *Schopenhauer as Educator* Nietzsche quotes Schopenhauer: "A happy
life is impossible; the highest that man can achieve is a
heroic life."[20]

Nietzsche never ceased to admire the honesty and courage that led Schopenhauer to break with the Western philosophical tradition. He never ceased to acknowledge his debt
and gratitude to Schopenhauer, who early guided him in his
own opposition to philosophical optimism. But Nietzsche is
a Schopenhauer pupil only in the sense that true veneration
must be connected with critique and that "the man who remains a pupil requites his teacher but ill."[21] While they both
start with the same fundamental presuppositions, their conclusions differ sharply. Nietzsche goes far beyond the pessimistic teaching of Schopenhauer and uses pessimism
merely as a premise that must be overcome in order to lead
to an ultimately positive philosophy wherein the emphasis
is on synthesis and creativity. Schopenhauer's philosophy, by
contrast, led to passive resignation and to what Nietzsche
called "weak pessimism."

Nietzsche's polemic against optimistic views is directed
against many philosophical positions, among them the

Hegelian belief in the progressive movement of history, and the proponents of a Darwinian theory of evolutionary progress. His arch-enemy, however, is Socrates. He attacks his teaching as containing a non-Dionysian false optimism that proved fatal to tragedy, and helped initiate an age of decadence and decline. Socrates is, to Nietzsche, "the archetype of the theoretical man . . . and theoretical optimism" who is responsible for the abolishment of myth and instincts, replacing them with logical schematisms and empty abstractions, and holding that everything which is not fully intelligible is devoid of all meaning. Socratism, Nietzsche claims, brought about a turning point in Western civilization; in place of doubt and suffering, and the heroic drive toward the unknown and unexplored, it put complacent trust in the omnipotence of man's logical powers from which in turn all moral and noble deeds are said to be derived. It equated knowledge with virtue and happiness and thereby, Nietzsche asserts, destroyed the instinctive impulses of the early Greeks, the deeper wisdom of the pre-Socratic philosophers and their superior culture, which was not optimistic but tragic. Thus Nietzsche says in *The Birth of Tragedy:*

> consider the consequences of the Socratic maxims: 'virtue is knowledge; all sins are based on ignorance; only the virtuous are happy'—these three basic formulations of optimism cause the death of tragedy. . . . For who can misjudge the optimistic elements in the nature of dialectics which celebrates a victory in every syllogism and can breathe only in an atmosphere of cool and conscious clarity? Once that optimistic element had penetrated tragedy, it gradually overgrew its Dionysian regions and brought about their annihilation.[22]

Socrates remains the arch-villain throughout all of Nietzsche's writings and is, together with Plato, held responsible for the perversion of the Greek tragic spirit. Nietzsche's polemic against Socratism as well as against Platonism is of central concern for his philosophical arguments and will therefore continue to play an important part in this study.

In addition to opposing all optimistic positions, Nietzsche equally strongly rejects what he calls "weak pessimism." It has often been overlooked that he makes an original and significant distinction between strong and weak pessimism. While he affirms the former as possessing positive elements, he attacks the latter as negative and uncreative. The failure to recognize this distinction has led many readers to the false conclusion that Nietzsche's teaching manifests a philosophy of despair and negativity. This is a misunderstanding for which Nietzsche himself must be at least partly blamed, since he often uses the term "pessimism" in this dual sense, without any specific qualification. It is therefore essential to analyze the meaning of weak and strong pessimism, as Nietzsche understands it.

Nietzsche finds the roots of weak pessimism in the teaching of Schopenhauer, in the spirit of romanticism, and in the transcendence of Christianity. As noted before, he acknowledges his debt to Schopenhauer, pointing particularly to the important contribution that Schopenhauerian metaphysics made to philosophical thought by its opposition to the false claims of optimistic traditions. But, Nietzsche argues, Schopenhauer's pessimism is weak, because it neglects one of life's most important challenges—that of "overcoming." Instead, it seeks escape from suffering and deliverance from the ever-struggling and striving will, because it holds non-being to be better than being, and the will to nothingness to be greater than the will to live. It is a philosophy of negation and resignation, which sees the highest attainment in the abolishment of all willing, all striving and desiring, a state which, according to Schopenhauer, can be achieved only in the artist's timeless contemplation and in the life of the ascetic man. Nirvana is the final goal, a state of perfect calm and nothingness in which, as Schopenhauer puts it, "what remains after the entire abolition of the will is for those who are still full of the will certainly nothing; but to those in whom the will has denied itself, this world which is so real with all its suns and milky ways is nothing."*

Schopenhauer, Nietzsche says, fails to grasp the true meaning of pessimism: suffering and struggle are productive powers that are not to be abolished but overcome, canceling out that which is passive and weak, but preserving and developing that which can become the basis for a pessimism of strength. Schopenhauer's pessimism is to Nietzsche a philosophy of defeat and resignation that must be refuted. In *The Birth of Tragedy* he quotes a passage from Schopenhauer's major work, *The World as Will and Idea:* "That which provides the power of transport in tragedy arises from the sudden recognition that the world and life fail to give any true satisfaction and therefore do not deserve our loyalty. This is the tragic spirit, which leads us to the final goal of resignation." And he goes on to say: "How differently Dionysus spoke to me! How alien all this resignation was to me!"[23]

Nietzsche's arguments against Schopenhauer, whose philosophy he often attacks as an expression of romanticism, are extended to the whole romantic movement, which he similarly accuses of weak pessimism. In view of Nietzsche's own sharp repudiation of romanticism, it is strange that many Nietzsche interpreters, among them Ernst Bertram, Karl Joel, and Thomas Mann, contend that Nietzsche was

---

* Arthur Schopenhauer, *The World as Will and Idea* (New York: Doubleday & Co., 1961), p. 421.

himself essentially romantic.* While I admit that parallels between Nietzsche and the romantic movement can be drawn, for they do share an emphasis on individualism, intuition and feelings, a revolt against rationalism, and the spirit of the Enlightenment, these similarities are, in my opinion, superficial and do not include the most essential features of their views on life. Indeed, Nietzsche is not only nonromantic, but anti-romantic. This is an opinion that is also held by the recognized Nietzsche scholar Walter Kaufmann.** Perhaps the differences in interpretation are largely due to a lack of agreement regarding the equivocal concept of "romanticism." However, we are not here concerned with the proper definition of romanticism, but with a clarification of what Nietzsche means by weak pessimism as it arises out of his own conception of romanticism.

Nietzsche distinguishes decisively between the romantic and the Dionysian world view and holds that the romantic vision of life is nontragic. Romanticism, says Nietzsche, is sick and decadent in spirit: it grows out of feelings of resentment and revenge, and expresses itself in tearful lament and, ultimately, in self-destruction. Above all, it negates life, seeking refuge from conflicts and pain in dreams and self-deceptions, and in a flight from the present into the past and the future; it glorifies night and death. In contrast, Dionysian faith is a Yes-saying to life and tragedy, an affirmation of the present, a "delight born of pain," a "strength of thought." It springs not from resentment, weakness, and "impoverishment of life," as does romanticism, but from "overfullness of

---

* Ernst Bertram, Nietzsche: *Versuch einer Mythologie* (Berlin: Bondi, 1918); Karl Joel, *Nietzsche und die Romantik* (Leipzig: Diederichs, 1905); Thomas Mann, *Last Essays* (New York: Alfred A. Knopf, 1959).

** Walter A. Kaufmann, *Nietzsche* (Princeton: Princeton University Press, 1950), p. 101.

life," from creative power and joy. In *The Gay Science* Nietzsche asks:

> What is romanticism? . . . It is perhaps remembered that I
> at first approached the modern world with some extreme errors
> and overestimations and, in any case, with great hopes. I
> understood . . . the philosophical pessimism of the nineteenth
> century as if it were the symptom of greater strength of
> thought, of bolder courage, of more victorious fullness of life
> than had characterized the eighteenth century, the age of
> Kant, Hume, Condillac and the sensualists. . . . One sees that
> I, at that time, misunderstood the essential character of phil-
> osophical pessimism as well as of German music—that is their
> romanticism. . . . Regarding all aesthetic values, I now use this
> main distinction: . . . Is it hunger or overflow which has here
> become creative? . . . The desire for destruction, change, be-
> coming can be the expression of superabundant power, big
> with future (my term for it is the word 'Dionysian'). But it
> can also be the hatred of the misfit, the poor in spirit, the
> destitute; it is hatred that destroys because it rebels against
> everything that exists, yes, against being itself. . . . This is
> romantic pessimism in its fullest expression, be it as Schopen-
> hauerian philosophy of the will or as Wagnerian music: —Ro-
> mantic pessimism . . . there could be another kind of pessimism
> which is classical . . . this vision belongs to me . . . I call it a
> pessimism of the future . . . Dionysian pessimism.[24]

Above all, Nietzsche judges Christian transcendence to be
the paradigm of weak pessimism, for Christian faith, he believes, devalues the temporal sphere and looks for a better
world in a timeless Beyond. It looks for a compensating
heaven where all suffering is redeemed by divine grace, and
all evil and injustice find heavenly recompense. "Dionysus
against the 'Crucified,' there you have the contrast. There

is no difference in respect to their martyrdom—it is a difference in the meaning of it. Life itself, its eternal fertility and recurrence, causes pain, destruction, the will to destroy. In the other case, suffering—the 'Crucified as the innocent one'— counts as an argument against this life, as a formula for its condemnation."[25] Nietzsche's polemic against Christian teaching and its transcendent tendencies, rooted in the Platonic tradition, occupies an important place in his philosophy and will continue to be a subject of discussion here. But Nietzsche asks:

> Is pessimism necessarily a sign of decadence, of failure and exhausted instincts, as it is now . . . with us modern Europeans? Or is there a pessimism of strength, an intellectual predilection for what is hard, evil and problematic in existence, arising from a plethora of health, plenitude of being? . . . Is there a pessimism of the future . . . the Dionysian pessimism?[26]

Strong pessimism represents to Nietzsche the heroic attitude of the higher individual who has the courage to stand alone and self-reliant, neither comforted by a compensating heaven nor protected by illusions. He recognizes that destruction and annihilation are part of the eternal cycle of life and death, and of the everlasting change that pervades all nature. He knows that contradiction, evil, and suffering belong to the very essence of life, to "the economy of the whole." And yet he does not turn away in hatred, resignation, or negation. In his very failure and despair the Dionysian man fulfills himself, recognizing that "it is out of the deepest depth that the highest must come to its heights."[27] He affirms life in spite of, or even because of, tragedy, understanding it in terms of its perils and potentialities, its nothingness and its greatness. "The saying Yes to life even in its strangest and hardest problems; the will to life, rejoicing over its inexhaustibility even in the very sacrifice of its highest types—that is what I call Dionysian."[28]

Pain and suffering become the central theme of Dionysus: "Only the disciple of suffering has produced all enhancement of man."[29] As with nearly every concept that Nietzsche analyzes in his dialectical method, so here, too, we must distinguish between two kinds of suffering. There are those "who suffer from overfullness of life and want a Dionysian art as well as a tragic insight and outlook on life . . . and then those who suffer from impoverishment of life and demand of art and philosophy calm, stillness, smooth seas or also frenzy . . . revenge against life itself . . . the most voluptuous kind of frenzy for those so impoverished."[30]

The first kind of suffering is connected with the concept of *Rausch*, "the psychology of the orgiastic as an overflowing feeling of life and power where even pain has the effect of a stimulus."[31] It is difficult to translate the German word *Rausch* adequately, since it combines connotations variously referring to states of alcoholic intoxication and to the orgiastic abandon experienced in impassioned dancing, sexual intercourse, and the performance of ancient religious rites. More specifically, Nietzsche uses the word *Rausch* to describe the ecstasy of the artist and the feeling of superabundance connected with the creative act. All of these states manifest a mixture of suffering along with feelings of vitality, joy, heightened sensitivity, and power. To the second kind of suffering belong the attitudes of Schopenhauer, Wagner, and, above all, Christianity. In *Nietzsche contra Wagner*, he repudiates Schopenhaur and Wagner, his early masters, and expresses his thorough disillusionment with their respective solutions of the problem of suffering through escape into Nirvana and the Holy Grail of Parsifal:

"They negate life; they slander it, hence they are my antipodes."[32] And in *The Will to Power* he contrasts the Christian meaning of suffering with that in his own tragic philosophy:

> The problem is that of the meaning of suffering: whether a Christian meaning, whether a tragic meaning. In the first case, suffering is supposed to be the road to a holy life; in the latter, life itself is considered holy enough to justify any immensity of suffering. The tragic man affirms even the hardest lot on earth.[33]

Suffering, under the sign of Dionysus, becomes a creative experience, a feeling of life and strength. "Only thus does man reach his heights, when lightning strikes him."[34]

Nietzsche's tragic philosophy, based on the "overcoming of pessimism," is in fact a method that turns "weak pessimism" into a "pessimism of strength." The weak characteristics of the pessimistic premise are eliminated, while those that act as stimulants are preserved, leading to the creation of a strong, heroic individual and a culture that is tragic. This tragic culture cannot be achieved without the realization that suffering, pain, and contradiction are essential elements in the productive activity of life and art, which, in order to create, must first destroy; in order to affirm, must first deny and annihilate. In doubt and despair Dionysus overcomes weak pessimism and reaches his deepest wisdom: the meaning of life is life itself; this life with all its paradoxes, evil, despair. There is a touch of truth in the irrational and paradoxical; there is the power of greatness in the very abyss of pain; there is an element of the divine in evil that "can yet turn every desert into luxurious farm land."[35]

IV

As previously noted, the roots of Nietzsche's tragic view are found in Greek tragedy. It is in the ancient drama of the Greeks that Nietzsche discovers the basic elements and defining properties of his concept of tragedy and uncovers the essence of the Dionysian spirit, whose revival he wants to bring about. Not the plastic arts which had been to the German classicists the highest manifestation of the Greek genius and their own Apollonian ideal, but Greek tragedy, is in Nietzsche's view, fundamental for the understanding of the classic spirit and his own tragic philosophy. Greek tragedy, by its fusion of dialogue and chorus, image and music, exhibits for Nietzsche the union of the Apollonian and Dionysian, a union in which Dionysian passion and dithyrambic madness merge with Apollonian measure and lucidity, and original chaos and pessimism are overcome in a tragic attitude that is affirmative and heroic.

While Attic tragedy exhibits the features of both "the Dionysian lyric of the chorus and the Apollonian dream world of the scene," Nietzsche stresses the fact that Greek drama grew out of the cult and worship of Dionysus and the spirit of music. Originally tragedy was nothing but chorus which, by means of Dionysian lyric and music, enacted the celebration of the god Dionysus and was an artistic substitute for ancient religious rites. And even in the tragedies of Aeschylus and Sophocles, when dramatic action was added and image and dialogue encroached upon lyric and music, the chorus retained its central importance. It is this fact, Nietzsche claims, which accounts for the superiority of Aeschylean and Sophoclean tragedies over those of Euripides, where the role of the chorus disintegrated, thereby destroying the true meaning of tragedy, namely, its Dionysian spirit of music.

Nietzsche, under the influence of Schopenhauer's aesthetic theories, assigns to music a genesis and character radically different from those of all other arts. To both Schopenhauer and Nietzsche, music is based on aesthetic principles and criteria of beauty that are unlike those of painting, sculpture, and epic poetry. While the latter arts represent an Apollonian individuating act, music transports us into a state in which the boundaries between individuals and the limits of space and time are broken down, and a sense of mystical unity with the universe is experienced. Music reveals a world that is unknown and unknowable to reason with its fragmentizing, isolating activity, but is grasped intuitively by feelings and instincts. It penetrates to the primal force of life, which is, to Schopenhauer and Nietzsche, the will itself. Thus Schopenhauer says:

> Music is by no means like the other arts the copy of ideas, but the copy of the will itself, whose objectivity the ideas are. This is why the effect of music is so much more powerful and penetrating than that of other arts, for they speak only of shadows, but it speaks of the thing itself.*

And Nietzsche states in *The Birth of Tragedy*:

> True Dionysian music represents to us a universal mirror of the world will: each particular event refracted in that mirror is at once enlarged into the image of an eternal truth. . . . Now the gospel of universal harmony is sounded, each individual not only feels united and reconciled with his fellow man, but at one with him, as if the veil of Maya had been torn apart and there remained only . . . the vision of mystical Oneness.[36]

---

* Schopenhauer, *The World as Will and Idea*, p. 269.

But again, Nietzsche does not follow his teacher Schopenhauer all the way. For Schopenhauer, the aesthetic experience in art, and particularly in music, leads to a pure mode of contemplation in which, even if only for moments, man is raised above all willing and all individuality. In the intuition of eternity he is freed from the ever-striving and desiring will. There is no more struggle, no more pain, but merely a state of pure will-less contemplation. However, in Nietzsche's view, the aesthetic experience in music does not lead to the negation of the will but to a feeling of oneness between the individual will and the world will. It does not liberate us, in the healing intuition of the eternal, from desire and suffering. Instead, what we actually experience in the dithyrambic rhythm of Dionysian music is a state of exultation, which includes suffering and pain as part of the primordial essence of all things. We feel a sense of joy and realize that "in spite of terror and pain, life is at bottom indestructibly powerful and creative."

Dionysian beauty does not exclude the discordant and ugly, as do the harmonious sculptural forms of a Praxiteles or a Phidias. Dionysian delight is not found in the serenity and peace of pure contemplation, or in the resignation and denial of the will, but is contained in the wisdom of Silenus, in the hero's painful dilemmas, in the constant activity of the striving will:

> Now we see struggle, pain, the destruction of appearances as necessary, because of the abundance of countless forms pressing into life, because of the boundless fecundity of the world will. . . . That primal Dionysian delight, experienced even in the presence of pain, is the origin common to both music and tragic myth.[37]

Although Nietzsche does stress the Dionysian musical element, it remains the fusion of both the Dionysian and the Apollonian to which he attributes the greatness of Attic tragedy. With the aid of Dionysian wisdom and its deeper insight into reality, Apollonian isolated images and the individual characters and events of tragedy reach deeper levels of existence and are enlarged to universal truths. On the other hand, with the aid of Apollo, the musical elements find expression in concrete representations, and Dionysian discord and dithyrambic excess are given harmony, clarity, and form.

Nietzsche's conception of Greek tragedy, and of the concept of the tragic in general, has much in common with that of Hegel.* This claim can be justified in spite of the many differences between them, such as the fact that in the Hegelian system the province of art is subordinated first to religion and ultimately to philosophy, while for Nietzsche a separation of the aesthetic experience from the religious and philosophical is not possible. However, significant parallels can be drawn, of which only a few are briefly mentioned here. To both, Greek tragedy is art par excellence, reaching a height never again equaled in any culture. To both, it is not Greek plastic art but Greek tragedy that expresses in the fullest manner the Greek genius, the essence of art and the greatness of the human spirit. To both, it is Aeschylus and Sophocles who most adequately represent the classical ideal and realize the fundamental principles of tragedy, while Euripides is considered closer to the modern conception of drama, which emphasizes the personal and subjective rather than the universal aspects of being. His dramas, in contrast to those of Aeschylus and Sophocles, are no longer Attic, they contend, but Hellenistic, marking a period of

---

* Hegel developed his theory of tragedy in his *Vorlesungen ueber die Aesthetik*. Further material can be found in his *Religionsphilosophie, Geschichte der Philosophie* and *Phaenomenologie des Geistes*.

transition and mediation between the classical and the romantic. Nietzsche, characteristically, is much stronger in his criticism of Euripides than is Hegel. He not only considers his dramas inferior to those of Aeschylus and Sophocles, but in *The Birth of Tragedy* he names Euripides, together with Socrates, as the destroyer of tragedy and initiator of an age of decline and decadence.

Nietzsche accuses Euripides of having brought about the destruction of tragedy by introducing rationalistic elements and thereby abolishing the Dionysian principle, the spirit of music and myth. He points out that, until Euripides, Dionysus was the major protagonist, not only in the earliest forms of Greek tragedy when it contained only a chorus, but also in its later development when the Apollonian nonmusical elements of dialogue and image were added. Prometheus, Oedipus, and all the other central characters of Aeschylus and Sophocles are, to Nietzsche, actually Dionysian masks, despite their Apollonian features, for their actions express the musical mood of the chorus. But Euripides, Nietzsche claims, drove Dionysus, the genius of music, from the tragic stage and tried to rebuild the drama on non-Dionysian foundations, giving it the Apollonian form of dramatized epic, and destroying the true meaning of tragedy, which can be interpreted only as a concrete manifestation of Dionysian conditions.

Most significant to Nietzsche is that the chorus, of central importance until Euripides, has, in his view, become subordinated to the dialogue and, deteriorating into a counterfeit and mere stage convention, is threatened with extinction. It is no longer dramatic, participating in the actions of the tragic hero and reflecting the eternal, universal aspects of being, but it is now narrative and decorative, standing aside as a cool and detached spectator. Euripides' characters are no longer universalized, deepened and illuminated from within by the power of music; instead, they portray indi-vidualized, single, character traits, which are projected into violent passions. Their suffering is in the highest degree personal and does not—as Dionysian tragedy demands—ex-press the eternal dialectic of the universal forces of nature and its inexorable laws. Pathos and lamentation replace heroic suffering and tragic action.

Thus, Nietzsche concludes, Euripides' plays become, in the absence of Dionysus, rational structures in which the mystical, musical mood and its powerful dramatic rhythm are replaced by logical argument, debate, and rhetoric. His plots and actions no longer grow out of the inevitable necessity of cosmic laws, but, being conceived intellectually, they are contrived and inorganic. Apollonian rationality, clarity, and lucidity replace the problematic, ambiguous, and mysterious depth of earlier tragedies. Language, the instrument of Apollo, takes the place of Dionysian music and builds artificial, rational constructs where there was once the living reality of myth. In the end, Nietzsche be-lieves, Euripides, by forsaking Dionysus, is in turn forsaken by Apollo. And now it is neither Dionysus nor Apollo who speaks in his dramas, but a new divinity and daemon called Socrates. Based upon the Socratic emphasis on reason and knowledge, Euripides's new aesthetic axiom is now stated by Nietzsche as "Whatever is to be beautiful must also be conscious and sensible."[38] Rationalism, the arch-enemy of myth and the spirit of music, finally brings about the death of tragedy and initiates an age that is unheroic, uncreative, and untragic.

V

Both Hegel and Nietzsche hold that Greek drama, prior to

Euripides, provides the key to an understanding of the essence of tragedy and what is to them its central theme: conflict and reconciliation. To Hegel the conflict is one of the spirit, of man's "ethical substance," which, in continuous dialectical development and self-division, seeks a synthesis through "a harmony of discords." For Nietzsche the central theme of tragedy is expressed in the duality of the Apollonian and Dionysian, their everpresent antagonism and strife and their everpresent acts of reconciliation.

The essential characteristics of tragedy, as paradigmatically exhibited in Greek drama, are to both Nietzsche and Hegel heroism, nobility, and universality. Tragedy is never based upon the kind of suffering that is sentimental and weak, nor is it motivated merely by an instinct for self-preservation. It is suffering based upon some sort of collision that springs from the deeper dimensions of Hegel's "spirit" and Nietzsche's "will to power." The belief in the greatness of man is for both inseparable from the idea of tragedy. In *The Birth of Tragedy* Nietzsche points out that it is not a paradox that tragedy flourished during the Periclean age of confidence and vitality, while it declined with the fall of the city states and the loss of the belief in the power and dignity of man. He asks:

> Was it not exactly in the most creative periods of their youth that the Greeks possessed the will to tragedy? . . . Was it not, to use Plato's words, frenzy and madness which brought about the greatest blessings for Hellas? And, conversely, was it not precisely during periods of dissolution and weakness that the Greeks became more and more optimistic, frivolous . . . gay, and scientific?[39]

And to Hegel, too, tragedy is the most adequate embodiment of the affirmative power of spirit, which, even in its deepest divisions and failures, does not lack positive elements of reconciliation, heroism, and nobility.

> They may be called heroes, inasmuch as they have derived their purposes and their vocation, not from the calm, regular course of things . . . [but] from that inner spirit still hidden beneath the surface. . . . If we go on to cast a look at the fate of these world-historical persons whose vocation it was to be the agents of the world-spirit—we shall find it to have been no happy one. They attained no calm enjoyment; their whole life was labor and trouble; their whole nature was naught else but their master-passion.*

To both Hegel and Nietzsche the Aeschylean and Sophoclean heroes exhibit the fullest expression of the tragic spirit. They do not lament and weep, but suffer the anguish and reversals of their destinies with strength and courage, and retain their dignity in failure and death. Sophocles conceived doomed Oedipus, one of the greatest sufferers of the Greek stage, as a pattern of nobility and human greatness, a greatness that extends beyond the narrow concerns of the individual, beyond the ordinary conception of good and evil, and reaches into the fundamental depth of the human spirit and of being itself. It is a spirit that Nietzsche sees lost in modern man, who has become weak and unheroic, possessing no intensity or magnitude, stirring no awe or reverence—but merely pity.

The essential function of conflict and negation is for Nietzsche, as for Hegel, contained in their positive and creative power. The aim of tragedy is neither defeat nor pity and fear, but the victory of the human spirit. Its ultimate reality is not opposition but synthesis and reconciliation,

---

* Hegel, *Philosophy of History* (New York: Willey Book Co., 1944), Introduction.

which may be present even where the end of the drama seems to be a catastrophe. Yet, a sense of ambiguity, conflict, and mystery remains the essence of tragic action and of the final reconciliation.

In stressing the heroic element, Nietzsche saw himself in opposition to the Aristotelian definition of tragedy, as interpreted by him. In *The Birth of Tragedy* he repudiates Aristotle's conception of tragedy as producing pity and fear and effecting the catharsis of such emotions. He argues that tragedy is not based on the "depressing" emotions of pity and fear, but attains a supreme state of heroism and exultation. It does not aim at catharsis, "that pathological release of which philologists do not know whether to place it among medical or moral phenomena," but achieves the highest stage of affirmation, where "even the greatest pain is justified out of an excess of health. . . . Whoever goes on talking about pathological and moral effects, which do not belong to the aesthetic sphere, may as well despair of his sensibilities."[40] The goal of tragedy is not "to be cleansed of dangerous emotions by vehement discharges . . . thus it was understood by Aristotle, but to become . . . beyond terror and pity the eternal lust of becoming."[41] The end of tragedy is to see greatness and beauty even in the face of the horrible and ugly, to exult over suffering and pain, and to affirm the creative powers of dithyrambic frenzy. Nietzsche points to the origin of tragedy, the ancient mystery rites, and claims that they celebrated the worship of Dionysus and expressed their orgiastic savagery, not merely as a means of catharsis, but as a spiritual regeneration and rebirth, a mode of acceptance and not of despair. "That life is essentially, in spite of all phenomenal change, indestructibly powerful and joyful, this solace was expressed most concretely in the chorus of satyrs, nature beings who dwell behind all civilization and

preserve their identity throughout every change of generation and history."[42]

Nietzsche's attack upon the Aristotelian theory of catharsis exhibits his tendency to unfair criticism. However, it
also shows the difficulties of the Aristotelian theory, which
has, in fact, led to age-long controversies about its meaning
and intention. Actually, Aristotle and Nietzsche seem, to me,
despite many differences, not far apart in some of their
views on tragedy.

Aristotle's catharsis has been interpreted as referring to
purification and purgation of passions. If it is purification,
to be "placed among moral phenomena," then in order to
understand the meaning of catharsis we have to consider
Aristotle's meaning of morality and goodness of character.
While his virtuous man is not "beyond good and evil," he is
not moralistic in the narrow sense. He possesses excellence,
and excellence is the realization of his highest potentialities.
He possesses pride, and "pride implies greatness."* He is
the "great-souled man" whose excellence, nobility, and pride
are indeed close to Nietzsche's "higher man." Purification of
passions thus means getting rid of what is petty and vain,
thereby freeing our emotions to realize their power and
appropriate excellence.

If, on the other hand, catharsis is to be interpreted as
purgation, to be "placed among medical phenomena," we
have to bear in mind the dynamic character of Aristotle's
philosophy and his concept of the mean. Then it becomes
clear that purgation for Aristotle cannot mean the extinction
of our passions or a reduction of their intensity to a state
of undynamic passivity. Instead, what it does mean is removal of excess in order to establish the balance upon which

---

* Aristotle, *Nicomachean Ethics*, 4. 3.

health of body and mind depends.* It aims at removal of the destructive and compulsive elements that passions possess, thereby releasing their formative powers and transforming them into free, active, and dynamic states—in Nietzsche's language, giving Apollonian form to Dionysian chaos.

While recognizing significant differences between Aristotle's and Nietzsche's theories of tragedy, further points of contact can be found, which not only achieve a rapprochement between the two philosophers, but also prove their closeness to modern psychological theories. The most important of these points of contact is perhaps their mutual recognition of the dangers of emotional repression and the necessity of emotional release. This recognition is expressed in Aristotle's theory of catharsis and in Nietzsche's Dionysian tragic spirit, in which instincts and impulses find formed expression, thus preventing them from deteriorating into the repressed *ressentiment,* envy, and hatred of the "impoverished," the spirit of the "herd man." The spirit of both Aristotle's and Nietzsche's views on tragedy is Greek, a blending of man's weakness and magnificence, his frailty and strength.

Having stressed the heroic element in Hegel's and Nietzsche's conception of tragedy, I return to the discussion of the aspect of universality. The problem of tragedy as conflict and reconciliation, as pessimism and its overcoming, is for both supra-personal in character. Without the relation to totality there is no tragic conflict but merely personal suffering that is weak and pathetic; without the universal element

---

* Aristotle, *Politics,* 8. 7. 5–6. "Passions which affect some temperaments violently, occur to some extent in all. There is simply a difference of intensity; so, for instance, with pity and fear, and again with religious ecstasy. By this last emotion some minds can be overpowered; yet we see their balance restored by sacred music of an orgiastic type, as if they had received medical treatment and catharsis."

there is no reconciliation or overcoming but merely resignation. True art and tragedy must transcend the narrow barriers of the individual and his subjective concerns; they must put upon the immediate present the stamp of the eternal. Hegel's and Nietzsche's emphasis on the universal is based upon an interpretation of tragedy that is anti-romantic in its essence. It is founded on the refutation of the entire romantic conception of the primacy of the narrow self and a rejection of what Keats called "the egotistical sublime." In *The Birth of Tragedy* Nietzsche says:

> To us, the subjective artist is always the bad artist, and we demand, above all, in every genre and kind of art a victory over subjectivity, deliverance from the self, the silencing of every individual will and desire; in fact, we cannot believe that any genuine art work could lack objectivity and disinterested contemplation.[43]

To Hegel, tragedy is essentially the journey of the subjective spirit as it approaches the universal. To Nietzsche, it is the union of Apollonian individuality with Dionysian primal unity, the *Ur-Eine*. While the subjective, individual aspects are expressed in image and dialogue, original oneness is experienced in the musical sounds of the chorus, which is not only the origin of tragedy, but its very core and essence. Music speaks a universal language that not only imitates single phenomena, but expresses reality itself. In Dionysian music the principle of individuation is shattered and a union with nature is celebrated. The tragic hero identifies with the foundation of being, its pain and contradiction; he becomes one with the forces of nature, suffering in their destructive power and rejoicing in their creative activity.

Nature speaks to us through Dionysian art and its tragic symbolism in a voice that is true and undisguised: "Be like me, the original mother who, under constant change of appearances is eternally creating and eternally giving birth and finding joy and satisfaction." . . . In spite of pity and terror we are happy in having life, not as individuals but as part of a life force with whose procreative lust we have become one.[44]

The aspect of universality is not only an essential characteristic of tragedy; it also plays an important part in Nietzsche's concept of freedom. While Nietzsche's idea of freedom is fully developed only in his later works, particularly in connection with his teaching of eternal recurrence and "amor fati," it is already present in his early writings on tragedy and in his interpretation of the actions of the tragic heroes in the Aeschylean and Sophoclean dramas. Oedipus, Orestes, and Antigone are not mere puppets of inexorable forces of fate and the will of the gods. The tragic hero of the Greeks is not medieval man, who did not question the existence of two separate worlds: the City of God and its ideal universal order, and the Earthly City of sin, guilt, and suffering; who did not revolt against the will of God and a fate that was imposed upon him, but accepted it in resignation and humility. The Age of Faith produced no tragic heroes, no Prometheus, no Oedipus.

The hero of Greek tragedy also recognizes the duality of the divine and human will; he, too, is torn by the antithesis between man and his divinities. "The individual in his heroic striving toward universality, and in his attempt to shatter the limits of individuation, experiences in himself the primordial contradiction of all things . . . he sins and suffers."[45] But he does not suffer in resignation and passivity. His titanic will defies the gods and commits an act of *hubris*. Nietzsche uses Goethe's words to express the boldness and agony of the Promethean man:

> Here I sit, kneading men
> In my image,
> A race like myself,
> Made to suffer, weep
> Laugh and delight,
> And forget all about you—
> As I have forgotten.[46]

Nietzsche points out that man's highest good must be bought with crime and paid for with grief and despair. But within his defiance and suffering the tragic hero experiences "an obscure sense of mutual dependency . . . and joins forces with his gods." He experiences a mystical oneness and universal harmony. "He feels himself to be godlike and strides with ecstasy and elation as the gods he has seen in his dreams. . . . In Dionysian rapture and mystical self-abrogation . . . his unity with the essence of the universe is revealed to him."[47]

The identification with the cosmic whole and its divinities brings about a sense of freedom. Fate is not something external that compels us to act against our will. "Ego Fatum." I myself am necessity and fate; I myself am Moira, that mysterious and inexorable force. By a heroic, titanic act of his will the tragic hero transforms an otherwise alien fate into his own. In spite of the conflicts between divine and human will, between nature and man, which must always remain part of that "primordial contradiction of all things," his spirit is not one of resignation and despair, but is free

and unconquered. In spite of adversities, doubt, and contradictions, the heroes of the Greek stage assert the freedom
and ultimate greatness and dignity of man and life, without
which tragedy is not possible for Nietzsche.

Nietzsche's conception of Greek drama and the Greek
spirit as a union of Dionysus and Apollo, and as "the overcoming of pessimism," is a profession of faith in the dignity
and nobility of man and a justification of life in its totality—
its greatness and smallness, its pain and its joy. It is an
interpretation of tragedy that not only is valid for the Periclean age, but has become a living faith and guiding principle of all Western culture. Nietzsche's attempt to return
to the classic ideal of the Greeks, and to reconstruct a faith
on the basis of a pessimism that is strong and heroic, makes
him not only a disciple of Aeschylus and Sophocles, but a
force that has influenced philosophical, religious, and aesthetic movements of contemporary civilization. In an age
when Zarathustra's pronouncement of the "death of God" is
heard with greater urgency than in Nietzsche's own time,
in a world that is deprived of traditional values, Nietzsche's
"strong classic pessimism" is indeed needed to overcome the
dilemmas and anxieties of modern man.

Nietzsche's desperate search for a new meaning in a godless world is continued in contemporary drama. We feel the
Aeschylean sense of tragic fatalism and the Sophoclean trans-
figuring nobility even in the seemingly debased characters
of the present stage. We detect Nietzsche's tragic spirit in
the plays of Brecht, Beckett, Ionesco, Osborne, and Pinter,
in their attempts to come to terms with the absurdity of
human existence, and in their efforts to preserve human
dignity in the face of a reality that seems paradoxical and
senseless. Whatever new forms dramatic art may assume,

the basic demands that Nietzsche advances in his analysis of tragedy must be preserved, if art and drama are to survive and remain meaningful.

In addition to its influence upon contemporary drama and art, Nietzsche's philosophy has had an impact upon almost every trend of twentieth-century thought. His tragic view is close to the temper of our own age, in which man has become fully and consciously problematic to himself. His philosophy is meaningful for the age of anxiety because it is based upon a reality that does not exclude absurdity and despair. While differing from it on many points, Nietzsche is a true precursor of contemporary thought. Under his influence the modern artist and existential philosopher become with him disciples of Dionysus, "the great ambivalent one," who denies and destroys, yet affirms and creates. Like Nietzsche, they do not regard absurdity and pessimism as ends in themselves, but as a realistic foundation upon which to build a new faith in life and man. Their call to revolt is a call to create. And thus Camus's words sound like a distant echo from Nietzsche's writings:

At the end of the tunnel of darkness there is inevitably a light for which we have to fight. All of us, among the ruins, are preparing a renaissance beyond the limits of nihilism.

—Camus, *The Plague*

2
NIHILISM

What is the meaning of nihilism? That the highest values are devaluated. There is no goal; no answer to the "why."[1]

Nihilism stands at the door. . . . What I relate is the history of the next two centuries. I describe what is coming, what can no longer come otherwise: the advent of nihilism.[2]

—Nietzsche

I

Nietzsche's philosophical teaching has been characterized by many interpreters as nihilistic, destroying the meaningfulness of being and the possibility of truth. Indeed, philosophical nihilism pervades all of Nietzsche's works, from the earliest to the latest periods of his creative life. An analysis of his conception of nihilism therefore becomes the *sine qua non* for an adequate understanding of his thought. Furthermore, Nietzsche's treatment of nihilism is of special interest to our own age and to contemporary man, whose encounter with nothingness is real and urgent. Indeed, Nietzsche was

right when, with remarkable insight, he predicted that nihilism in various guises and forms would haunt the twentieth
century. No longer do we trust our gods and our traditional
values and goals; no longer do we believe in the power of
reason and science. Religion and morality are in a state of
crisis, faced with what Martin Buber called "the eclipse of
God." The concepts of rationality, progress, and freedom are
held to be principles of interpretation and not facts. Nothingness is the main theme of our existential philosophies, our
literature, and our art. In sum, an empty void threatens to
destroy our culture and the quality of our lives. But, as
Nietzsche teaches, this void not only represents disintegration of values, emptiness, and despair; it also offers challenges
and opportunities. It can also represent a great intellectual
task, to recast the image of man and the values by which he
lives and to rediscover the humanity that has become lost
and frustrated in our technological civilization. And it is in
this task—which is at once critical, retrospective, and creative
—that Nietzsche's novel interpretation of nihilism can be of
aid to us.

While Nietzsche's teaching has been correctly termed
nihilistic, it is so only in the specific sense Nietzsche gives
the term. This meaning is contrary to the traditional interpretation of nihilism as connoting total negativity and emptiness. Nietzsche introduces an entirely new concept of nihilism
which is not negative but tragic. It possesses that double
meaning and Janus-faced duality which are the essential
characteristics of Nietzsche's conception of the tragic, being
both destructive and creative, both negative and affirmative,
both "fertile and frightful at the same time, looking at the
world with that twofold gaze that all great insights possess."[3]

Nietzsche's conception of nihilism as a tragic phenomenon
is based on his belief that negation and destruction are

merely a *Zwischenstadium*, a stage of transition which must
be overcome. This stage of transition, however, is a necessary
basis for all creative activity. It contains the potentials for
growth and the essential elements for building a positive
position of strength. Without first breaking down outworn
traditions, a revaluation of values is not possible. Nihilism
and negation always precede affirmation and always remain
part of it. In the words of Heidegger, in whose philosophy
the concept of "nothingness" plays a central role, "Nothingness does not remain the indeterminate contrast to being,
but it reveals itself as belonging to being as such."*

While Nietzsche judges that the traditional concept of
nihilism refers to a "system of growing weakness" that is
decadent and totally destructive, he sees his own tragic form
of nihilism as a "system of growing strength." This nihilism
is the basis of a tragic culture and not the destruction of
culture. The central problem of Nietzsche's philosophy is to
get beyond the initially negative stage and make the concept
of nihilism meaningful and creative. Although in a letter to
his friend Erwin Rohde he calls himself, together with Taine
and Burckhardt, an extreme nihilist, he adds significantly:
"I myself never doubted that I could find the exit and the
hole through which one arrives at something."[4]

As previously noted, Nietzsche calls the process by which
"weak nihilism" is transformed into one of strength and vitality "overcoming." I agree entirely with Karl Jaspers, who
speaks of Nietzsche's philosophy as the "overcoming of
nihilism," and says: "At no time was Nietzsche merely a
nihilist; already his pathos is contrary to nihilism. The pronouncement 'God is dead' creates a constant task."** Negation

---

* Martin Heidegger, *Was ist Metaphysik?* (Frankfurt a.M.: Klostermann,
1955), p. 5.
** Karl Jaspers, *Nietzsche* (Berlin: De Gruyter, 1950), p. 252.

is never the final aim, but it must precede affirmation and, what is most essential for our understanding of Nietzsche's thought, it must always remain part of it in the act of over-coming—an act earlier compared to Hegel's synthesis in which the elements of the thesis and the antithesis are not abolished but *aufgehoben*. Negation replaces Cartesian doubt as the new methodology of the tragic philosopher and becomes the prolegomena to a future philosophy.

The term *nihilism* is used more often as a political or social doctrine than as a strictly philosophical one. In this sense it was introducd in connection with the early Russian form of revolutionary anarchism and first used by Turgenev in 1862 in his novel *Fathers and Sons*. But Nietzsche's nihilism has little to do with the political connotations of the term. Also, as argued before, his interpretation of nihilism as a tragic system is in contrast to the philosophical tradition wherein it denotes a totally negative attitude that denies the very possibility of truth and value. In the latter sense, critique and doubt do not aim at a revaluation of values, but at the destruction of any possible foundation and meaningfulness of being, knowledge, and morality.

The first and, in the strictest sense, perhaps the last real nihilist of the Western tradition was the sophist Gorgias of Leontini, whose famous dictum expresses his extreme position: "Nothing exists; if anything did exist, it would be un-knowable; and if it existed and were knowable, the knowl-edge of it could not be communicated to others." Often mentioned as another strictly nihilistic position in Western philosophy is Schopenhauer's pessimistic conception of life as eternal suffering, from which the reasonable man seeks escape through the annihilation of his forever-striving indi-vidual will. Interestingly, this teaching has much in common with some aspects of the Buddhistic doctrine of Nirvana, which holds that this world is an illusion and possesses no ultimate reality. But, while nihilistic elements are indeed present, I believe that Schopenhauer's total philosophy cannot be termed nihilistic. It is particularly in his ethical theory that one indeed finds positive elements.

The doctrine that the visible phenomenal world we live in is unreal and represents only a mirror of the inner, true nature of reality leads Schopenhauer to the conviction that our separate individual wills are merely transitory, temporal phenomena of the true, unified will. The true meaning of the multiplicity of selves with their private interests and desires is revealed only in the metaphysical unity of the cosmic will. And with this identification of the individual will with the will as a whole, virtue begins. The tormentor and the tormented become one; the suffering of the whole world is felt as one's own. The moral man begins to see his face in the other's, to identify the "I" with the "Thou"; his actions reveal the metaphysical unity that lies beyond the illusory multiplicity of individual wills. Schopenhauer's ethical theory, which can here be mentioned only briefly, is sufficient ground for a contention that his total philosophy cannot be termed nihilistic in the strict sense of the term.

Less strictly defined, the term nihilism has been used to denote sceptical positions, such as those of the ancient sceptic Pyrrho, the medieval philosophies of Duns Scotus and William of Ockham, and the critical analysis of Hume. Scepticism, however, must be distinguished from nihilism, as used in both the sophistic and the tragic senses. It does not represent a total, radical denial of the possibility of truth and the meaningfulness of existence. Its emphasis is on doubt and limits. It denies man's ability to comprehend the ultimate nature of things "behind" phenomena, and attain knowledge that is complete, absolute, and certain.

It is critical of the dogmatic teaching of scholasticism and its concern with a remote transcendental reality, with eternal verities and an abstract realm of values. It rejects rationalistic system-building with its unproved postulates and its claim of the certainty of knowledge. But scepticism does not deny the possibility of knowledge in general, provided this knowledge is based upon a realistic appraisal of the bounds of human understanding, and is limited to the methods of a thoroughgoing empiricism. However, while scepticism is less negative and radical than the sophistic nihilism of Gorgias of Leontini, it is by no means equal to Nietzsche's positive position, where nihilism is interpreted as an ultimately creative concept.

Most typically, the term *nihilism* has been used by realists in their polemic against idealism. In this sense it was first introduced in 1799 by F. H. Jacobi* in his attacks on Fichte, and later by the Scottish metaphysician William Hamilton.**

Nietzsche himself introduces radically new elements and perspectives on nihilism in his analysis of its origin and meaning. To this analysis he devotes the first book of *The Will to Power;* further references can be found mainly in *The Gay Science* and *The Genealogy of Morals.*[5] However, whether treated directly or not, nihilism in its various meanings is of central concern to all of Nietzsche's writings, and remains a necessary part of his tragic philosophy.

II

To reach a clearer understanding of Nietzsche's conception of nihilism, the following two passages are of impor-

---

* Friedrich Heinrich Jacobi, *Sendschreiben an Fichte* (Hamburg: Fr. Perthes, 1799).

** Quotations from Hamilton's *Lectures on Metaphysics* can be found in *Vocabulaire de la Philosophie* (Paris: Presses Universitaires de la France).

tance. In *The Will to Power* Nietzsche asks: "What is the meaning of nihilism?" And he answers: "That the highest values are devaluated."[6]

And in *The Gay Science* the cry of the madman announces the death of God and with it the rise of a nihilistic age:

> Have you not heard of that madman who lit a lantern in the bright morning hours, ran to the market place and cried incessantly "I seek God! I seek God!" As many of those who do not believe in God were standing around just then, he provoked much laughter. "Did he get lost?" said one. "Did he lose his way like a child?" said another. "Or is he hiding? Is he afraid of us? Has he gone on a voyage, or emigrated?"— Thus they shouted and laughed. The madman jumped into their midst and pierced them with his glances. "Whither is God?" he cried. "I shall tell you! We have killed him—you and I! All of us are his murderers!"[7]

For Nietzsche, the problem of nihilism arises out of the discovery that "God is dead." By "God" Nietzsche here means the historical God of the Christian tradition. But more importantly, in a wider philosophical sense, God symbolizes the whole Platonic-Christian realm of a transcendent reality and its supersensible, absolute values that have dominated the Western tradition.

The "event" of the death of God and the analysis of its causes and consequences dominate all of Nietzsche's later works. But this idea is already present in writings preceding the famous statement of 1882 from *The Gay Science*. In a passage from the years between 1869 and 1872 (published posthumously in the *Nachlass*), he says: "Either we die because of our religion or our religion dies because of us. I believe in the old Germanic saying: All gods must die."[8] Indeed, the pronouncement of the death of God must have been a familiar theme for Nietzsche, the son and grandson of Lutheran ministers, who, in his early youth, must have heard Luther's chorale "Gott selbst ist gestorben" sung many times in church. And later he must have been acquainted with Hegel's and Pascal's use of this pronouncement, as well as those of Jacob Boehme and Meister Eckhart. Nietzsche's statement, however, assumes its own specific meaning and does not belong in the sphere of the religious in the narrow sense. It is neither an atheistic statement, nor a cry for the revival of the old faith, nor a Hegelian attempt to celebrate in the abyss of nothingness a new speculative resurrection of God.* Instead, it represents a repudiation and comprehensive critique of the whole Platonic-Christian tradition of transcendence as well as a diagnosis of nineteenth-century civilization that—while no longer believing in this tradition—still gave it lip service.

In the dictum "God is dead," Nietzsche wants to characterize the historical movement that was initiated by Platonism, passed through centuries of Christian teaching, and reached its climax and crisis in his own time. This movement "is still on the way." It is a movement that Nietzsche calls nihilistic because it is either based upon false, transcendent values that deprecate this life, or it accepts the void and emptiness that resulted from the collapse of these values. Nietzsche's analysis of nihilism clearly establishes an indictment of Western civilization, and is a revolt against its transcendental metaphysics and dualistic moral order. But— and this is all too often overlooked—his analysis is, above all, an attempt to help lead the nineteenth century out of the void that resulted from the fall of its traditional values and achieve what he calls a "revaluation of values."

---

* G. W. F. Hegel, *Glaube und Wissen* in *Gesammelte Werke*, 4 vols. (Berlin: Duncker & Humblot, 1832), 1: 157.

The "highest values," the acceptance and subsequent loss of which are the "meaning of nihilism," originate from the Platonic-Christian tradition, which placed philosophy "under the guidance of morality."[9] They are the eternal, immutable values of Plato's realm of ideas, and the transcendent, supersensible norms of Christianity, which transformed the Platonic "Good" into the Christian God. These values are, according to Nietzsche, nihilistic because they are based upon a false foundation: a conception of being that is static and immutable, existing in a transcendent realm of universal essences. This view denies reality to the world we live in, the world of the senses, of change, and opposition, and degrades it into a secondary world of semblance and illusion. But the fall of these values creates a situation that Nietzsche considers equally nihilistic, since this fall does not in itself lead to a revaluation of values, but merely to a void and crisis.

God is dead—the highest values are devaluated. The world has lost all meaning and content. Nietzsche saw with deep insight the dilemma and despair that resulted from modern man's loss of faith. He recognized that the "death of God" did not have only intellectual and theological consequences, but—and this was of primary concern and urgency to him— also penetrated the deepest strata of man's total psychic life. While the advance of science had brought about the collapse of the transcendent ideals by which men had lived for centuries, it offered no substitute. Science could not replace the religious experience, having no equivalent for the religious symbols and images that had earlier pervaded man's whole life from birth to death. Being confined to the experience of the natural world, it could not replace the individual's concrete religious connection with a transcendent realm of being that had provided comfort and promise. Instead, it offered a universe that was neutral and alien to man's deepest aspirations and needs, a universe in which man felt alone and homeless.

In the first chapter of *The Will to Power*, Nietzsche names as the "highest values" the concepts of unity, purpose, and truth, and he describes the dilemma and emptiness that result from the devaluation of these categories.

With the loss of the belief in unity, the universe is no longer understood as an absolute, unchanging, eternal whole that possesses permanence and substance. The old metaphysical concept of being is destroyed and with its destruction man loses his identification with something higher and more unified than the constant change and becoming apparent to his senses. The relation between individual self-consciousness and the universal "all," between human existence and "being-as-such," is destroyed. The eternal, absolute essences and forms by which man had found and measured his own values are abandoned. He is alone and faces a void.

With the loss of a sense of purpose, resulting from the denial of a teleological universe, the foundation of a moral world order is shattered. Man no longer possesses ideals and absolute goals toward which to strive. He has lost all direction and purpose. In despair and fear he faces the dilemmas of existence without the comfort and security of eternal goals, norms, and categorical imperatives. He is lost, without a God and without the promise of a better world.

The devaluation of the categories of unity and purpose brings about the destruction of the traditional vision of a metaphysical world that is whole, ordered, and eternal, and that exists as the "true" world of being beyond change and becoming. What is left is a world of mere appearance and semblance, possessing no certainty or permanence, having no goals, no unity, no truth, no being. A "horror vacui" seizes man, whose basic trait it is that he needs a goal and "that he would rather will nothingness than not will at all."[10]

> What indeed has happened? The feeling of valuelessness was attained when one realized that the total character of existence must not be interpreted by means of the concept "purpose," or that of "unity" or "truth." . . . There is no unity in the multiplicity of happenings: the character of existence is not "true" but false. . . . Briefly, the categories "purpose," "oneness" and "being," with which we gave value to the world, are withdrawn by us—and now the world looks valueless.[11]

Nietzsche calls the concepts of unity, purpose, and truth "cosmological values," while also referring to them as "subjective categories of reason." As cosmological values they are those "higher values" which the Platonic-Christian tradition falsely endowed with objective validity, whereas they are in fact merely subjective categories, created to satisfy the psychological and practical needs of man. Nietzsche's "subjective categories" are not only in opposition to the rationalistic tradition in its various forms, but they also are opposed to Kant's conception of the categories. Although both Kant and Nietzsche are forerunners of twentieth-century pragmatism, Nietzsche's position is much more radical and closer to the contemporary interpretation of pragmatic theory. He is certainly greatly influenced by Kant's critical philosophy, which limits the categories of understanding to the phenomenal world. But his rejection of the rationalistic claims is, unlike Kant's, uncompromising, denying the Kantian view of the categories as being *a priori* forms of the mind that make objective science possible.

Kant's and Nietzsche's respective conceptions of the categories reveal the fundamental difference between the critical and the tragic approach. Kant's critique leads him into the realm of pure reason and man's moral consciousness; Nietzsche's tragic philosophy leads him into nihilism. Nietzsche's polemic against Kant, as well as his full position in regard to the problem of truth, is the subject of the next chapter. But what must here be stressed is Nietzsche's demand that the "highest values," which were falsely projected into the world, be "devaluated" and "withdrawn." Now the world no longer has unity, purpose, truth. Result: "The belief in the categories of reason is the cause of nihilism. We have measured the value of the world by categories which refer to a merely fictitious world."[12]

With the loss of the belief in the objective validity of the categories, the so-called "true" world of the Platonic-Christian tradition loses its meaningfulness. Its metaphysical foundation is destroyed, together with all the ideals, norms, and values erected on the basis of it. The true world that Plato had held accessible to the sage by an intellectual ascent to the Good no longer exists. The true world that the Christian church had promised to the pious and repentant sinner —a world beyond suffering and evil—becomes an illusion. There is no authority, neither that of faith nor that of reason. Together with the death of God goes the collapse of the whole Platonic-Christian teaching, whose philosophical thought and culture were built upon the belief in a harmonious, teleological universe and an immortal soul. The "true" world becomes a "fable . . . let us discard it."[13]

III

Nietzsche's radical critique of Platonic-Christian teaching has left us with an empty void and nothingness. The fall of the Western tradition has brought about the crisis of nihilism. "The time has come when we have to pay for having been

Christians for two thousand years. We lose the support which gave meaning to our lives."[14] But having led, in his analysis of nihilism, to a state of negativity and emptiness, Nietzsche now has the task of finding "the exit and hole through which one arrives at something," to construct a new culture that can lead mankind out of the crisis of nihilism. "How to philosophize with a hammer" is the subtitle of *The Twilight of the Idols*. But the hammer is not only a tool of destruction; it is also an instrument of reconstruction. As Nietzsche never ceased to stress, both functions are involved in the creation of new values: "And whoever wants to be a creator . . . must first be an annihilator and break values."[15]

By bringing about the fall of what he considered to be the long tradition of a pseudometaphysics that had grounded the temporal in the eternal, the spatial in the infinite, and the human in the divine, Nietzsche carried Western metaphysics, as Heidegger points out,* to its ultimate conclusion and thereby brought about its turning point, "die Umkehrung des Platonismus." By proving the falseness of the "higher values," Nietzsche also wants to prove the falseness of Plato's division of all being into two worlds of unequal ontological rank: the "true," transcendent world of ideas, and the inferior world of the senses and nature. The distinction between a true and an apparent world now becomes meaningless. Along with the devaluation of the highest values goes the fall of Plato's "true" world; what is left is the apparent world, which is now the only world that exists and thus becomes the true world. The reversal of Platonism is accomplished. The world of the senses, of change, contradiction, and suffering is no longer a mere shadow and illu-

---

* Martin Heidegger, "Nietzsches Wort 'Gott ist tot,'" in *Holzwege* (Frankfurt a.M.: Klostermann, 1957); also in his *Nietzsche*, 2 vols. (Pfullingen: Neske, 1961).

sion, a descent into darkness; it is the only reality we possess and must live in. Transcendent metaphysics is replaced by a metaphysics of life and existence, by a new ontology which alone can be meaningful for modern man and his existential concerns.

The empty void into which Nietzsche's critique had led gains new significance. Nothingness is no longer a mere absence of content, an indeterminate contrast to being, but is revealed as possessing a positive relation to being. Nothingness belongs to the creative act of overcoming, through which we must first abolish old idols and superstitions in order to achieve a significant revaluation. Nietzsche's novel and original interpretation of the concept of nothingness plays an important part in twentieth-century existential philosophies, particularly in Heidegger's new ontology. Further related aspects will be discussed in Part II, Chapter 3.

But while Nietzsche is indeed an important precursor of contemporary existential thought, his critique of traditional metaphysics contains elements that are absent in later thinkers. And it is these elements which give his critique its truly tragic dimension. Nietzsche's revolt against Western philosophical systems is not only distinguished from all previous critiques of sceptical and critical philosophies by its complete lack of compromise, its passion, despair, and awareness of crisis, but it also differs from later anti-metaphysical thought by its greater complexity. Nietzsche was a man of great imagination and perhaps even greater religious and metaphysical yearning. In spite of his violent polemic against transcendent metaphysics, his break is never complete. His tragic philosophy represents both a revolt against these traditions as well as a deep involvement in them.

While Nietzsche himself, in contrast to Hegel who regarded his system as the culmination of all previous philosophical traditions, claims that his own philosophy is a new beginning, an attempt to create a new "free spirit" of the "dangerous perhaps,"[16] he remains, in fact, rooted in Western traditions. His relation to them possesses the complexity and ambiguity that are characteristic of his Dionysian tragic concept. His "philosophizing with a hammer" is mingled with a longing for the very values that he destroys. While, by his reversal of Platonism, he creates a metaphysics of change and becoming, the yearning for the eternal and universal remains part of his thought. He vehemently attacks all attempts at transcendence that claim to penetrate behind phenomena and grasp the absolute; he reduces traditional metaphysics to a fiction of the intellect in which unity, totality, and permanence are but subjective categories of the mind, which man reads into nature. But, at the same time, he is filled with a deep metaphysical longing to break the principle of individuation and "tear asunder the veil of Maya," to behold the vision of primal oneness behind appearances.

This longing is evident not only in his early writings, but—as will be shown below—it is also present in his later, mature thought, although to a much lesser degree. While not always acknowledged by Nietzsche himself, the conflict between his radical doubting and metaphysical longing is never resolved, and contributes to the complexity and ambiguity of his philosophical thought as well as to the difficulties of interpretation. This conflict must also have been responsible for the deep suffering and despair that accompanied Nietzsche's search for meaning and truth. Indeed, perhaps his violent diatribes and his excessive language are, at least in part, caused by his own inner conflicts and frustrations, derived from his inability to make a complete break with traditions he intellectually rejected but was deeply involved in psychologically. Nietzsche's dilemma is shared by many today. The abolishment of the transcendent world and its absolute values does not solve the problem of the human spirit, but merely brings into desperate relief the pathos of the human situation. The death of God and loss of faith does not remove our longing for those higher values. With Samuel Beckett and his tragic, absurd heroes Estragon and Vladimir, we wait for Godot to come*—Godot, of whose identity we have no knowledge and of whose justice and benevolence we despair.

IV

The act of overcoming the negative consequences of Nietzsche's radical critique is not simple. In addition to elements already mentioned, there are others, of which the concepts of "amor fati" and "eternal recurrence" are the most important. While a fuller and deeper understanding of the process of overcoming nihilism requires a clarification of these concepts, a significant analysis would be difficult to undertake at this point and must therefore be postponed to a later discussion.

What must be noted here, in the context of Nietzsche's analysis of nihilism, is his distinction between various stages of nihilism. He stresses three forms: weak or passive nihilism, incomplete nihilism, and strong or classic nihilism. These various forms are not completely separate and independent stages; they interpenetrate, with each stage containing elements of the other, while also destroying some and adding new ones—thus achieving an act of overcoming, the Hegelian "aufheben" that cancels, preserves, and elevates.

"Weak nihilism" is passive and tired, a sign of fear and

---

* Samuel Beckett, *Waiting for Godot* (New York: Grove Press, 1954).

defeat. Here one finds the disillusioned individual who has lost belief in traditional values and goals, and cannot bear this life of suffering and pain without the hope and promise of a truer and better world, without the direction of goals and moral imperatives. This world of evil and suffering remains a world of nonbeing and error to him. His negation has brought him no freedom, no strength, no growth. His spirit is exhausted and broken. The only alternatives left to him are: to stick to the old traditional values in spite of the fact that he no longer believes in them; to create new authorities and idols that will replace the old ones that have fallen; or to negate life altogether in resignation and defeat. Nietzsche gives this succinct description of the weak nihilist. "A nihilist is a man who judges that this world as it is should not exist and that the world as it should be does not exist. Therefore existence has no meaning: the pathos of the 'Umsonst'."[17]

Weak nihilism, which Nietzsche calls "the decline of the power of the spirit,"[18] is, he claims, as old as philosophical thought. It is represented in the pessimistic views of Schopenhauer and the romantics, which are based on passivity, resignation, and resentment. It is expressed in Kant's transcendental world which, Nietzsche asserts, was invented only in order to create a ground for his own new idols of freedom, morality, and a God whose existence could not be proved but still must remain a possibility in the supersensible sphere of the "beyond of reason."[19] It is contained in Hegel's attempt to replace the old God with "the will to the deification of the All in whose contemplation and exploration peace and happiness can be found."[20]

"Incomplete nihilism" is a state of transition, "in the midst of which we live."[21] Here man has found the will to negate more fully and meaningfully, to deepen the problem, but he has not yet found "the strength to revaluate values and to deify and affirm the apparent world of becoming as the only world."[22] He is not yet the "higher man" who reaches the stage of active and complete nihilism.

Nietzsche sees his own age as a period of transition, an age that recognizes the falseness of established values and traditions but has not yet broken with their spirit. It is an age that is still filled with the longing for absolute goals and purposes, a longing that is deeply rooted in the nature of man. "God is dead; but as is the way with human beings, there will perhaps be thousands of years yet in which his shadow will be seen in caves. And we must also defeat his shadow."[23] The madman who cries "God is dead" is one of the "preparatory men [who] cannot yet leap into being out of nothing . . . but who prepares this age for one yet higher."[24] Conscious of his dilemma, he cries out in anguish: "Whither are we moving? Away from all suns? . . . Are we not straying through an infinite nothing? . . . Has it not become colder? Is not night and more night coming on all the time?"[25]

The madman is no longer one of the multitude in the marketplace who have lost their faith but do not suffer or probe deeply; who laugh and mock and refuse to face the consequences of the death of God but cover up the truth with veils of illusions and hypocrisies in order to preserve their "green pasture happiness," their customs and comforts:

At last [the madman] threw his lantern on the ground, and it broke and went out. "I come too early," he said then; "my time has not yet come. This tremendous event is still on its way, still wandering—it has not yet reached the ears of man. Lightning and thunder require time, the light of the stars requires time, deeds require time even after they are done, in order to be seen or heard. This deed is still more distant from them than the most distant stars—and yet they have done it themselves."[26]

"This tremendous event is still on its way" today. Like Nietzsche's age, our own can be termed an age of transition. The madman's cry is heard in the wasteland of our cities, in our churches and universities, and, above all, in the gatherings of the young. It is heard with anguish and despair against the mockery and disdain of the complacent and uncommitted. Again, the madman who is one of the "preparatory men" came too early. And again, it will require time before revolt, negation, and despair can be turned into affirmation. The preparatory men, while "preparing this age for one yet higher," are not yet the "higher men," the "free spirits" who are creators of new values and a new tragic age. They are not yet representatives of a nihilism that is strong and active.

"Classic [or] active nihilism" is to Nietzsche "a phenomenon of strength and of the heightened power of the spirit."[27] Here weak nihilism is overcome. The strong, heroic individual not only recognizes the artificial and deceptive character of traditional values—as the madman did—but has the strength to free himself from the need for these deceptions. He has the courage and power to accept and affirm life as it truly is and achieve a revaluation of values. "God is dead"; now man himself is responsible for creating his own values, grounding them, not in a transcendent realm, but in his own existence. In its heroic and affirmative spirit strong nihilism is, to Nietzsche, the foundation for a new philosophy of the future and a revival of the tragic age. The tragic circle is completed: the rise of nihilism and its overcoming. The problem of nihilism is "the problem of weakness or strength . . . : the weak are broken by it; the stronger destroy what does not break; the strongest overcome the need for goals and norms. This together constitutes the tragic age."[28]

The strong, "ecstatic" nihilist grasps the fullest meaning of the cry of the madman who came too early for the masses of the marketplace and has himself not yet risen to the truly positive and creative aspects of his pronouncement. The ecstatic nihilist senses behind the madman's cry of lament and despair a feeling of joy and liberation. "We philosophers and 'free spirits' feel at the pronouncement of the death of God the rays of a new dawn. . . . At last the horizon appears free again . . . at last our ships can sail again . . . the sea, our sea is open again; perhaps there was never before such an open sea."[29] The old God has died; the old values are lost. The true world becomes a fable. "Which world remains? The apparent world? . . . End of longest error; zenith of mankind. Incipit Zarathustra."[30]

The void that the death of God and the fall of the Platonic-Christian values have created is not mere nonbeing and darkness. Nietzsche interprets this void as the greatest challenge in human history, for now man himself becomes fully responsible. The void is a space of freedom, a freedom to create new values. The deepest dimensions of Nietzsche's conception of freedom will emerge in the course of this study, after various other aspects of his philosophy, primarily that of *amor fati,* have been introduced. But whatever other elements belong to it, Nietzsche's conception of freedom grows out of his nihilistic position. Freedom can be achieved only after a destruction of old idols and empty traditions, after a radical critique of the Christian and Kantian views, where freedom exists only in the transcendent world of the Christian heaven or the Kantian noumenal realm, and is based on metaphysical and moral beliefs and attitudes that "condemn life." Nietzsche's new freedom exists "beyond good and evil," independent of traditional moralities and their transcendent metaphysics. It is not based on a dualistic world order, but is meaningful for this life only, the life of the senses, of conflict and despair.

The void that was caused by the death of God becomes for the Nietzschean "higher man" the foundation of a new faith and piety. He no longer reveres a transcendent God, but worships life itself despite its suffering and contradictions. "That which differentiates us is not that we find no God, neither in history nor in nature nor behind nature . . . but that we do not feel that what has been revered as God is godlike."[31] The new divinity that replaces the God who has died is life itself and the greatness of man—his heroic will to destroy and, in destroying, to build and create. "All beauty and majesty which we have loaned to real and imagined things, all this must be returned as the property and product of man."[32] Nietzsche expresses this thought poetically in *The Gay Science*:

There is a lake which one day refused to flow off and erected a dam where it had hitherto flowed off; ever since, this lake has been rising higher and higher. Perhaps this very renunciation will also lend us the strength to bear the renunciation itself; perhaps man will rise ever higher and higher when once he ceases to flow out into God.[33]

Nietzsche's conception of nihilism as a process of destruction and overcoming is vitally connected with his concept of the "will to power." The will to power becomes the new foundation and essence of life, which Nietzsche substitutes for the dethroned God. "Where I found life, I found will to power . . . where the power to create, to will, has grown to such heights that it has no more need for false interpretations and fictitious constructions."[34]

The will to power replaces the lost categories of purpose, unity, and truth. It is a creative force that has no purpose and goal, unless it is the goal within itself, the will to create within its own contradictions and its own productive powers, the will to grow and overcome itself. The will to power does not possess the categories of harmony and unity, unless there is harmony and unity in the tension and the dynamic play of its antithetical forces. It does not possess truth and being, unless it is tragic truth that is full of conflicts and contradictions, based upon a metaphysics of being as eternal destruction and eternal creation.

> And do you know what the world is to me? . . . An immensity of power, without beginning, without end . . . this Dionysian world that eternally creates itself and eternally destroys itself; this secret world of double bliss, this "beyond good and evil". . . . This world is the will to power . . . and nothing else.[35]

The concept of the will to power becomes the "exit and hole" through which Nietzsche passes from the supersensible realm of eternal ideas and the disillusionment of its fall to a new affirmation and faith. "God is dead"; let us worship life and the will to ever more life. The "true" world has fallen; let us revere the world of the senses, of change and contradiction. Let us revere the will to negate and to overcome.

V

The various stages of nihilism that Nietzsche distinguishes

are, as noted before, not static and separate from each other, but interact and interpenetrate in the development of the individual and the history of mankind. Nietzsche conceives history as a dialectical movement in which periods of decline continuously interchange with those of height and where, in fact, the highest cultural achievements must, at the same time, also contain elements of negativity. The event of nihilism, in its various forms, is not limited to any particular period of history or to any particular nation. It is a constantly effective historical force that, in different degrees, is at work in all periods and all ages. Nietzsche sees nihilism as a basic law of history, a necessary, inescapable phenomenon that pervades the entire history of mankind and Western civilization. It is a power that is present in all cultures as a driving force, a part of the curve of life as it rises and falls. It is ever-present, having no beginning or end, and is "still on the way."[36] "What I relate is the history of the next two centuries. I describe what is coming, what cannot come otherwise: the rise of nihilism. Its history can already be told: necessity itself is here at work."[37]

Nihilism as a historical movement is for Nietzsche not destructive but tragic, containing within its critical and analytical activity the very basis for reconstruction. "We need new values, a counter-movement which presupposes nihilism logically and psychologically and can come only out of nihilism."[38] A nihilistic movement is present in every creative period of history in which a high cultural level is achieved. It was present in ancient Greece and the Renaissance, both of which Nietzsche names as examples of strong, creative ages. "The symptoms of decline belong to times of enormous growth; each creative, powerful movement of humanity has at the same time produced a nihilistic movement."[39]

Nietzsche's views are contrary to optimistic conceptions

that understand the historical process in terms of straightforward development and progress. He repudiates both the Christian theistic view of history as the steady advance of mankind toward a far-off divine event, and the Darwinian conception of evolution as meaning progress rather than simply change. He similarly rejects Hegel's conception of the world process as the progressive development of the human spirit and self-consciousness toward ever greater stages of freedom and ever higher levels of consciousness, where every age, nation, and civilization is but the embodiment of an idea that unfolds progressively throughout time.

World history, to Nietzsche, does not relate a story of progress.

> Mankind does not represent a development toward something higher or better or stronger in the manner in which it is thought today. Progress is only a modern idea, that means a false idea. . . . Humanity does not advance. . . . The total aspect is that of a vast, experimental laboratory where a few things succeed, scattered throughout all ages, and immensely many fail, where all order, logic, connection and obligation are absent.[40]

What is later in time is not necessarily more valuable. The highest, strongest historical periods and the most creative individuals are not products of a steady advance and development. Thus the culture of the ancient Greeks and its revival in the Renaissance were, according to Nietzsche, never surpassed or even ever reached again, whereas the nineteenth century is, to him, an age of decadence, an untragic age of weakness and defeat. "The goal of humanity does not lie in the end,"[41] in the completion of a progressive, evolutionary movement, but it lies above history in the supra-historical events of mankind. These events may have occurred three thousand years ago in the culture of an ancient people or in the attempt to revive that culture. "The European of today remains in his values far below the European of the Renaissance; the course of history is not necessarily a development to higher stages."[42]

Nietzsche conceives the function of history as threefold: critical, antiquarian, and monumental. Critical history "judges and condemns"; antiquarian history is "conservatism and reverence"; and monumental history contains the active, creative elements that are provided by the heroic actions of the strong individual. History in this threefold function is like a timeless theme in which supra-historical forces are forever at work, "condemning, revering, and creating." This is exactly the meaning of nihilism and tragic culture: to cancel, preserve, and elevate, and thus turn a weak nihilism into one of strength. Nihilism becomes the basic law of history, present in all ages and all civilizations.

Critical history must precede as well as remain part of an age of strength and productivity. It must provide the elements of doubt and despair that lead to a radical critique of the past and present. It must diagnose and condemn what is sick and decadent, and thus bring about the destruction of false and hollow pseudo-cultures. Without critique and fundamental change every culture would deteriorate into an undynamic state of stagnation and sterility. "Man must have strength to break up the past. . . . He must bring the past to the bar of judgment, interrogate it remorselessly and finally condemn it."[43] Critical tendencies are, as Nietzsche sees it, most fully developed in the most creative periods of history and in the strongest, highest individuals. But to these critical elements those of antiquarian and monumental history must be added in order to achieve the highest culture that Nietzsche designates as tragic. Ultimately, it is always the development of the higher individual, his strength and creative will to power, that is the meaning of history for Nietzsche. "The goal of humanity does not lie in the end, but in its highest specimen."[44] It lies in a Phidias, an Aeschylus, Heraclitus, or Michelangelo, in the greatness of the individual and his creative powers.

Nietzsche's analysis of the origin and causes of nihilism is primarily an attempt to find a new meaning in a world that has lost faith in its old values and traditions. It is an attempt to reconstruct the basis of a culture that Nietzsche claims was destroyed when Platonic-Christian concepts of being and morality became dominant in Western thought, a culture that is tragic, containing the elements of both negation and affirmation, both despair and exultation. Whether Nietzsche succeeded in achieving his aim cannot be determined at this point, and indeed it may remain an unanswered question at the end of this study. But whatever our judgment may be, the passionate concern of Nietzsche's undertaking cannot be doubted. Nor can we doubt the affirmative spirit which, in spite of negation and doubt, pervades his passionate search for truth and meaning throughout his attempt at a revaluation of values.

> I probed into the causes and origins and thus I lost my reverence. . . . It grew strange and lonesome around me; but that which is to be revered in me, secretly it bore fruit . . . and a tree grew in whose shadow I sit, the tree of the future.[45]

3
THE PROBLEM OF TRUTH

The belief in truth begins with doubt in all previously held "truths."[1]

"Truth" is not something that is there to be found and discovered, but something that must be created and can be called a process, or better, a will to conquer which has no end . . . a process ad infinitum. . . . It is a word for the "will to power."[2]

I

Nietzsche's philosophy has been interpreted as nihilistic, but it is particularly his treatment of the problem of knowledge that has been attacked as producing a radical nihilism. His critics claim that not only does Nietzsche fail to solve particular epistemological problems, but he destroys the notion of truth itself. Pronouncements such as "nothing is true," or "the lie is more divine than truth"[3] are often quoted as examples of his radically nihilistic stand.

In contrast to these accusations, I contend that Nietzsche's philosophy represents a passionate search for truth, with conclusions that do not at all destroy the meaning of truth, but only the traditional conceptions of it. His revolt against traditional systems does not lead to radical nihilism, but to a new conception of knowledge. This view has become fundamental for twentieth-century thought, making Nietzsche a precursor of contemporary epistemological theories in their pragmatic and existential interpretations.

Since Nietzsche's concept of truth evolves within the framework of his tragic philosophy, it is indeed based upon a nihilistic foundation. But what has been overlooked by critics of his epistemology is the same fact that led to misconceptions of his philosophy in general, namely, that here, too, he makes a significant distinction between "weak nihilism" and a "nihilism of strength." Whereas both forms of nihilism agree in rejecting optimistic philosophies and in claiming a metaphysical foundation for their pessimistic world views, they differ in their evaluation of this pessimistic foundation. In weak nihilism it is seen as negative and destructive, whereas it is positive and creative in a nihilism of strength.

This failure to recognize the distinction between a nihilism that merely destroys and one that arrives at a revaluation of values is in large part responsible for the erroneous conception of Nietzsche's epistemological investigation as being radically destructive. But the blame is not entirely on the side of the Nietzsche reader. Nietzsche himself contributes much to the misunderstanding by his inconsistency in the use of the word "truth." Like many other terms, he uses "truth" in two senses, without clarifying which one he is referring to: the old, traditional meaning, which he rejects, or the tragic meaning, which he affirms. Thus, for instance, when he demands "the doubting of all truth,"[4] he refers only to a conception of truth as absolute and certain and not to one that takes into account the fact that "the highest values" of the Western tradition "have fallen."

Karl Jaspers gives a further example of the double meaning of the Nietzschean use of the term *truth* when he analyzes the statement from *The Genealogy of Morals,* "Nothing is true; all is permitted," and says:

> There is something ambiguous about this sentence. At first it sounds as if Nietzsche were dropping into a hole. . . . Conversely, however, the sentence may be seen in a meaning altogether different from this destructive one. It may make room for the most genuine roots of man. If such can be its bearing, the "weakness" which sinks into chaos is to be conquered by a "nihilism of strength." "Nothing is true, all is permitted" shall bring forth a deeper truth than any which has ever been known. *

Nietzsche's new approach to truth raises many questions and also many doubts as to its ultimate outcome, but it can never be denied that his will to truth is diametrically opposed to a nihilism that merely attacks. Nor can it be doubted that he desperately tries to find a way out of the dilemma into which his search for truth leads him—a search that is guided by an almost fanatical intellectual honesty and integrity—and occupies him throughout his entire philosophical life.

Nietzsche does not present us with a systematic theory of knowledge. Any attempt to construct one on the basis of his scattered remarks, aphorisms, poetry, and myth would be a difficult, if not impossible, task. It would, above all, be contrary to the intention of his thought and lead to a

---

* Karl Jaspers, *Nietzsche and Christianity* (New York: Henry Regnery Co., 1961), p. 83.

distortion of his views. Nietzsche, as Walter Kaufmann rightly asserts, is not a system builder, but a problem thinker.* His treatment of knowledge and truth raises problems and doubts that are not always solved or solvable. It leads into paradoxes and labyrinths in which one often feels inextricably lost. But while this lack of coherent form and definiteness makes it exceedingly difficult to discern a systematic development and clear direction, there does exist a dominant pattern in Nietzsche's epistemological investigation just as in his metaphysical and ethical thought. This pattern is that of a nihilism of strength in its double function: the task of "breaking old tables" and thus establishing the pessimistic foundation, and the consequent task of making this work of destruction meaningful and creative.

Thus Nietzsche's treatment of the problem of knowledge must and does begin with establishing the nihilistic basis through a merciless critique of traditional philosophical systems. "The belief in truth begins with the doubt of all previously held 'truths.' "5 Pessimism and doubt are necessary premises; "nihilism is the logical and psychological presupposition" for a new metaphysics of life and being, as well as for a new tragic conception of truth. Nietzsche's critique is not entirely without precedents, owing some of its fundamental concepts to the philosophical traditions of Bacon, Locke, and, above all, Hume and Kant. Nietzsche is heir to Hume's scepticism, which limits the power of pure reason to analytical truths; he is heir to Kant's critical philosophy, which restricts the categories of the understanding to the phenomenal world. It is within the Humean and Kantian tradition that Nietzsche becomes the leader of the revolt against classical rationalism, which is the dominant

---

* Walter A. Kaufmann, *Nietzsche* (Princeton: Princeton University Press, 1950), p. 61.

motif of twentieth-century critical philosophy. Even those philosophers who, like Husserl, aim at a reaffirmation and "reconstruction of reason" have done so on the basis of a critique initiated by Kant and continued by Nietzsche.

But Nietzsche is not a mere mediator. His critique is extreme and radical, and distinguished from all previous ones by a passion and urgency that can be compared only with Kierkegaard's writings, with which, however, he was barely acquainted. It is directed not merely against one or another particular conception of truth, but against the very existence of truth in its traditional meaning. It does not only attack a particular epistemological system, but all systems, which, he claims, are based on unproven premises and empty deductions. It is not a Kantian critique, which aims at compromise and synthesis; rather, Nietzsche wants to demolish the very bases and presuppositions of all traditional epistemological views.

His violent, uncompromising critique expresses more fully than any preceding one the whole impact and crisis of rationalism, and is of specific importance and meaningfulness for the existential concerns of twentieth-century man. His mode of thinking is close to the modern age of anxiety and its conception of truth that borders on the edge of chaos and despair. His revolt against rationalism and the traditional conceptions of truth and knowledge is of particular importance to the "great negation" of our rebel young, whose thoroughgoing rejection of reason aims at a liberation of the nonrational forces of the human personality. Like Nietzsche, they challenge the scholar's ideal of objectivity and his cool, uninvolved mode of inquiry. With him, they search for alternative methods that will express the richness and versatility of our total experience of life—methods that will lead not to empty abstractions and statistical generalizations, but to the inner depth of our particular, immediate experiences, our passions and instincts, our fantasies and intuitions. But Nietzsche would warn against a confusion between creative passions that arise from controlled "strength" and are given Apollonian form, and those which remain unsublimated and, given complete license, can lead to barbarism.

II

Nietzsche's critique of traditional epistemological systems has been called a "historical critique of pure reason."[*] Indeed, with the pre-Socratics as the single exception, Nietzsche attacks the basic concepts of ancient thought, of scholasticism, of modern science and philosophy. "Falsehood and forgery pervade the whole history of philosophy."[6] He judges the whole foundation and structure of Western thought to be false and artificial, and attributes the blame to a philosophical and scientific ideal that was inherited from Socrates and Plato and ever since has dominated Western thought and Christian beliefs. He sees a tradition that is guided, not by a desire for truth, but by moralistic concerns and prejudices: by Plato's "divine dialectic," which equates knowledge with virtue, and by Christian teaching, which makes knowledge subordinate to the salvation of the soul. "The sense of truth is itself one of the highest and most powerful efflorescences of the moral sense."[7] All traditional conceptions of truth—including those of Kant, Hegel, and Schopenhauer—"the sceptical, epoch-making, as well as the historicizing and pessimistic attitude, have a moralistic origin."[8]

Motivated, according to Nietzsche, by moralistic interests,

---

[*] George Allen Morgan, *What Nietzsche Means* (Cambridge: Harvard University Press, 1943), p. 243.

traditional philosophy arrives at two central presuppositions: the absoluteness and certainty of knowledge, and the primacy and superiority of pure reason. It is these two basic claims that are the chief targets of Nietzsche's radical critique.

The problem of knowledge is, for Nietzsche, a metaphysical one. As Heidegger points out, it is "eine Frage des Seienden," a question of being. The idea of truth as eternal and absolute—the whole quest for certainty—goes hand in hand with, and presupposes, the belief in a universe that is static and fixed. Traditional truth, says Nietzsche, is but a form of "the ascetic ideal," which stands and falls with the Platonic concept of being and the Christian idea of God. Absolute truth, like absolute morality, presupposes the existence of another reality beyond the finite world of the senses, of change and opposition, which was held to be merely a world of "appearance and semblance." It assumes a reality that truly is, existing unchanged in a transcendent realm, be it the Platonic realm of eternal ideas or the Christian heavenly sphere.

With the development of new scientific concepts which reveal a reality that is dynamic and dialectical, the old truth as absolute, certain, and unconditional becomes meaningless, and must be replaced by one that is in accordance with this new interpretation of reality. Yet, Nietzsche complains, "it is still the old metaphysical belief upon which the belief in science rests. . . . We knowers of today, we unbelievers and anti-metaphysicians, we still take our fire from the flame which was lighted by a faith that is thousands of years old."[9] While accepting the dictum "God is dead," modern scientists and philosophers fail to accept its implications and continue to cling to values and beliefs that are based upon presuppositions they deny. They merely replace the theological spirit with a rationalistic one and transform the old scholastic idols into modern ones, based no longer on transcendent realms but on the supremacy of reason. In place of the scholastic belief in the certainty of revealed truth, they claim the certainty of individual consciousness; in place of a priori "clear and distinct" ideas, there is now the alleged certainty of the axioms of geometry, the principles of logic, and the laws of causality.

Nietzsche demands that modern philosophy genuinely face the fact that "God is dead," and with it the whole transcendent, supersensible realm and every philosophical view, ideal, and norm that have been erected on its basis. The world of the senses, of change, and of becoming is now the only world. It thus becomes the "real" and the "true" world. A new concept of truth must be created that accords with this changed conception of being and grows out of the dialectical pattern of life itself. It is a truth that is dynamic and problematic and contains change and contradiction, as does life itself. "Untruth must be derived from the 'true' character of things themselves."[10] "The falseness of a given judgment does not constitute an objection against it. . . . To renounce false judgments is to renounce life, to negate life."[11]

With the abolition of the transcendent "true" world, the distinction between reality and appearance falls, and with it the essential antithesis between false and true. And just as Nietzsche accomplished a revaluation of values and created a tragic morality beyond good and evil—wherein evil is a necessary part of good—so he creates a theory of knowledge beyond truth and falsity, where error is a necessary part of truth. With Hegel, and versus Kant, a logical conception of truth, in which only one of two contraries can be true, is

denied. Truth and falsity are now both part of every judgment, just as they are part of life. Thus Nietzsche asks:

> Whatever forces us to assume that there is an essential dif-
> ference between "true" and "false"? Is it not sufficient to
> assume different levels of semblance, lighter and darker
> shadows and tones of semblance—different values in the
> painter's sense of the term? . . . If you wanted to get rid of
> the world of semblance, there would be nothing left of your
> truth either.[12]

We ask with Nietzsche: "But how is truth possible in spite
of the fundamental untruth in knowledge?"[13] How can contradiction and error be called truth? How is it conceivable
that "the lie and not truth is divine"? It seems as if Nietzsche's attempt to prepare the negative premise of his tragic
conception of knowledge leads us into an abyss where the
possibility of truth itself is denied. And indeed, Nietzsche
goes on to deny not only the possibility, but also the desirability of a truth that is static, absolute, and certain.

The consciousness of certainty lacks the fundamental elements of tragedy and strong nihilism, the elements of doubt
and negation. Certainty leads to stagnation and the destruction of the will to create. "It is a prejudice that certainty
is more valuable than uncertainty and open seas."[14] "Perhaps
it is in this respect that our language sounds strangest."[15]
But this is the essence of strong nihilism: doubt, contradiction, and error are not negative, but positive, creative elements. They open new possibilities and new vistas and lead
to a more fruitful search for truth. Truth is not static and
lifeless, merely there for us to discover; it is changing and
dynamic and must ever be created anew by man. It has no
closed boundaries and definite solutions, but leads in its

limitless, unending course to invention and experimentation. It is in this sense that "the lie is more divine than truth," since truth in the traditional sense destroys the will to create.

The denial of absolute truth is, to speak with George A. Morgan, not an absolute denial of truth.* The new, tragic philosopher no longer needs synthetic judgments *a priori* to provide certainty and universality. He accepts a truth that is replete with uncertainties and ambiguities. He does not want to abolish error and falseness, but uncover their meaning and necessity. Error and falseness, in the tragic sense, must, according to Nietzsche, be distinguished from the meaning given them by traditional philosophers. In the latter they have a psychological basis in cowardice and fear; the fear of giving up old habits and beliefs, and facing "open seas." In contrast to this negativity, the tragic philosopher endows error and falseness with a metaphysical as well as an epistemological meaning. In both senses their essence is creativity. Error is derived from being itself, its continuous change and fundamental duality. "To renounce false judgments is to renounce life."[16] Error is further the creative tool of the "perilous philosopher of the perhaps," in his limitless, fearless road of experimentation. "Life is the condition of knowledge. To err is the condition of life. . . . The knowledge of errors does not cancel them out. We must love and cherish error. It is the very foundation of knowledge."[17]

The limits that Nietzsche sets to knowledge are very different from those of sceptical and critical philosophies. They are not the limits of the Lockean "historical plain method" and its paralyzing demand "to be content with what is attainable to us in this state." They are not those of Hume's atomistic account of knowledge, which lacks passion and

---

* Ibid., p. 256.

despair. They are not the limits that the critical philosophy of Kant arrives at. Unlike Kant, Nietzsche does not need a "Copernican revolution" in order to provide knowledge with certainty and universality. He does not ask "How are synthetic *a priori* propositions possible?" but "Why are synthetic *a priori* propositions necessary?" While previous philosophers, even when sceptical and critical, had still been guided by a deeply rooted longing for certainty, Nietzsche breaks completely with the concept of certainty and prepares the ground for what Charles Peirce calls a "new maturity," which replaces certainty of knowledge with various degrees of probability. He accepts a truth that is contradictory and changing, implying a never-ending search, a never-ending will to create. "Truth as something . . . which signifies process, or even more, a will to overcome which has no end."[18]

The limits that Nietzsche set to knowledge have become accepted limits in the twentieth century, which has finally caught up with Nietzsche in admitting that uncertainty is attached to any human enterprise. The sciences, precisely as Nietzsche had urged and anticipated with profound clarity, repudiate the possibility of rational certainty and predictable causality, and acknowledge the need for a revision of the meaning and function of truth. With the discoveries of Heisenberg concerning the principles of physics and Goedel concerning mathematical ambiguity, the sciences have arrived at the state where they breed paradoxes for reason itself. Philosophy, breaking with the classical, rationalistic tradition, redefines the concept of truth. In its pragmatic and existential orientations it rejects a truth that is conceptual, abstract, universal, and instead postulates a truth that is concrete and individual, filled with passion and intensity and rooted in the fundamental condition of human existence. Psychology, reflecting the changes in both science and philosophy, learns, from Freud, that man is largely nonrational in his motives and actions. Literature and art, discrediting the certitudes and unshakable basic assumptions of former ages, depict a world of shattered beliefs whose center is not rationality, clarity, and certainty, but only absurdity.

III

After attempting to destroy the optimistic beliefs of previous philosophers concerning the certainty of knowledge, Nietzsche attacks their second presupposition: the absolute primacy and superiority of man's reason. Max Scheler credits Nietzsche and Wilhelm Dilthey with having first recognized the fact that "reason was but an invention of the Greeks" and that the notion of "homo sapiens" had become what is most dangerous for any idea, namely, self-evident.* Indeed, Nietzsche traces the roots of rationalism to the teaching of Socrates and Plato. Socrates is for him the "father of rationalism," the archetype of the "theoretical man" who destroys the instinctual powers of man; who becomes the enemy of myth and tragedy, and the initiator of a decadent age in which the power of reason becomes "self-evident." Nietzsche would largely agree with Dilthey, who writes:

> The rationalistic position is rooted in the whole religious and metaphysical attitude . . . it takes reason to be the principle of world order and not an episodic fact on earth. Yet, today no one can escape the fact that this magnificent, religious, metaphysical background is no longer self-evident. One can no longer reject an opinion which considers the sovereign

---

* Max Scheler, *Philosophische Weltanschauung* (Bonn: Fr. Cohen, 1929), p. 25.

intellect of Descartes a passing and unique product of nature.
. . . The power of this reason to take possession of reality
through thought becomes a hypothesis or a "postulate."*

The alleged supremacy of man's reason is destroyed. *Homo
sapiens* is replaced by what Scheler calls *homo faber,* a creature of drives and practical needs.** Reason cannot gain
insight into the intelligible order of things and discover objective and absolute truth. Rather, it is an organizing power
that imposes upon the amorphous reality of changing phenomena its own logical forms as a means to order, synthesize,
and manipulate experience. The categories of the mind do
not possess objective validity. "We have no categories to
distinguish a 'world in itself' from a 'world of appearance.' "[19]
They are fictions which are created for two reasons: to satisfy the psychological and the pragmatic needs of man.

The psychological basis for the belief in the objective
validity of the categories, Nietzsche claims, is the same as
that for the belief in the certainty of knowledge: man's need
for order, permanency, security. It is this need, and not objective reality, that creates the belief in the unity of self-
identity, the permanency of an unchanging substratum, and
the existence of universal causal connections. The categories
are our own constructions; they have no basis in fact, but in
nonrational impulses and fears, in hopes and wishes.

This painting—which we call life and experience—has evolved
gradually . . . because we have, through millennia, looked at
the world with moral, aesthetic, religious claims, with blind
inclinations, passions or fears; because we have so wallowed

---

* Wilhelm Dilthey, "Erfahrung und Denken" in *Gesammelte Schriften,*
12 vols. (Leipzig: B. G. Teubner, 1921–58), 5: 88.
** Max Scheler, "Zur Idee des Menschen," in *Die Wissenschaft und die
Gesellschaft* (Leipzig: Der Neue-Geist, 1926).

in ill breeding of illogical thought, the world has gradually become variegated, tremendous, rich in meaning and spirit; it has acquired color—but we were the colorists. The human intellect has caused the appearances to appear and has projected our erroneous presuppositions into things.[20]

The categories in their pragmatic meaning are described as tools that science uses to order the manifold of experience, which in itself does not possess unity, permanency, or causality. "In the formation of the categories it was the following need that was decisive: not the need to know, but the need to connect, to schematize for the purpose of understanding and experience."[21]

Nietzsche thus advances a pragmatic criterion of truth. Knowledge becomes a subjective interpretation, a fiction of our mind, created by our needs. The world we know is a world of our own making and not an objective order that exists antecedently to the ideas and theories we form about it. Science is an invention rather than a discovery. It is merely a "finding again of that which we ourselves put into things."[22] All logical axioms are means to create the concept of reality. They do not contain criteria of truth, but are only "imperatives about that which must be considered as true."[23]

Nietzsche's conception of the categories of the mind is in many respects close to Kant's analysis of the categories of the understanding. Nietzsche did not himself acknowledge this link. He was, on the whole, a severe critic of Kant's philosophy of pure reason. However, in his early works, we find an enthusiastic recognition of Kant's contribution to the development of philosophical thought. In the first *Untimely Meditation, David Strauss,* he says: "For the Philistine . . . a Kantian philosophy does not exist. He does not have any conception of the fundamental antinomy of idealism and the relativity of all science and reason."[24] And in *The Birth of Tragedy*, Nietzsche speaks of Kant's victory over the optimistic foundations of logic and pays the highest tribute to Kant when he calls him "the initiator of a tragic culture."[25] But later, in *Twilight of the Idols*, Nietzsche identifies Kant's dualism with that of Christianity, whose spirit he calls pessimistic and decadent, and in sharp contrast to that of a tragic and Dionysian philosophy.[26]

There can be no question that Kant and Nietzsche differed widely, not only in their ethical and metaphysical views, but also in their theories of knowledge. Attempts to bring about a rapprochement of both philosophers often resulted in a distortion of their views. Thus Hans Vaihinger, in his *Philosophy of the "As If,"** attempts to prove the Kantian origin of Nietzsche's "doctrine of illusion" by a comparison of Kant's ideas of pure reason, as treated in the "Dialectic" of the *Critique of Pure Reason*, with Nietzsche's interpretation of the categories as fictions of the mind. However, in spite of the fact that Kant's ideas of pure reason and Nietzsche's categories of the mind might indeed, with Vaihinger, both be called "heuristic fictions," it is precisely here in the "Dialectic" that Nietzsche finds the basis for his attack upon Kant. The Kantian ideas—among them the concepts of God, freedom, and immortality—exist beyond experience in the realm of noumena, and function as moral facts that guide our beliefs and actions. It is this element of transcendence which Nietzsche so violently rejects in his own philosophy of life and existence, and which makes it impossible to draw both philosophers closer together.

Any rapport between the philosophies of Kant and Nietzsche cannot, I believe, rest upon Kant's "Dialectic" and

---

* Hans Vaihinger, *The Philosophy of the "As If"* (New York: Harcourt Brace, 1929).

theory of pure ideas, which lead beyond science to the *Critique of Practical Reason* and problems of ethics. But if we limit ourselves to Kant's and Nietzsche's views on knowledge and compare Nietzsche's analysis of the categories to Kant's categories of the understanding, as treated in the "Analytic" of the *Critique of Pure Reason,* we can achieve a rapprochement between them. Here both Nietzsche's and Kant's categories can be interpreted as tools to order and schematize experience, without which the possibility of science, and indeed of all knowledge, would for both be destroyed. Unlike the ideas of pure reason, Kant's categories of the understanding are not "illegitimately" extended into the sphere of noumena, which we can never know. While the ideas of reason are both transcendental and transcendent, originating in human consciousness but transcending the limits of all possible experience and understanding, the categories are only transcendental and not transcendent.

It is difficult to understand why, in his later writings, Nietzsche so completely rejects Kant's teaching and ignores his debt to a philosophy that limits knowledge to the phenomenal world. As Vaihinger has pointed out, one reason is certainly to be found in their temperamental differences. Nietzsche's poetic passion, which transformed all ideas into an inner drama and intellectual adventure, lacked an affinity with a method that was abstract and architectonic. But in addition to such an explanation on the basis of temperament, it is also possible to point to a real misunderstanding on Nietzsche's part. The misunderstanding centers in the concept of the transcendental. Nietzsche overlooks the special meaning of Kantian terminology and sees no distinction between "transcendental" and "transcendent," using both as synonymous terms. Categories are for Nietzsche either "diesseitig" or "jenseitig," on this side or the other side, and thus the Kantian categories are attacked as empty, transcending and "independent of all experience, originating in pure reason . . . a pure idea."[27] But "transcendental" is not "transcendent." Kant's transcendental categories of the understanding do not originate in a world beyond, but within self-consciousness; they are not legislative to a noumenal realm of religion and morality, but to the phenomenal world of experience. They are, like Nietzsche's categories, tools of knowledge that order the manifold of experience and construct a world of our own making, the world of phenomena.

But while significant similarities do exist, the fact must not be overlooked that the relation between Kant's and Nietzsche's conception of the categories is a much more complex one. It is primarily Kant's dualism that created a dilemma for himself as well as for those influenced by his critical philosophy. While both the sensuous and the rational are necessary for the Kantian complex of knowledge, his categories contain only the rational element. They are not built up from experience or influenced by it, as the British empiricists had critically maintained, but they exist independently of experience and prior to it, constructing an intelligible and orderly world out of the sensible manifold and bestowing certainty and universality upon the complex of knowledge. For Nietzsche, however, reason, as separated from our senses and drives, is a fiction, a meaningless abstraction. "The categories have merely a sensuous origin."[28]

A further difference arises when Kant points to a causality between phenomena and things-in-themselves. While, on the one hand, he had stressed that a deduction from an appearance to its cause is not based upon facts and knowledge, he nevertheless does not eliminate the possibility of a causal connection between noumena and phenomena. Nietzsche, however, rejects the whole concept of the "Ding an sich" as representing true reality in the noumenal realm, and thus he also denies the possibility of any connection between the noumenal and the phenomenal world, knowable or otherwise. The phenomenal world is the only world that exists. "The contrast to this phenomenal world is not the 'true world,' but the formless, undefinable world of sensuous chaos . . . thus another kind of phenomenal world, one which is not knowable to us."[29]

A comparison of Kant's and Nietzsche's conception of the categories reveals, in spite of similarities, the fundamental difference between a critical and a tragic spirit. The spirit of Kant's critique is one of optimism, synthesis, and reconciliation, which prevents any distrust in reason, and merely delimits and curtails its function. "Awakened from his dogmatic slumber," Kant still belongs to those "knowers of today who take their fire from the flame which was lighted by a faith that is thousands of years old." He still endows the categories with the qualities of certainty and universality; he still looks for a return to the "true world," be it no more than the consolation of a possibility. Truth, for Kant, cannot contain contradiction. His concern with the antinomies of reason does not lead him to the tragic recognition of their necessity and fruitfulness, but to a separation of reason and understanding, to the duality of pure and practical reason in order to overcome the contradictions. Kant's fundamental optimism is far removed from the spirit of the tragic philosopher who accepts uncertainty, semblance, and contradiction as inevitable aspects of reality and truth.

While it must be admitted that Nietzsche had many justified reasons for seeing, on the whole, only the untragic and unproblematic in Kant, there is another side to Kant—not evident in the "Aesthetic" and the "Analytic" of the *Critique of Pure Reason*—that Nietzsche was not aware of. He did not detect behind the dry, unimaginative style and the architectonic method, Kant's inner dialectic, and what Kant himself called the "restless endeavor of reason." He failed to recognize that Kant's wider conception of reason, which included not only the understanding and the faculty of ideas but also the perception of the beautiful, was able to go to the limits where the free interplay between the categories of the understanding, the imagination, and ideas of reason enter a world that does not exclude the experience of both the terrible and the sublime.

Despite fundamental differences, Kant's and Nietzsche's theories of the categories of the mind establish both philosophers as forerunners of pragmatism, although neither the Kantian nor Nietzschean theory can be equated with twentieth-century pragmatism. Nietzsche, however, is much closer to the contemporary interpretation, although he would scorn any narrowly utilitarian approach. His pragmatic interpretation of knowledge is influenced not only by Kant but also by Ernst Mach.* Both Nietzsche and Mach followed Kant in limiting knowledge to phenomena and in stressing the synthesizing and organizing function of the categories; but they differed from him in their rejection of synthetic *a priori* judgments, which allegedly make an objective science possible. To Kant's phenomenalism they added Hume's scepticism. Their categories are not Kant's *a priori* static forms of the mind, which bestow certainty and universality upon knowledge. They are fictions—what Vaihinger called "the most expedient forms of error"—but they are fictions that serve life and, as such, they are truer

---

* Nietzsche himself does not refer to Mach's writings, but his sister Elizabeth Foerster-Nietzsche relates in *Das Leben Fr. Nietzsches,* 2 vols. (Leipzig: Naumann, 1895–1904) that he studied Mach's *Die Mechanik in ihrer Entwicklung* in 1884 in Zuerich and was greatly influenced by it.

than traditional truths which weaken life. "The falseness of a given judgment does not constitute an objection against it. . . . The real question is how far a judgment furthers and maintains life."[30]

IV

Thus Nietzsche has prepared the pessimistic premise: truth is not certain, absolute, eternal, but subjective, relative, forever changing and erring. Reason is not an inborn faculty that possesses the power to grasp the absolute and eternal. The categories of the mind do not give us objective knowledge, but are simply pragmatic tools for ordering the phenomenal world. With the fall of the absolute authority of reason, the validity of all rationalistic and conceptual systems of knowledge is destroyed. They are merely artificial structures which are built on the basis of unproven presuppositions and have led to empty, meaningless deductions that are far removed from the tangled, painful complexities of life and existence. The will to truth of traditional philosophers was, in fact, a will to illusion, motivated by lack of courage and integrity, and guided by the unconscious desire to justify and preserve the moral and religious prejudices and values of their time.

Having reduced intellectual knowledge to the level of subjective and relative symbolism, Nietzsche discovers a new source of knowledge: Intuition. The instinctual forces of man are seen as having the power to reach a more genuine comprehension of truth. They disclose reality in its living, dynamic form and reach into deeper dimensions, closed to science and logic. Although Nietzsche made his own important contributions to the study and understanding of man's instincts, which greatly influenced twentieth-century depth psychology, the emphasis on instincts in the process of knowledge does not originate with him. It is a thesis that had been advanced by the "Sturm und Drang" movement, by Hamann and Herder, in opposition to the rationalism of the Enlightenment. In 1873 Nietzsche read Hamann at the suggestion of his friend Ritschl, and was thus not acquainted with Hamann's works when he wrote *The Birth of Tragedy* in 1872.[31] He had, however, already read Herder at that time.

Further influences include Eduard von Hartmann's *Philosophy of the Unconscious*, to which Nietzsche refers in letters to his friend Rohde.[32] In *The Gay Science* Nietzsche says: "For the longest time, thinking was considered as only conscious; only now do we discover the truth that the greatest part of our intellectual activity is unconscious."[33] Both Nietzsche and Hartmann follow the voluntaristic theories of Schopenhauer and his teaching of the primacy of the will over the intellect. The unconscious becomes a source of wisdom and knowledge that can reach into the fundamental aspects of human existence, while the intellect is held to be an abstracting and falsifying mechanism that is directed not toward truth but toward "mastery and possession."

In his early writings, Nietzsche speaks of two separate elements, instincts and reason. The instinctual powers of man are represented by the Dionysian principle, the intellect by the Apollonian. In *The Birth of Tragedy* he tries to prove the superiority of instincts over reason. The highest knowledge is reached in Dionysian rapture and ecstasy when primordial passions and drives are aroused to a state of frenzy. Nietzsche attributes the superiority of the early Greeks to the supremacy of instincts, and the decline of Greek culture to the victory of Socrates over Dionysus, of reason over instinct. Decadence was initiated by the rise of rationalism and the deterioration of the instinctual mythical forces. "It has been proved impossible to build culture upon the foundation of rationalistic knowledge."[34]

In his later writings, however, Nietzsche attempts to abolish the traditional dualism of reason and impulse and achieve a union of both. Reason is no longer seen as an entity in itself, but rather as a state of relations between different passions and desires. In *Beyond Good and Evil* he defines thinking as "nothing but the interaction and interrelation of our drives."[35] And in the *Nachlass* he says: "The intellect is the instrument of our drives and nothing more; it is never free. It is sharpened in the struggle of the various instincts and therefore deepens the activity of each instinct."[36] "Each passion and drive contains within itself its own quantum of reason."[37]

The new unified instrument of knowledge that Nietzsche introduces is the "will to power," of which both reason and instincts are manifestations. The will to power, the basis of his metaphysics, becomes the foundation of his theory of knowledge. "The will to truth is the will to power."[38] All our categories of thinking—thing, attribute, cause and effect, reality, appearance—all are interpretations to be understood in terms of will to power. It is a power that must be clearly distinguished from "power" as meant in Bacon or Hobbes or any utilitarian interpretation. It is not a power to control nature, or a power that serves as a tool of utility, but is a creative instinct, an inner drive toward growth and expansion that is not void of rational elements in their specific Nietzschean meaning as functional principles of organization and form. The will to truth, which is part of the will to live, is defined as "the most spiritual will to power."[39]

The real philosophers are commanders and law-givers. . . . They grasp with creative hands toward the future, and every-

thing that is or was becomes to them a means, a tool, a hammer. Their knowing is creating, their creating is lawgiving,
their will to truth is will to power.[40]

Nietzsche's conception of the role of intuition, and of the
hoped-for union of Apollo and Dionysus in the field of knowledge, is fraught with difficulties and contradictions. Intuition becomes a truly tragic concept. The intuitive powers
are not only instruments to grasp the phenomenal world of
change and becoming, but they are also referred to as means
to "shatter the *principium individuationis*" and to achieve
a deeper Dionysian insight into "reality itself." This latter
claim is in contradiction to Nietzsche's general position,
which revolts against transcendent metaphysics and any
epistemology derived from it.

As is the case with many of Nietzsche's inconsistencies,
here, too, the basis can be found in the fact that his critique
of traditional philosophy is tragic in the fullest sense of the
term. In spite of its passionate polemic, it does not achieve
a complete break with traditional philosophical views, but
merely "overcomes" them. While Nietzsche introduces nearly
every philosophical trend of twentieth-century thought, he
still remains deeply rooted in the traditions of the past. His
critique is a profoundly tragic experience. It is not a passive
and detached analysis and refutation, but represents an in-
tense involvement, filled with passion and despair, and a
longing to revere what it destroys. Although he abolished
transcendent metaphysics, he continued to yearn for the
eternal and universal.

Nietzsche's problem is not entirely different from that of
Kant, whose dualism he so violently attacks. It is not only
Kant but also Nietzsche who is guided by a deep metaphysi-
cal longing and still "takes his fire from a flame that was

lighted by a faith that is thousands of years old." Neither is content with a reason that merely synthesizes and schematizes, but cannot reach into "reality itself." Thus, although Nietzsche rejects Kant's noumenal realm, the "Ding an sich," and any search for it as meaningless, he continues to refer to the "Ur-Eine," the primal oneness of things. It is true that this concept changes in the course of Nietzsche's philosophical development. It is first close to Schopenhauer's interpretation as based upon Kant's separation of the noumenal and phenomenal. Later, the *Ur-Eine* is "another kind of phenomenal world, one which is not knowable to us." But whatever its interpretation at different stages of Nietzsche's development may be, the *Ur-Eine* represents his tortured longing to reach the deeper dimensions of being "which are not known to us."

The metaphysical impulse leads Kant to the realm of "Practical Reason," where the Absolute is reached not by logical demonstration, but by a postulatory leap. It leads Nietzsche into difficulties and contradictions in which intuition assumes an ambiguous and dual role. The conflict between Nietzsche's radical doubting and his metaphysical longing is never fully resolved. His relation to the traditions of the past possesses the complexity and ambiguity of his Dionysian tragic philosophy, in which each concept and truth contains within itself its opposite and is as divided and contradictory as life itself.

V

Nietzsche may have succeeded in preparing the pessimistic premise and destroying the possibility of truth in the traditional sense. But "we know that the destruction of an illusion does not yet result in truth, but merely in a bit more ignorance, a widening of empty space, an increase of waste."[41] The question is: Has Nietzsche, in spite of already-noted problems, succeeded in overcoming the nihilistic foundation and created a new conception of truth that is based upon a "nihilism of strength?"

The basis for Nietzsche's attack upon previous philosophers centers primarily on two points: first, the illusory character of their concept of truth and, second, its destructive effect upon life. As already noted, the claim as to the certainty and absoluteness of knowledge is an optimistic illusion that is erected upon a false metaphysics, which ignores life as it is, degrading it to "mere appearance": it is motivated not by a will to truth, but by a psychological need for order and security, and the unconscious wish to preserve the religious and moral prejudices of their age. But more important, for Nietzsche, is the fact that these illusions are not only false, but that they weaken life and man's creative faculties. The belief in a truth that is static and eternal lacks the fundamental tragic elements of questioning and doubting. It leads to sterility and stagnation and destroys man's will to power, his will to create.

Nietzsche demands a truth that is creative and serves life. But it may at first seem doubtful whether Nietzsche has not in turn arrived at the same dilemma as did traditional philosophers: the dilemma of the fundamental antithesis between truth and life, which leads to the need for illusions. Is not this new truth that is full of error and contradiction, and must in its ever-changing character forever elude us, equally destructive to life? Nietzsche admits the danger and says: "We make the experiment with truth . . . perhaps humanity will perish as a result of this."[42] Does he further, in order to avoid this dilemma, not create his own illusions, the categories of the mind which are admitted to be pragmatic fictions, necessary for life? Here, too, "it is our need that interprets the world, our instincts and their consent and disapproval."[43]

What, then, are the essential differences between the old, traditional errors and illusions that Nietzsche rejects and those of the tragic philosopher who aims at a nihilism of strength?

The differences that evolve out of Nietzsche's writings are based, I believe, on three fundamental characteristics which, Nietzsche claims, are missing in traditional philosophers, but are imperative for the tragic philosopher, and account for the creative element in the latter's conception of truth. These elements are those of passion, courage, and integrity.

The desire for certainty lacks the passion to question and suffer deeply; it lacks "an inner need and deep necessity. . . . To stand in the midst of the *rerum concordia discors* and the whole wonderful uncertainty and ambiguity of existence and not to ask, not to tremble in the eagerness and joy of questioning . . . that is what I despise."[44] Moreover, adherents of neither the rationalistic systems nor the scholastic dogmas possess the courage to face a reality and truth that is full of conflicts and paradoxes. Guided by fears of uncertainty and "open seas," they build sanctuaries in the transcendent divinity and in the absolute authority of reason. Finally, they lack the honesty and integrity to acknowledge the illusory character of their truths, and thus endow them with the status of absoluteness and certainty. In their false optimism they weaken man's instincts and destroy his will to life and truth.

Even the sceptical and critical philosophies, along with theories of "weak" pessimism, do not achieve the tragic insight that the traditional concepts and values are not only false but, above all, undesirable. They are still under the guidance of Plato's "divine dialectic" and the domination of Platonic-Christian values. "The sceptical, epoch-making, as well as the historicizing and pessimistic attitudes, have a moralistic origin. Since Plato, philosophy has been under the domination of morality."[45]

Nietzsche asks for a new type of philosopher, a "free spirit" who possesses passion, courage, integrity. He is not a "scientific laborer" to whom philosophy is a matter of detached speculation, but he is driven by an inner necessity, a passionate Dionysian striving for truth. He has the courage to bear the tragic recognition of a reality and truth that are basically nihilistic in character, and yet not to seek escape either in the comfort of false optimism or in the resignation of weak pessimism. "In every will to know there is a drop of cruelty."[46] The question is: "How much truth can one bear, how much truth can one risk?"[47]*

The tragic philosopher has the honesty and integrity to admit the illusory and transient character of his so called truths, refusing to endow them with absoluteness and certainty. Above all, he has the courage and insight to accept and affirm falsehood and illusion as inevitable and as creative. His errors arise not because of a false, transcendent, static conception of being, but because metaphysically the world is one of change and becoming, of destruction and creativity. His illusions do not have a paralyzing effect, but serve, in their continuously changing form, as pragmatic tools of science and as stimulants to the creative urges of

---

* It is perhaps Freud more than any other later nineteenth-century innovator who understood the meaning of that question. He insisted on exposing pious illusions so that men must "confess to the instincts that are at work in them, face the conflict, fight for what they want, or go without it." *The Complete Psychological Works of Sigmund Freud,* standard ed. (London: Hogarth Press, 1953), 11: 150.

life. They are not based on lazy optimism or weak pessimism, but on a pessimism of strength. "Knowledge in the service of the highest life. We must even want illusion, this is the meaning of the tragic."[48] The will to power is the will to illusion, the will to struggle and create. It leads to suffering and pain, but also to the highest joy of creation.

To Nietzsche, knowledge cannot be contained in a closed, static system, but is a process, and thus involves ceaseless questioning. " 'Truth' is not something that is there to be found and discovered—but something that must be created and can be called a process, or better, a will to conquer which has no end . . . a process *ad infinitum*. . . . It is a word for the 'will to power.' "[49]

In this unending process Nietzsche hopes to find the solution to the fundamental dilemma that confronted the traditional as well as the tragic philosopher: the need for a synthesis of life and truth. The process of truth shows the same characteristics as life itself: struggling, erring, and finally overcoming. "The will to know and the will to err are ebb and flow. . . . Life is the condition of knowing, erring is the condition of life."[50]

The Nietzschean synthesis is, however, not to be understood as a dissolution of all conflicts and contradictions concerning the problem of truth and life. It is a synthesis that preserves the dynamic, dialectical elements, without which the search for truth would be lifeless and uncreative. The awareness of the dilemma between life and truth, the consciousness of limitations continue. The nihilistic premise is not abolished, but "overcome." The road to truth continues to be one of struggle, risks, and dangers; it is never free of frustrations and despair. And thus Zarathustra laments in the "Nightsong":

Night has come, now all fountains speak more loudly. . . . Light
am I: ah, that I were night! But this is my loneliness that
I am girt with light. . . . This is the passion of the light against
what shines: merciless it moves in its orbit. . . . Night has
come: ah, that I must be light! And thirst for the nocturnal!
And loneliness.[51]

Zarathustra's "Nightsong" is Nietzsche's poetic description of man's Dionysian longing for the burning and consuming light of truth, a truth which, when fully possessed,
threatens to destroy life. It is the tortured expression of the
seeker of truth, who in loneliness and suffering despairs of a
truth that he can never fully possess. "Such things have never
been written by poets, never been felt, never been suffered:
thus only a god Dionysus suffers. The answer to such a
dithyramb on the sun's isolation in light is Ariadne."[52]
Nietzsche uses the ancient myth of Theseus and Ariadne
to symbolize man's passion for truth and his never-ending
search, which, if pursued with courage and honesty, may
lead to the destruction of both truth and life. "It may be
that mankind perishes in its passion for truth."[53]

"Ariadne," said Dionysus, "You are a labyrinth: Theseus has
lost his way in it, he has no more direction." . . . Ariadne answered: "I do not want to pity when I love; I am tired of pity.
All heroes shall perish in me. That is my deepest love for
Theseus: I destroy him."[54]

Nietzsche does not clearly define Ariadne's role in his
tragic philosophy. But we know that she is the goddess of
vegetation and spring and that her festivals at Naxos represented both the spirit of sadness and dissolution as well as
joy and rebirth. But perhaps she is also the *Liebeshass* that

pervades Nietzsche's writings, which attacked without pity or compromise and destroyed what he loved and revered.* In the stillness and loneliness of night a new truth is born, a truth that does not console and comfort, but affirms dangers and risks, and accepts the pain, the burning light, and loneliness—the totality of all—this is Ariadne's deepest love. Ariadne, like Dionysus, is perhaps a symbol of Nietzsche's central theme of tragedy: to destroy in order to rebuild, to perish in order to be reborn.

A new truth is created within the forever-erring process of life and the recognition of the semblance of all truth. Truth is no longer a transcendent, abstract concept, but a judgment that grows out of the tangled perplexities of life. Reason is no longer a changeless, supernatural essence that forms universals and constructs syllogisms, but it is part of our basic instincts and drives, part of our "will to power." The tragic philosopher turns away from abstractions and logical deductions to a truth that is meaningful as an element within life. Truth becomes a power, a vital function that is formed in the act of existence.

Dionysus becomes Faust, the weary scholar who despairs of the futility of abstract knowledge and the barrenness of learning. He turns to life and concrete experience in order to satisfy his hunger for truth. Through pain and joy, through love and crime, he wanders with Mephistopheles, the spirit of evil and negation who yet creates the good, until in his hour of greatest agony he sees the final truth: Truth is not a definite end and goal that can ever be reached, but it is contained in the suffering and in the glory of actual

---

* Nietzsche's position in regard to the emotion of pity can be compared to that of Spinoza: "Pity in a man who lives according to the guidance of reason is in itself evil and unprofitable" (*Ethics* [New York: Hafner Publishing Co., 1955], pt. 4, Prop. L).

existence, and in the never-ending struggle and striving of man's will to truth.

According to the legend, Faust's soul was to belong to the devil after the expiration of a specific period. But in Goethe's drama, the pact between God and the devil is given a deeper meaning. A condition is added. Only then shall Faust belong to the devil, if Mephistopheles should succeed in stilling Faust's longing and in satisfying his striving. It is here that we find the contradiction and absurdity of the pact, as well as the central meaning of the *Faust* drama. Mephistopheles could succeed only if Faust should cease to be himself; for it is the very essence of man to continually reach for higher and higher goals and truths, and never attain the consummation of his desire.

Faust's striving will and Nietzsche's will to power are Spinoza's "conatus," the drive and power toward self-preservation, in the full meaning of preserving and developing. But "the effort by which each thing endeavors to persevere in its own being is nothing but the actual essence of the thing itself."* If this essential aspect disappears, the thing ceases to be. It is clear that God must win the wager.

The road to truth has no end. Its meaning is found in the eternal striving for truth. "Verily, I say unto you: good and evil [truth and falseness] that are everlasting do not exist. True to their own essence, they must ever surpass themselves anew."[55] Jaspers expresses the spirit of this tragic search for truth when he says: "Nietzsche does not show us a way, he does not teach us a faith. . . . Instead, he grants us no peace, torments us ceaselessly, hunts us out of every retreat and forbids us all concealment."** Nietzsche himself compares his position to that of Lessing when he says in

---

* Ibid., pt. 3, Prop. VII.
** Karl Jaspers, *Nietzsche and Christianity*, p. 104.

The Birth of Tragedy: "Lessing, most honest of theoretical men, dared to say that the search for truth was more important to him than truth itself and thereby revealed the innermost secret of inquiry."[56]

Dionysus, the patron of Nietzsche's philosophy, has been seen as having many aspects. He is the ancient god of destruction and fertility; he is the essence of tragedy and the symbol of contrariety at the center of the universe; he is the artist's creative "Rausch," and the titan's defiant will; he is height and abyss, nihilism and its overcoming; he is the will to question more deeply and persistently than has ever been questioned before; he is the will to power.

Finally, Dionysus is Nietzsche's own mask, expressing the profound complexity of his own personality. Thomas Mann compares Nietzsche to Hamlet's torn and dual character. He points out that Nietzsche was by nature deeply "respectful," and that his mind was "shaped to revere pious traditions." "But what [he asks] was it that drove Nietzsche upward into the pathless wastes, lashed him on to the torturous climb and brought him to a martyr's death on the cross of thought?"* And Mann answers that it was his destiny and his destiny was his genius. But, above all, it seems to me that it was Nietzsche's deep passion for honesty and integrity that drove him to the path of destruction and negation even while he longed for affirmation. It is this almost fanatical passion which explains his radical criticism and often desperate cruelty against traditions which he felt profoundly involved in. But this passion and cruelty also turned more directly against himself, against his own ideas and creations. At no time did he offer these as final solutions,

---

* Thomas Mann, *Last Essays* (New York: Alfred A. Knopf, 1959), pp. 141f.

but continued to probe and doubt with a relentlessness and agony which finally destroyed him.

And thus we detect a note of sadness and despair when Nietzsche says: "And what are you in the end, my written and painted thoughts? Not long ago you were so brightly colored, so wicked and full of thorns and secret spices . . . already you have taken off your newness and some of you, I fear, are ready to turn into truths, so immortal do you already look, so heartbreakingly proper, so boring."[57] "Whatever I create and however much I love it . . . soon I must become its adversary and oppose my love."[58]

In the end we still question: Who is Dionysus, the "Ambivalent One?" And we go back to Nietzsche's early writings of 1870–71, and the basic metaphysical thought that was with him all his life: "If contradiction is true being . . . then in order to understand the world in its deepest meaning is to understand contradiction."[59] Later, in *Dawn*, written in 1881, he quotes Hegel: "Contradiction moves the world; all things contradict themselves."[60] And he writes:

Contradiction, the last and final reality? "Yes," says Dionysus, "that I might make man stronger, more evil and deeper than he is." "Stronger, more evil and deeper?" I asked, shocked. "Yes," he said once more, "stronger, more evil, deeper, and also more beautiful" . . . and saying this, he smiled his Halcyon smile, this Tempter-God.[61]

PART II

The Eternal Recurrence

Immortal is the moment in which I created the eternal recurrence.
Nietzsche, Nachlass (XII, 371)

Behold, we know what you teach: that all things return eternally and we ourselves with them, and that we have already been here an eternal number of times, and all things with us.
Nietzsche, Zarathustra (VI, 321)

THE DOCTRINE'S IMPORTANCE

The teaching of the eternal recurrence is the turning point of history.[1]

—Nietzsche

The importance of the theory of eternal recurrence within the framework of Nietzsche's thought has been a subject of dispute among Nietzsche scholars. Some dismiss the idea as a subjective, religious experience, a deceptive illusion that has no philosophical significance.* Others acknowledge its

---

* Ernst Bertram, *Nietzsche, Versuch einer Mythologie* (Berlin: Bondi, 1918). Alfred Baeumler, *Nietzsche, der Philosoph und Politiker* (Leipzig: Reclam, 1931); Walter A. Kaufmann, *Nietzsche* (Princeton: Princeton University Press, 1950), pp. 279 ff. Kaufmann does not stress the importance of the idea of eternal recurrence in Nietzsche's thought and asks: "Why does Nietzsche value this most dubious doctrine, which was to have no influence to speak of, so extravagantly?" He claims that the answer must be found in the fact that the eternal recurrence was to Nietzsche less an idea than an experience, an experience of joy in which the powerful man affirms life in its totality, "backward, forward and in all eternity." Kaufmann, however, does not see any contradiction between the fundamental concepts of Nietzsche's philosophy, as do the below-cited interpreters, among others. Instead, he stresses the close relation between the conceptions of the eternal recurrence and the overman. Both, he points out, are based upon Nietzsche's supra-historical point of view, on his denial of infinite progress, and on his dual affirmation of the value of the moment and the individual.

129

importance, but find it in irreconcilable opposition to other central concepts of Nietzsche's philosophy, primarily the will to power.* Nietzsche himself believed this doctrine to be of utmost importance for his total philosophy, and devoted his most productive years in the 1880s to its analysis and development. He stressed the essential connection between the will to power and the eternal recurrence. These two basic concepts belong to the same creative period and are never presented as contradictory or mutually exclusive by Nietzsche.

I here contend that the idea of the eternal recurrence is not only of central importance, but that it presents a vital and essential unity through which the various aspects of Nietzsche's thought are synthesized. It is a teaching that expresses in the fullest sense Nietzsche's tragic, Dionysian philosophy, possessing the same Janus-face that characterizes all his thoughts: the will to nothingness and the will to eternally recurring life. It grows out of his conception of nihilism as a dialectical movement and basic law of history and being. "Let us think this thought in its most extreme form: existence, as it is, without meaning or goal, but inevitably recurring without end into nothingness: 'the eternal recurrence.' This is the most extreme form of nihilism: nothingness forever."[2] But at the same time "the eternal recurrence is the highest formula of affirmation that can ever be reached."[3]

The "Eternal Recurrence" expresses Nietzsche's critique and repudiation of the Platonic-Christian tradition and the destruction of its values. But it also leads to the creation of

---

* Ludwig Klages, *Die Psychologischen Errungenschaften Nietzsches* (Bonn: H. Bouvier, 1958); Georg Simmel, *Schopenhauer und Nietzsche* (Leipzig: Duncker & Humblot, 1907); Oscar Ewald, *Nietzsches Lehre in ihren Grundzuegen* (Berlin: Hoffmann, 1903).

new values. It denies the timeless eternity of a supernatural God, but affirms the eternity of the ever-creating and destroying powers in nature and man. "This idea contains more than all religions which despise this life as unreal. . . . It is the religion above all religions."[4] It celebrates the union of man with the creative forces of nature and expresses the highest apotheosis of life. "The eternal recurrence, the Yes-saying pathos par excellence which I call the tragic pathos."[5]

The most important treatment of the theory is found in *The Gay Science* and in *Zarathustra*.[6] Nietzsche calls the eternal recurrence the fundamental conception of *Zarathustra*: "I now relate the story of Zarathustra, the basic conception of this work, the eternal recurrence."[7]* Above all, it is the *Nachlass* that contains a wealth of references to the idea of eternal recurrence and the related concept of the will to power.

The opinions as to the origin of the idea of eternal recurrence, "this abysmal thought," vary. Nietzsche himself does not make it clear whether we can trace its origin to the influences of previous thinkers, or whether we are dealing with an absolutely unique idea, conceived independently in the pure air of the Engadin, "six thousand feet above man and time." Lou Andreas-Salomé relates that Nietzsche mentioned the idea in one of his letters and spoke of it "as a silently whispered secret."** In *Ecce Homo* we find the following passage: "The idea of the eternal recurrence belongs in the month of August 1881; it was written on a page with

---

* The idea of the eternal recurrence is already mentioned in Nietzsche's early works (*Fate and History; The Tragedy of the Will and Fate*, both in *Juvenilia*, vol. I of the Musarion ed., *The Use and Abuse of History for Life*, I, 298; *Philosophy in the Tragic Age of the Greeks*, X, 101f). References to the idea can also be found in *Beyond Good and Evil* (VII, 183) and *The Antichrist* (VIII, 212, 382).

** Lou Andreas-Salomé, *Friedrich Nietzsche in seinen Werken* (Wien: Konegen, 1894), p. 222.

the words: 'six thousand feet above man and time.' I walked on that day through the woods at the lake of Silvaplana . . . where the thought came to me."[8] And in *Zarathustra* he speaks of "the moment of noon in which time is abolished, in which eternity is experienced and perfection is reached."[9]

However, in other passages Nietzsche names earlier thinkers who taught the idea of eternal recurrence. Thus he says in *Ecce Homo*: "The doctrine of the 'eternal recurrence,' that is, of the unconditional and infinitely repeated circulation of all things . . . this teaching of Zarathustra might in the end already have been taught by Heraclitus. At least the Stoics, who inherited almost all their fundamental ideas from Heraclitus, show traces of it."[10] In the second *Untimely Meditation, The Use and Abuse of History*, he names the Pythagoreans as teachers of the doctrine of recurrence, but he repudiates their interpretation of the idea as a recurrence of events within a span of known history and not, as he sees it, as "an unconditional and infinitely repeated circulation of all things."[11]

According to Jaspers, the idea of eternal recurrence was conceived by Nietzsche completely independently of any historical connections, and has its roots neither in Greek nor Christian thought. It is not an "intellectual thought, but the existentialistic experience of a moment which, by producing the idea, was given by means of it a decisive, metaphysical meaning."[*] As noted before, Alfred Baeumler also stresses the existential and personal aspects of the Nietzschean idea; but, in contrast to Jaspers, he denies it any philosophical significance.[**] However, Baeumler fails to take into account that Nietzsche is a philosopher of life and existence who, in opposition to traditional systems of abstract thought, de-

---

[*] Karl Jaspers, *Nietzsche* (Berlin: De Gruyter, 1950), p. 354.
[**] Alfred Baeumler, *Nietzsche, der Philosoph und Politiker*, p. 81.

mands the thinker's passionate involvement. His ideas are not conceived "clearly and distinctly" in the Cartesian manner, which allegedly excludes all doubt, but they come on "dove's feet," in the solitude of Sils-Maria, in the "most silent hour . . . when one hears, one does not see."[12]

The idea of eternal recurrence is not demonstrated in logical deductions; it is expressed in poetic symbols and metaphors. But the symbols and metaphors, most vivid in *Zarathustra*, are not merely artificial devices for making discourse vivid; they are means by which the creative mind perceives and communicates new ideas and new relationships. Although it cannot be denied that Nietzsche's idea of eternal recurrence contains deeply personal, subjective, and also religious elements, this fact does not diminish its value and philosophical significance. If, with Nietzsche, we endorse or accept criteria of truth and value that contain existential meaning, we also must conclude that Descartes's "clear and distinct ideas" cannot always express enough. Nietzsche, we have seen, would of course claim that they can express nothing about reality adequately.

Nietzsche presents the idea of eternal recurrence in many forms and under many aspects. Here I will discuss its special importance as viewed from scientific, metaphysical, and ethical perspectives.

THE SCIENTIFIC BASIS OF NIETZSCHE'S THEORY OF ETERNAL RECURRENCE

Everything has been here before innumerable times insofar as the total field of energy always returns.[1]

—Nietzsche

I

Most of Nietzsche's scientific ideas are discussed in the *Nachlass* of the eighties, the many notes and fragments intended by him to be the basis for his magnum opus, the *Will to Power*. In these notes he calls his doctrine of eternal recurrence "the most scientific of all possible hypotheses" and stresses the possibility of a scientific proof.[2] However, he also realized that he did not then possess sufficient knowledge to provide such a proof. In a letter to Franz Overbeck, written September 1881, he complains: "I know so little about the results of the sciences. . . . The realities are missing in my knowledge, and the idealities are not worth a rap."[3] And

134

as reported by Lou Andreas-Salomé, he planned in the fall
of 1882 to withdraw from all creative writing and devote the
next ten years to the study of mathematics and natural
sciences.*

We know that Nietzsche's early education had been a
humanistic one and that his professional and philosophical
interests were not primarily scientific. But a concern with
the results of the sciences did nonetheless exist prior to 1881
and independently of the need to systematize his theory of
eternal recurrence. In fact, his interest in the sciences began
at Schulpforta, and continued at the University of Leipzig
under the influence of Friedrich Zoellner. It was deepened
by his studies of the pre-Socratics, primarily Democritus and
Heraclitus. During the years in Basel, he studied numerous
scientific books, among them, according to his sister, those
of Wundt, Helmholtz, Riemann, and Caspari.** But while
present earlier, Nietzsche's scientific interest reached its
height in the last creative period, the time of Zarathustra
and the eternal recurrence. Thus in 1884 he wrote to Franz
Overbeck: "I must now go step by step through the whole
row of disciplines, as I have decided to devote the next five
years to the elaboration of my philosophy for which I have
built a 'Vorhalle' in my Zarathustra."[4]

Nietzsche's scientific theories and hypotheses have found
little recognition and acceptance and have, on the whole, not
been taken seriously by either scientists or philosophers. He
remains the philosopher of culture, the Zarathustra prophet
whose temper is not scientific, but imaginative, artistic, and
speculative. In his introduction to the Musarion edition,

---

* Lou Andreas-Salomé, *Friedrich Nietzsche in seinen Werken* (Wien:
Konegen, 1894), p. 128.
** Elizabeth Foerster-Nietzsche, *Das Leben Friedrich Nietzsches*, 2 vols.
(Leipzig: Naumann, 1895–1904), 2: 316.

Richard Oehler speaks of Nietzsche's development from a philologist to a moralistic critic and philosopher, from an immoralist and anti-Christ to a creator of new values, but says nothing about Nietzsche as a philosopher of nature.

Nietzsche's writings, however, manifest his continuous attempt to reach a scientific understanding of the processes of nature. Particularly in his theory of eternal recurrence he exhibits characteristics that are close to a scientific temper: a desire to find uniformities and order in the cosmic processes, a belief in the eternal, immutable laws of the universe, and a longing to transcend particular, individual human existence in order to find a nexus between man and nature. Admittedly, his scientific insights are intuitive rather than systematic; however, his intuitive ability to grasp the basic problems of science is indeed outstanding. He not only gained a truly remarkable understanding of the sciences of his day, but drew conclusions, particularly in the field of atomic theories, that science itself did not make until the end of the nineteenth or the beginning of the twentieth century.*

My purpose in this study is, however, not to evaluate Nietzsche's contributions to the natural sciences. It is to prove, on the basis of his scientific hypotheses, that his theory of eternal recurrence does represent a unified doctrine, containing none of the alleged contradictions many interpreters have stressed.

II

Nietzsche's doctrine of the eternal recurrence is based upon the following presuppositions, which he states in the

---

* Alvin Mittasch, *Friedrich Nietzsche als Naturphilosoph* (Stuttgart: Alfred Kroener Verlag, 1952). Mittasch attempts to prove Nietzsche's importance as a philosopher of nature.

Nachlass: time is eternal and infinite; space is limited and finite; the number of atoms, the constituent elements of the universe, is determined and finite. From these presuppositions it follows that only a finite number of configurations and combinations of atoms is possible and that, therefore, in a sufficiently long period of time, a recurrence of past configurations becomes necessary.[5]

> The present configuration must be a repetition and also the one which bore it and the one which originates from it and so backward and forward eternally. . . . An infinite number of new changes and combinations of a limited energy is a contradiction . . . there are no infinitely new changes, but a cycle of a limited number of the same recurs again and again. Activity is eternal; the number of its products and configurations is limited.[6]

Nietzsche finds the scientific basis for the theory of the eternal recurrence in the principle of the conservation of energy. "The principle of the conservation of energy demands the eternal recurrence."[7] The teacher of eternal flux and change, the heir of Heraclitus adds the principle of permanency and endurance to the concept of becoming. Being and becoming are not opposites, but being contains both change and endurance. Both principles are inherent in the nature of things and recur in every particular embodiment. Mere change without conservation would be merely a passage from nothing to nothing; there must be something that endures throughout change, something that adds content to bare activity.

Nietzsche, as later Whitehead, looks for a meaning in the otherwise "senseless dance of categories," and he finds it in the principle of eternal recurrence. The antithesis between being and becoming is abolished in a synthesis of Heraclitus and Parmenides, in the doctrine which "impresses upon becoming the character of being. . . . That all recurs is the most extreme approach of a world of becoming to one of being."[8] On the basis of the validity of the law of conservation and under the assumption that the total number of the constituent elements of the universe is finite, the theory of a recurrence of past states and configurations of atoms in a sufficiently long period of time becomes necessary.[*]

The important question that now arises is: How are Nietzsche's presuppositions to be interpreted? What are these atoms and their configurations whose finite number and infinite recurrence Nietzsche claims?

If these presuppositions are interpreted on the basis of mechanistic theories of explanation and classical atomism, then the conclusion could be drawn that Nietzsche's cyclical theory refers to particular identical fixed states that will, after a sufficiently long period of time, recur in exactly the same way as they have already occurred an infinite number of times in the past. This conclusion is drawn by most Nietzsche interpreters who, on its basis, are then confronted with apparently irreconcilable contradictions between the cosmological and the ethical meaning of the theory, as will be discussed below.

It is my contention that Nietzsche's theory is not based upon the classical atomism which still prevailed at his time, but upon a dynamic-energetic explanation of nature. This leads to a different interpretation of his conception of atoms

---

[*] Milic Capek, "The Theory of Eternal Recurrence in Modern Philosophy of Science with Special Reference to C. S. Peirce," in *Journal of Philosophy*, 57, no. 9: "The identical recurrence of the past . . . this is what was intuitively grasped by Nietzsche in the middle eighties of the last century and a few years later proved by Henri Poincaré. Poincaré proved that every mechanical system, no matter how complex it may be, provided it is made up of a finite number of elements, must, in a sufficiently long interval of time, pass an infinite number of times through a configuration which is infinitely close to that through which it had already passed. The proof of this so-called 'theorem of phases' was later simplified by Zermelo and Caratheodory."

and thereby to conclusions which also differ from interpretations of the theory as a return of exactly the same static, unchanging states.

On the basis of Nietzsche's writings and posthumously published notes, a theory of nature can, I believe, be constructed that proves Nietzsche to be a precursor of twentieth-century dynamism. He calls the ultimate constituents of the world "quanta of energy." Energy becomes the fundamental notion of the universe, displacing matter. These quanta of energy are no longer the rigid particles of Democritus, Gassendi, and Dalton. They are not the material, indivisible particles whose mechanistic movements determine the configurations of the world and whose essential property is their immutability. Nietzsche's quanta of energy are profoundly different from the corpuscular entities of classical atomism. "The atom as a fixed point is without content and never exists. . . . The dynamic interpretation of the world with its denial of empty space and corpuscular atoms will shortly gain power over the physicists."[9]

Nietzsche's concept of "Kraft" (power) is, in its dynamic qualities, close to the energy theories of contemporary physics. He breaks with the materialistic and mechanistic explanation of the world that reduces all natural phenomena to a change in position of intrinsically immutable particles. The world is not a "block universe," made up of an aggregate of corpuscular atoms that persist through all time. Nor is it a pack of cards that, if shuffled long enough, must eventually, by pure chance, turn up the same card again.[*] Nietzsche's universe is close to that of Bergson, James, and Whitehead, in which atoms are not immutable bits of matter, but "cen-

---

* Hans Reichenbach, *The Direction of Time* (Berkeley, Calif.: University of California Press, 1956), p. 99: "When we shuffle a pack of cards . . . long enough, we must by pure chance eventually come back to the original state, because the probability of arriving at such an arrangement is larger than zero."

ters of energy whose essence is fluid" and whose function it is to organize its own incessant activity.

However, it cannot be denied that Nietzsche is not completely uninfluenced by the scientific world view of his age. There are passages in his writings that still point to a mechanistic theory of nature. But wherever these passages are found, they are always connected with the recognition that "the mechanistic explanation must be considered imperfect and merely a temporary hypothesis."[10] They are always given with his admission that the mechanistic explanation is a deception, motivated by a need for clarity and simplicity. "The mechanistic explanation of the world is an ideal: to explain as much as possible with as little as possible, that is to bring it into formulas."[11] "In order to understand the world, we must be able to calculate it, to have constant causes; since we have no such constant causes in reality, we invent them . . . the atoms. This is the origin of atoms."[12]

It must be further acknowledged that Nietzsche's intuitive insights, which pointed the way toward the twentieth century's dynamic view of nature, were not independently conceived in the heights of the Engadin. Nietzsche lived in a period of scientific transition. While the nineteenth century had primarily a mechanistic background, the struggle between the mechanistic and the dynamic conception of the world had already begun. Nietzsche himself mentions being influenced by Faraday, Boscovich, Caspari, Zoellner,[13] and, above all, Robert Mayer, whose theory of the conservation of energy and *Ausloesungsbegriff* made an important impression upon Nietzsche.* Nevertheless, Nietzsche's originality

---

* Robert Mayer, *Mechanik der Waerme*, "Ueber Ausloesung." Nietzsche writes to Gast (*Die Briefe Peter Gasts an Friedrich Nietzsche*, 2 vols., [Muenchen: Verlag der Nietzsche-Gesellschaft, 1923–24], 1:110), April 16, 1881: " 'Ueber Ausloesung' is for me the most essential and valuable part of Mayer's book."

and unusual ability to intuit and anticipate future developments and trends must be fully recognized despite the many influences by scientists of his own time as well as influences of earlier thinkers, such as Leibniz and Goethe. Although the mechanistic theory of nature was already undermined in Nietzsche's time, it was not until the end of the nineteenth and the beginning of the twentieth century that definite conclusions were drawn.

Whitehead credits modern science with being the challenger of classical materialism, and specifically credits William James as being the destroyer of the Cartesian Ego.* He could have named Nietzsche as the challenger of both: the destroyer of Descartes's ego, which was based upon a false psychology that "mistook a feeling of power for a cause";[14] and the destroyer of Democritus's and Dalton's atom, and therefore the whole basis of mechanistic science.

III

Nietzsche's revision of the traditional concepts of atom and mass thus replaces the traditional concepts of static, material quantities with the dynamic quanta of power and energy that are constantly acting and reacting. A quantum of power is characterized by the effect that it exerts and that it resists. "The quantity of power is constant, its essence is fluid."[15] Activity and process become the fundamental concepts, as they were indeed for Whitehead. The universe becomes a field of force, a field of incessant activity.

The principle of the conservation of energy, which Nietzsche accepted as the basis of his theory of eternal recurrence,

---

* A. N. Whitehead, *Science and the Modern World*. Whitehead, in naming William James as the challenger of the Cartesian Ego, points to James's *Does Consciousness Exist?*, which appeared in 1904.

expresses a law of conservation which now takes place within change and process, a change that is not based upon a mechanistic principle, but the new, dynamic principle of energy. Thus he says in the *Nachlass*:

> Not only constancy of energy, but the will to become stronger in each center of energy as the only reality. . . . It is a struggle between two elements unequal in power: a new adjustment is arrived at according to the measure of power each possesses. . . . In the smallest organism, energy is constantly formed and must be constantly released; either by itself, if there is fullness, or an incentive from outside must be added.[16]

Since Nietzsche's dynamic world view disputes the mechanistic, materialistic principles of his time, the following questions must be asked: Does not an interpretation of Nietzsche's theory as a return of exactly the same states rest upon a materialistic, mechanistic principle of explanation and fall with the rejection of this principle? Can Nietzsche by eternal recurrence mean return of exactly identical particular events in the eternal monotony which he himself calls "die ewige Leier" (the eternal sameness of an organ-grinder), and which he rejects in *Zarathustra* as the teaching of the dwarf and the animals?[17] In the light of his dynamic views, can the recurring states be defined as configurations of simultaneously existing material, static, immutable elements, or must they not rather be understood as simultaneously occurring values of energy? It is clear that each of these questions requires explanation.

With our rejection of materialistic mechanism as the basis of Nietzsche's doctrine of eternal recurrence, an interpretation of Nietzsche's theory as a return of exactly the same fixed states must also be abandoned. This interpretation had presupposed not only the existence of a finite number of the fundamental constituent elements of the world within limited space and infinite time, but it also presupposed that these elements are distinct, static, and immutable. However, when it becomes meaningless to speak of a particular, definite, fixed state of the universe, it is likewise meaningless to speak of the return of such a state. If there are no permanent, self-identical, static elements—and to Nietzsche there are none—there are no recurring configurations of these elements. The theory of the eternal recurrence of exactly the same is an instance of Whitehead's fallacy of "misplaced concreteness."

A different interpretation of Nietzsche's theory must be constructed, based not on classical atomism, but on his own dynamic, vitalistic world view. That which returns is not any definite, particular fixed state of the universe; what returns is the total pattern of life, "der Gesamtcharacter des Lebens." "The Yes-saying to the total character of life as that which remains constant within all change."[18]

Nietzsche asks: "Is the existence of diversity and the absence of complete circularity in the world around us not sufficient counter-evidence against a uniform cycle of all that is?"[19] And he answers: "The same quantity of energy means something different on a different level of development. . . . Everything has been here before innumerable times insofar as the total field of energy (*Gesamtlage der Kraefte*) always returns. Whether aside from this anything identical has existed, is entirely indemonstrable."[20]

The eternal recurrence of the same is the return of the "Gesamtlage der Kraefte," in which energy is continuously formed and continuously released. It is the return of the dynamic pattern of nature and life, which is eternally active and eternally the same. Thus the principle of conservation cannot and does not refer to the conservation of a static, unchanging, fixed state, but refers to the preservation of the "field of energy," which contains within itself the elements of change and activity, tension and release, repulsion and attraction, destruction and creation. What returns is the tragic pattern of life as it rises and falls in eternal necessity and inevitability. "The energy of the totality of becoming rises to the highest point and falls again in an eternal cycle."[21]

6

THE ETERNAL RECURRENCE
IN ITS METAPHYSICAL
PERSPECTIVE

The only power that exists is that of the will.[1]

—Nietzsche

I

In the *Will to Power* Nietzsche says: "The triumphant concept of 'energy' . . . must yet be supplemented. It must be given an inner will which I designate the 'will to power'."[2] The will to power becomes the basic principle of nature, the fundamental drive that underlies everything, and in terms of which everything can be understood. It is the basis of his metaphysics which is both a rejection of the traditional concept of reality as well as a creation of a new philosophy of being. It is the foundation of his theory of eternal recurrence. "My theory contends that all productive energy is will to power and that there is no physical, dynamic or psychological force beside it. . . . The only power that exists is that of the will."[3]

Despite his genuine scientific interests, Nietzsche remains primarily a speculative thinker, the tragic philosopher who recognizes the limits of science and searches for totality and unity. While he attempts to provide a scientific basis for his doctrine of eternal recurrence, he nevertheless contends that scientific categories and abstractions cannot fully grasp the inner essence of being and the complexities of life. They must be supplemented and deepened by a voluntaristic interpretation and its basic concept, the will to power.

Nietzsche is often called a philosopher of life, and a distinction is hereby indicated between a philosophy of life and metaphysics, between life and being as such. But even Plato, the founder of a metaphysics, which Nietzsche rejects as static and transcendent, asks in the *Sophist*: "Can we ever be made to believe that motion and life and soul and mind are not present in perfect being? Can we imagine that being, devoid of mind and life, exists in awful unmeaningness, an everlasting fixture?" And Nietzsche asks: "Being . . . we have no other conception of it than 'life'. How could it be anything dead?"[4]

Despite alleged incompatibilities, Nietzsche's philosophy of life is indeed a metaphysics of being. Heidegger is correct in calling Nietzsche a metaphysician, and the eternal recurrence a doctrine where "being is thought in its deepest sense."[*] Wherever Nietzsche rejects metaphysics, it is only in its Platonic-Christian interpretation, which understood being as unchanging and transcendent," . . . in truth therefore not a rejection of all metaphysics, but only of a metaphysics of a fixed and static world."[5]

Just as Nietzsche, the "immoralist," is in reality a tortured seeker of moral values "beyond good and evil," just as the atheist is in fact consumed by a deep longing for a new God,

---

[*] Heidegger, *Nietzsche*, 2 vols. (Pfullingen: Neske, 1961), 1: 262, 369.

so the anti-metaphysician is, in his teaching of the eternal recurrence, the creator of a new metaphysics of life and existence. Nietzsche's critique is never merely negative and destructive. He attacks with violence and passion; he breaks old tables and lands in nihilism and despair, not in order to merely destroy and annihilate, but in order to overcome, in the Nietzschean sense of preserving and deepening while attacking and annulling. As mere counter-movement, Nietzsche's critique remains, like all opposition, bound up with that which it opposes. Even where not acknowledged by Nietzsche himself, there are many influences of the past in his philosophy, and many aspects of his new metaphysics can be traced back to previous philosophers. He himself names Heraclitus, Spinoza, Schopenhauer, and Goethe as his precursors and educators. Thus, although his metaphysics is a repudiation of the Western tradition and its emphasis on the supersensuous and transcendent, it by no means represents a complete break with the history of Western thought. And, indeed, despite his radical polemic against Socratic and Platonic teaching, he does not succeed fully in liberating himself from what he so violently attacks. The "Gegendenker" is at all times also the "Nebendenker."

But while Nietzsche's new metaphysics is not completely free of traditional elements, it does represent a conception of reality that also bears the mark of a distinctly modern temper and makes its author a true precursor of twentieth-century thought. Nietzsche's new reality does not dwell in a realm beyond nature and time, but it is lived, experienced, and suffered. It can no longer be understood by reason alone, because it touches the very depth of the human personality. It possesses existential meaningfulness in dealing with the concrete individual being and the pressing, urgent problems of his unique life.

Nietzsche's metaphysics, based on the repudiation of the Platonic-Christian tradition, represents a "reversal of Platonism," ("die Umkehrung des Platonismus"). In the dictum of the *Gay Science*, "God is dead," Nietzsche expresses the fact that the Platonic-Christian tradition and its so-called "true" world had collapsed, and with this collapse its supersensuous, eternal ideas and values had lost their meaning. The result of this "event" was at first the creation of a void, a world without sense, without permanency, without purpose. "The contrast between the apparent and the true world is reduced to a distinction between 'world' and 'nothingness.' "[6] Nothingness, however, is no longer conceived as nonbeing, as unformed matter, powerless to form itself into being. Nothingness becomes a space of freedom, the "open seas" of the new philosophical "free spirit" who creates a new metaphysics of being. The "true" world of the Platonic-Christian tradition is abolished. "But no! With the true world we also abolished the apparent world."[7] The true world is now this Earthly City in which we live and sin and suffer. The reversal of Platonism is accomplished.

The reversal of Platonism finds its fullest expression in the teaching of the eternal recurrence, which represents a denial of the beyond, the timeless, and is an affirmation of this life and the moment. Change, contradiction, and strife are no longer something outside being, but are necessary aspects of being itself, and of the tragic rhythm of life that eternally returns with all that is great and all that is small.

Heidegger calls Nietzsche's metaphysics a metaphysics of values. These values are, however, not those of traditional philosophy. They are transmoral, and reach into the sphere of being itself. Nietzsche's categories of being, morality, and aesthetics cannot be separated; they all merge in a total world view that is beyond good and evil, beyond the beautiful and ugly, beyond truth and falsity. This merging of ethics and metaphysics is true not only of Nietzsche's philosophy, but is a characteristic shared by existential thinkers, particularly by Heidegger, who is greatly influenced by Nietzsche.

In their stress on concrete individual existence and the primacy of personal experience over abstractions, in their concern with the unique facts of the human personality, both Heidegger's and Nietzsche's metaphysical teachings stress existential uniqueness and individuality. Yet, at the same time, both are transcending the particular and individual in what Heidegger calls authentic ontology. This transcendence is, however, performed on different grounds by both philosophers; and it is here that difficulties arise in Heidegger's understanding of Nietzsche, as we shall see in connection with the ethical interpretation of Nietzsche's theory of eternal recurrence. Heidegger's transcendence of "Dasein" into "Being as such" never seems quite to leave the "ontic" stage of the individual's personal experience. His categories of care, dread, and resolve seem to remain existential and human, although he insists upon a distinction between the ontological significance of his principles and their merely ontic application to particular, actual situations. Nietzsche's starting point, on the other hand, is not "Dasein," the individual's concrete existence, but nature. The individual does not create the "Umwelt" and give it meaningfulness; rather, man is placed within nature and gains meaning only within the totality of the cosmos. Life, for Nietzsche, means the unity of man and nature. The world we live in is not created anew each moment by a human decision. It is the human individual who must accept and identify with the laws of nature, its eternally destroying and creating activity, and its fundamental principle of the will to power.

II

The two basic concepts of the will to power and the eternal recurrence seem at first to be in sharp opposition. In fact, many interpreters have stressed the existence of a contradiction between a teleological "will to power" and a nonteleological "eternal recurrence," between eternal development and eternal sameness. However, it is my contention that the two concepts are closely interconnected and must be understood as a unity. Nietzsche's fundamental law, the "Ur-Gesetz" of being, must be interpreted in its double aspect of the will to power and the eternal recurrence.

These two opposed positions result from fundamental differences in interpretation. The Schopenhauerian foundation of Nietzsche's voluntaristic conception of reality, as well as the reversal of that foundation, are generally acknowledged. But disagreement exists as to the manner of and reason for the reversal of Schopenhauer's will to live to Nietzsche's will to power. This disagreement leads to different positions in regard to the acceptance or denial of a unity between Nietzsche's basic concepts of the will to power and the eternal recurrence.

Schopenhauer is without doubt the major influence in Nietzsche's voluntaristic interpretation of being, in which the will becomes the ultimate constituent of reality. However, his teaching provided only the starting point. Particularly in the later periods of Nietzsche's creative life, in which the concepts of the will to power and the eternal recurrence were fully developed, Nietzsche turned away from his former teacher. His conception of reality at first seems more pessimistic and negative than Schopenhauer's. Both lived in the shadow of Kant's critical philosophy, which made naïve, dogmatic metaphysics impossible. The distinction between what is and what appears to us had to be acknowledged. However, Schopenhauer believed that the noumenal realm, which exists in a state of primal unity, is not completely closed to us. It can, even if only in a limited sense, be reached by the annihilation of the objectified will. Nietzsche, on the other hand, denied the knowability of the "Ding an sich" (the "thing-in-itself") and abolished it as a metaphysical foundation. Not only are objects unknowable independently of the experiencing subject, but they also do not exist outside the human mind. In the *Will to Power* Nietzsche says: "All being is interpretation; there are no things in themselves, no absolute knowledge; the perspectivistic, deceiving character belongs to existence."[8] And in *Beyond Good and Evil* he adds:

> Philosophers are in the habit of speaking of will as if it were the best-known thing in the world. Schopenhauer, in fact, gave us to understand that will alone is really known to us, completely known, known without deduction and addition. But it seems to me that Schopenhauer also in this case did only what philosophers usually do: he took over and exaggerated a popular judgment. Willing seems to me to be, above all, something complicated, something that is a unity in word only. . . . In every willing there is first of all a multiplicity of feelings; . . . second, . . . in every act of the will there is a thought which gives commands; . . . third, the will is not only a complex of feeling and thinking, but above all it is a passion—the passion of commanding.[9]

The will, the foundation of all being, becomes a mere human category. Schopenhauer's distinction between the noumenal and empirical will is abolished. What remains is only "ein vermenschlichtes Metapher" (a humanized metaphor).

Nietzsche's position, however, is not always clear. In

spite of his denial of the knowability and existence of the noumenal realm, he could not quite bring himself to give up the hope that there was a world outside our sense experience and the articulation of the mind. The longing to penetrate "behind" phenomena into a primal state of unity is never completely absent from the complexity of Nietzsche's thought. Plato's "Eros" and Kant's "Dialectic" are present and at work, even if this is never acknowledged by Nietzsche himself. References to the "Ur-Eine" are not restricted only to his early writings, where he still accepted the Kantian distinction between the noumenal and the phenomenal, and the Schopenhauerian separation of the world as will and idea, primal unity and its objectifications. There are also references to primal Oneness, the "Ur-Eine," in his later works. But, on the whole, Nietzsche's position must be interpreted as a denial of the duality of the empirical and the noumenal will. This is particularly true after 1881, the period during which the concept of the eternal recurrence was developed.

With the abandonment of this duality, Schopenhauer's primal state that is free and determined by nothing outside itself, that knows no change and multiplicity, but exists in a state of unity and peace, becomes meaningless. Thus a return to a primal state by the annihilation of the objectified will becomes impossible. There is no hope for a reentry into a primordial state of peace; there is no salvation for the artist or saint, as Schopenhauer had claimed. All that is left is the phenomenal world, a world of ceaseless striving and pain. It is the only world that exists. There is no possibility of escape.

For Schopenhauer, on the other hand, this world of striving in which the primal will has objectified itself into a multiplicity of contradictory wills, is an illusion from which we must and can escape. The real world exists beyond space and time and causality, beyond pain and strife. It offers peace and salvation.

But Schopenhauer's liberation from the blindly striving will, which the saint allegedly accomplishes, is meaningless for modern Western man and his existential concerns, even were it possible. Nietzsche, whose philosophy stands under the symbol of Dionysus, wants to find an answer which does not lead to resignation and Nirvana, to what he calls "weak pessimism." He reverses Schopenhauer's metaphysical teaching, not by negating and abolishing its pessimistic premise, but by interpreting it Dionysiacally. Schopenhauer's blind, striving "will to live" becomes Nietzsche's positive and creative "will to power." It is a will that does not merely struggle for existence, but aims at stronger and fuller existence, at "growth and conquest and supremacy." It is a will that is equally active and aggressive, but no longer blind and without direction.

III

In *The Will to Power* Nietzsche says:

There is no willing that is not a willing to something; the goal must not be eliminated from the process of willing, which must always be connected with a command; . . . a general state of tension through which a quantum of power attempts release is not yet willing. . . . One has abolished the essence of the will, the "whither." This is, most of all, the case with Schopenhauer. What he calls "will" is only an empty word.[10]

It is here that difficulties and ambiguities of interpretation arise. The question is: What does Nietzsche mean by "whither" and "goal," which accomplish the reversal of the "will to live" into the "will to power?" If "goal" is interpreted in the traditional meaning of the word as an end toward which being develops and moves, if it is in any way connected with ideas of progress and morality, Nietzsche's own meaning is misunderstood and contradictions between his central concepts of the will to power and the eternal recurrence are thereby created. Instead, one must understand "goal," as used here, as an inner principle of form.

It is Nietzsche himself who here, as in many other instances, contributes to the misunderstanding of his theories by giving antithetical meanings to the same word, using it in the traditional sense as well as in the new meaning of his own philosophy. Although Nietzsche's concepts grow out of an entirely new way of thinking, he uses traditional, conventional terms to express his radically different ideas. In a "Backward Glance" to *The Birth of Tragedy* he himself admits:

> How much I regret the fact that I did not have the courage to create my own language in keeping with my own, radically novel ideas. . . . Using terms borrowed from the vocabularies of Kant and Schopenhauer, I tried laboriously to express value judgments which were in basic contradiction to the spirit and taste of these men.[11]

Indeed, I agree with Nietzsche. The use of his extraordinary mastery of the German language to create a new terminology would perhaps have prevented many misunderstandings. On the other hand, it might have led to its own difficulties and obscurities, as Heidegger's writings demonstrate. Again Nietzsche's own words have to be considered when he adds in the same "Backward Glance": "I did not have the courage to risk a fresh language . . . or shall I say the immodesty?"

By interpreting the word "goal" in the traditional rather than the Nietzschean sense, many of his critics have been led to see a contradiction between the nonteleological teaching of the eternal return of the same and the teleological will to power, in which development is understood as progressive movement, and creativity as novelty. Among those who interpret Nietzsche in this manner are Simmel, Oehler, and Vaihinger.* Their traditional interpretation of the word "goal" leads them to the conclusion that it is Darwin whose influence is responsible for Nietzsche's reversal of Schopenhauer's metaphysics:

> Between Schopenhauer and Nietzsche is Darwin. . . . Nietzsche's philosophy is the poetic, philosophical expression of Darwin's theory of evolution.**

> Nietzsche's teaching is the positive reversal of Schopenhauerianism and this is accomplished under the influence of Darwin. This is the thesis that I advance.***

However, Nietzsche's own statements express an often repeated rejection of Darwin's concepts of development. Although some passages in Nietzsche's writings do seem to indicate an agreement with certain aspects of Darwinism, this agreement is merely apparent. Such is the case with Darwin's principle of the "survival of the fittest," which Nietzsche calls "a conception of the first order."[12] But Darwin and Nietzsche mean something different by "survival"

---

* Georg Simmel, *Schopenhauer und Nietzsche* (Leipzig: Duncker & Humblot, 1907); Richard Oehler, *Nietzsche und die Vor-Sokratiker* (Leipzig: Duerr, 1904); Hans Vaihinger, *Die Philosophie des Als-Ob,* last chapter (Leipzig: Meiner, 1911); idem., *Nietzsche als Philosoph* (Berlin: Reuther & Reichard, 1902).

** Oehler, *Nietzsche und die Vor-Sokratiker.*

*** Vaihinger, *Nietzsche als Philosoph,* p. 43.

and something different by the "fittest." To Nietzsche "survival" is not mere self-preservation, but preservation of power. His fundamental principle of conservation, developed under the influence of Robert Mayer, contains the elements of inner growth and expansion. Life is not mere struggle for existence, but struggle for increase of power. "Wanting to preserve oneself is the expression of a distressed condition, a restriction of the fundamental instinct of life which aims at expansion of power. . . . Not distress, but abundance and extravagance predominate in nature."[13]

Likewise, Nietzsche's "fittest" are not those whose basic instinct is self-preservation; they are not the "herd" men who, guided by utilitarian principles, are "more clever . . . and have more ingenuity—by ingenuity I understand . . . timidity, patience, cunning, disguise."[14] The fittest is the higher individual, the "free spirit" who affirms struggle as a creative force and aims at intensification of power. This higher individual, the genius, is, according to Nietzsche, "the most sublime and therefore the most fragile machine. . . . The higher type presents an incomparably greater complexity— a greater sum of coordinated elements: thereby disintegration also becomes incomparably more probable."[15] In the struggle for mere existence it is not the genius, the exceptionally gifted, who stands out and survives, but the mediocre, the "herd" man. The principle of natural selection does not result in a continued evolution. "Species do not grow in perfection: the weak always master the strong—that is because they are the larger number; also they are more clever . . . cunning."[16]

Nietzsche's fundamental concepts are clearly opposed to Darwin's mechanistic and utilitarian principles of evolution, essentially because the latter lack elements of creativity. Thus he says in *The Will to Power*:

"Useful" in Darwinian biology means: to prove advantageous in the struggle with others. But it seems to me that true progress is already contained in the feeling of increase of power which is quite independent of its usefulness in the struggle; from this feeling alone originates the will to struggle.[17]

The will to power is a dynamic, creative force that does not aim at goals external to itself, but creates from within and organizes the dialectical powers of its own being. It does not aim at evolution and progress in the Christian theistic, Hegelian, or Darwinian senses. "The goal of humanity does not lie in the end, but in its highest specimen,"[18] in the greatness of the individual and his creative will. The will to power creates in the manner of the artist, not toward goals and purposes and utilitarian considerations, but out of an inner need for balance and form. Nature acts "not out of poverty and distress, but out of the fullness of its potentialities and an artistic urge."[19] It is "eine reine, freie Natur" (pure and free nature) which possesses "purposiveness without purpose."

The concept "goal," as traditionally understood, is to Nietzsche merely a Kantian regulative idea, a category of human invention that has no objective significance. "We have invented the concept goal; in reality there is no purpose."[20] In sum, "goal" as understood by Nietzsche is not external to the will, nor does the will go beyond itself in its striving for expansion. Its goal is the intensification and unfolding of its own powers—"power as the essence of the will and not as its goal."*

If the will to power is interpreted in this way, its unity with the concept of the eternal recurrence of the same can be accomplished without apparent contradiction. The will

---

* Heidegger, *Nietzsche*, 1: 52.

to power thus interpreted is the "Gesamtlage," the field of force, as discussed in the preceding section, and the Dionysian tragic pattern of life whose clarification was attempted in the first chapter. It is a center of energy that contains the forces of tension and release, of polarity and enhancement. And it is this *Gesamtlage* of the wills to power in their inner striving which returns again and again in eternal recurrence. "The eternal recurrence of all things lacks all goals and purposes: let us beware of attributing a goal to the cycle of eternal return."[21] "The energy of the totality of becoming rises to the highest point and falls again in an eternal cycle."[22]

IV

Nietzsche's reversal of Schopenhauer's "negative pessimism" into a positive, creative "strong pessimism" is in no way based upon the influence of Darwin, but upon that of Heraclitus, Spinoza and Goethe. "To place Darwin next to Goethe means to offend majesty, *majestatem genii.*"[23]

Nietzsche's concept of the will to power is influenced by Spinoza's and Goethe's nonteleological conceptions of being, his eternal recurrence by their concepts of unity. In what follows below, as well as in the last part of this study, I will emphasize the manifold connections that exist between Nietzsche's thought and that of Spinoza and Goethe. I believe that these connections will help illuminate aspects that are often overlooked in the writings of Nietzsche, whose style lacks the architectonic structure of Spinoza's philosophy and the classic clarity of Goethe's works. In particular, I hope that out of this comparison the concept of unity—which I hold to be central in Nietzsche's thought—will evolve with greater clarity and depth.

The Spinozistic elements in Nietzsche's thought are not always sufficiently recognized and their analysis has been largely neglected in the Nietzsche literature, where the emphasis is upon the influences of the early Greeks, Schopenhauer, Wagner, Reé, Stirner, and Emerson. However, Spinoza's influence is clearly evident in Nietzsche's writings, although it is often only indirectly exerted through the Spinozism of Goethe. It is primarily through the mediation of Goethe, whose poetic temper was closer to Nietzsche, that elements of Spinoza's philosophy were integrated into Nietzsche's thought. But additionally, Goethe and Nietzsche share many ideas that differ from what Spinoza taught.

Spinoza's influence upon Goethe has been fully recognized by Goethe scholars. Goethe himself also acknowledges his debt to Spinoza and his admiration for him remained constant throughout his life. First expressed in the *Ephemeriden,* it is still evident in his later works and in his last conversations with Eckermann. In *Poetry and Truth* he calls himself a "passionate disciple and convinced admirer" of Spinoza.* Nietzsche's attitude to Spinoza is, however, inconsistent; it ranges from ecstatic admiration to complete rejection. Thus he calls Spinoza his "educator and precursor"[24] and, in a letter to Franz Overbeck, he writes: "I have a precursor and what a precursor. . . . I find myself again in five fundamental points of his doctrine. . . . He denies freedom of the will . . . ends and goals . . . the moral world order, egoism, evil."[25] But more frequently Nietzsche criticizes Spinoza's philosophy severely as being too passive, too rationalistic, "too close to the old God in his concept of unlimited power."[26]

Nietzsche's attitude toward Goethe is even more complex and ambiguous. It is significant that, while he admired

---

* Goethe, *Dichtung und Wahrheit,* in *Saemtliche Werke,* 131 vols., 4 secs. (Weimar: Herman Boehlau, 1870–1918), sec. 1, 28:289.

Goethe's qualities of harmony and totality, which he himself did not possess but longed for, he paradoxically ignored those elements that they did share: the daemonic, the problematic, and the tragic. Thus the Goethe of the "Sturm und Drang," and Goethe as the titanic, Promethean poet are repudiated by Nietzsche, while the classical, "contemplative man in the grand style" is admired as being an embodiment of totality and unity.

But whatever their individual attitudes may have been at different stages of their philosophical development, important similarities in the views of all three thinkers do exist despite the many significant dissimilarities. The agreements are, however, often obscured by radical differences in temperament, in modes of thought, and in their writing styles. Spinoza's ultra-deductive, mathematical system, his all-harmonizing peace, his abstruse and technical language are an extreme contrast to Goethe's poetic intuition and Nietzsche's passionate striving and aphoristic style. The rationalistic teaching of "non ridere, neque lugere nec detestari, sed intellegere" is opposed to the poet's feeling and expression, as well as to the philosopher "with the hammer" who "writes with his blood." However, despite the intellectual differences that exist among the three thinkers, a genuine kinship can be established. Goethe's and Nietzsche's own insights are of significance here. In *Poetry and Truth* Goethe remarks: "The closest ties link us to that which is most opposite to ourselves."* And in *Beyond Good and Evil*[27] Nietzsche speaks of Spinoza's mathematical, deductive system as a "mask" that was necessitated by the scientific and philosophical demands of his time and has often led to a misunderstanding of his teaching.

---

* Ibid.

If we remove the "masks," the rationalistic geometer, the intuitive, "naïve" poet and the impassioned, unrestrained philosopher become "Wahlverwandte." Goethe becomes the true disciple of Spinoza and the precursor of many of Nietzsche's ideas; and Nietzsche becomes the tortured upholder of many philosophical views of Spinoza and Goethe.

The mode of thought of each thinker is dialectical and does not present clear, unambiguous answers. This is most evident in Nietzsche who, while aiming at coherence and unity, opposes dogmatic completeness and affirms the principle of contradiction as fundamental in metaphysics, epistemology, and ethics. Goethe, too, although admired by Nietzsche for his measure and harmony, is a truly problematic thinker who stresses the daemonic. But in regard to Spinoza, we must first remove the "mask" in order to uncover the dialectic of his thought, a dialectic that is deeper in Nietzsche and Goethe, but nevertheless is by no means absent in Spinoza. This dialectical element in Spinoza's philosophy has been largely ignored, so that he is generally considered to be a true rationalist who believes that a rational order exists in the universe and that man's reason can achieve certainty. Not only is he held to be unaware of the inconsistencies in his own system, but also of the fundamental antinomies that are inevitable in any metaphysical investigation. But in fact he, too, shares the eternal spirit of all great metaphysicians from Plato on who, in striving for totality and unity, become unavoidably involved in the ambiguities that are inherent in this quest. Karl Jaspers in *Die Grossen Philosophen* denies that Spinoza is a "cool and simple thinker" who presents "precise and unambiguous answers." He calls Spinoza a "durchgluehender Denker" and his philosophy "ein Hinsprechen zum Geheimnis."

V

As noted before, Nietzsche's basic metaphysical principle of the will to power is influenced by Spinoza's conception of being, as mediated by Goethe. The will to power has many elements in common with Spinoza's fundamental concept of substance. Both Spinoza's substance and Nietzsche's will to power are active, dynamic, nonteleological powers. However, while the nonteleological elements in the ideas of Spinoza, Goethe, and Nietzsche have been fully recognized and are indeed beyond dispute, scholarly agreement concerning the dynamic elements exists only in regard to the ideas of Goethe and Nietzsche. Some critics interpret Spinoza's world as conceived in the spirit of the Eleatics: undynamic, timeless, powerless, and static, in contrast to the dynamic pantheism of the Renaissance. But others, Goethe among them, acknowledge the vitalism in Spinoza's philosophy. To these interpreters, Spinoza's substance is not a dead and inert entity, but an active unity which is not only all inclusive, but also infinitely productive of an infinity of things. Substance as *causa sui* is expanded into *causa efficiens omnium rerum* that is active in all modes of being.

The logico-mathematical relations of ground and consequent become in fact the relations of real and productive powers. Spinoza's mathematical system is linked to the vitalistic spirit of the Renaissance and the dynamic pantheism of Giordano Bruno, which stress the inner productivity of nature in all its fullness and multiplicity. Spinoza's fundamental principle of *conatus*, which is active in every particular phenomenon as part of the divine force, assumes some of the characteristics of Goethe's concept of the "Eternal Feminine," the symbol of unlimited, creative activity, and

Nietzsche's "will to power."* These fundamental forces contain not only the impulse toward self-preservation—the endeavor to persist in their own being—but also a drive toward enhancement and growth, toward heightening of power.

As pointed out above, Nietzsche often misunderstood Spinoza. This is particularly so in regard to the principle of self-preservation, for Nietzsche did not recognize that Spinoza's notion is indeed similar to the will to power. It not only includes the element of self-preservation, but also the elements of growth and development. Nietzsche did not take into consideration that Spinoza's "conatus" contains three elements: conservation ("suum esse conservare"); the striving for perfection ("id omne, quod hominem ad majorem perfectionem—ducit, appetat"); the striving for heightening of power ("quod nostram agendi potentiam auget"). Thus he says, in complete misunderstanding of Spinoza's fundamental metaphysical principle:

> Spinoza's "principle of self-preservation" would set a halt to all change; but this is false, the opposite is true. Everything that is alive shows clearly that it does everything not in order to preserve itself, but in order to become more.[28]

However, even when the dynamic aspects of Spinoza's teaching are acknowledged, they cannot be fully identified with Goethe's, and less so with Nietzsche's, where elements of negation, opposition, and strife are additionally present. Spinoza's substance is still far removed from Nietzsche's will to power, insofar as the latter also contains the contradic-

---

* Goethe's concept of the "Eternal Feminine," the idea of the mothers as the symbol of creation and divinity, was inspired by Paracelsus and Plutarch, as he points out in a conversation with Eckermann, January 3, 1830.

tory, the irrational, and the unconscious. It is Goethe's principle of "polarity and enhancement" ("Polaritaet und Steigerung") that, while influenced by Spinoza, provides for Nietzsche those elements which Spinoza's philosophy did not adequately express: the elements of tension and opposition.

Goethe's principle of polarity is a basic, formative law that pervades all nature. But, for Goethe as for Nietzsche, polarity does not represent a negative and hostile antagonism. It expresses an opposition that seeks equilibrium and contains within it the capability of enhancement and intensification. Goethe adds a second principle to that of "Polaritaet" and calls it "Steigerung." But this second principle must always be understood as an inseparable part of the first. The essential function of conflict and negation for Goethe and Nietzsche, as for Hegel, is contained in their positive and creative power, which can achieve harmony and unity only as an outcome of opposition and strife.

Goethe, like Nietzsche, sees life and nature as eternal becoming and striving, as an eternal cycle of destruction and creation, of living and dying. The polar, dialectical forces which pervade all life and nature work in a perpetual rhythm of uniting and separating, of coming to be and passing away. In a conversation with Eckermann, Goethe says: "I compare the earth and her atmosphere to a great living being, perpetually inhaling and exhaling."* He acknowledges the fact that it was Kant who influenced the development of this concept:

> In Kant's scientific writings, I had grasped that idea that attraction and repulsion are essential constituents of matter and that neither can be divorced from the other. This led me to the recognition of polarity as a basic feature of all creation,

---

* Eckermann, *Gespraeche mit Goethe* (Stuttgart: Cotta), April 11, 1827.

a principle of permeating and animating the infinite range of phenomena.*

And in his *Theory of Color* he observes that everything of a phenomenal nature must suggest either an original multiplicity, capable of being merged into unity, or an original unity capable of becoming a multiplicity, "separating what is united, and unifying what is separate is the life of nature."**

Goethe's principle of "Polaritaet und Steigerung" and Nietzsche's "Wille zur Macht," both dynamic and active, both full of tension and polarity, share one further important feature: they are both nonteleological forces. It is here that Spinoza's influence upon Goethe and Nietzsche is strongest and the similarity between Spinoza's substance and Goethe's and Nietzsche's cosmic powers is most significant. All three thinkers conceive their basic concepts of energy as a nonteleological force that creates according to its own laws and without any final causation.

With the rejection of a transcendent God there is also a break with the traditional concepts of ends and purposes. Reality as a whole is devoid of ends and moral values. Nature, in possession of divine attributes, does not strive toward goals external to it; it realizes itself within its own being by the intensification and unfolding of its own powers. It does not aim toward ever higher and higher goals and ends, but every moment is of equal importance within the unity of the whole, and possesses the attributes of necessity and eternality. "Nature does nothing for the sake of an end, for that eternal and infinite Being whom we call God or

---

* Goethe, *Campagne in Frankreich*, November 17, 1782.
** Ibid., *Zur Farbenlehre* in *Saemtliche Werke*, 40 vols. (Stuttgart: Cotta, 1840), 38:39.

Nature acts by the same necessity by which He exists."*
Goethe and Nietzsche acknowledge their debt to Spinoza's view of an anti-teleological world. Goethe, also giving credit to Kant, writes to Zelter:

> It is an unbounded service of our old Kant that, in his *Critique of Judgment*, he effectively placed art and nature side by side and granted both the right of acting in accordance with great principles without purpose. Spinoza had earlier inspired me with a hatred for absurd final causes. Nature and art are too great to aim at ends.**

And Nietzsche says: "When I think of my philosophical genealogy, I feel in agreement with the anti-teleological, that is the Spinozistic movement of our time."[29]

Again it is Goethe who contributes to Nietzsche's understanding of Spinoza's anti-teleological world view by replacing the ultra-deductive, mathematical system with an artistic interpretation of life. For both Goethe and Nietzsche, the forces of nature work in the manner of the artist, creating freely without ends and purposes, out of the duality and fullness of their own being. They operate in a perpetual rhythm of separating and uniting, perishing and coming to be, a rhythm that Nietzsche calls tragic, full of polarity and tension but also of enhancement and power. There are many other important aspects of Goethe's and Nietzsche's anti-teleological views; they will be discussed subsequently, in connection with their aesthetic interpretations of the universe.

VI

Nietzsche's teaching of the eternal recurrence, whose

---

* Spinoza, *Ethics*, pt. 4, Preface.
** Letter to Zelter, January 29, 1830, in *Goethes Briefe*, 8 vols. (Berlin: O. Elsner, 1902–5).

basic concept of the will to power is closely linked to Spinoza's and Goethe's anti-teleological conceptions of being, is, additionally, influenced by their concept of unity—a unity that exists in spite of the infinite complexity and multiplicity of things.

Spinoza's pantheistic view, with its stress on the immanence of the creative principle, is the foundation of Goethe's and Nietzsche's universe. For both Goethe and Nietzsche, God exists in the creative activity of nature and man. "Existence is God."* Both find in the dynamic forces of the cosmos and their eternal cycle of destruction and creation, death and rebirth, the unity of God, nature, and man. In the pantheistic views of all three thinkers, nature gains a new significance. That which is real does not dwell in a Platonic-Christian transcendent realm, but within nature, of which man is an integral part. Many of the predicates which were once attributed to a transcendent God are now contained in nature. There is nothing outside nature, no creator or ruler who is different in kind and guides and directs man's destinies. "Deus sive natura." Nature is *causa sui*, eternal, infinite.

Goethe's conception of the universe as a unity of God, nature, and man is expressed in all his writings: his poems, dramas, letters, biographical notes, and scientific essays. In a letter to Jacobi he states: "When philosophy makes separation its chief aim, I find it impossible to derive any gain from it; . . . but when it integrates or rather when it heightens and strengthens our original feeling of unity, then I welcome it."** In the *Metamorphosis of Plants* he speaks of a primal plant, the "Ur-Pflanze," which represents to him an arche-

---

* Ibid., Letter to F. Jacobi, June 10, 1785: "Existence is God." Also see Eckermann, February 20, 1831; Nietzsche calls his teaching of the eternal recurrence "the religion of religions" (12:415).

** Letter to Jacobi, November 3, 1812, in *Goethes Briefe*.

type, an original unity, from which, as a result of gradual metamorphosis, all varieties and complex formations of organic life develop. This fundamental unity, much like an Aristotelian entelechy, contains within itself the potentiality of infinite modifications and is an inner principle that determines the organization of all living forms.

Nietzsche expresses the idea of unity most fully in his doctrine of the eternal recurrence, which grew out of the pronouncement of the "death of God," and the repudiation of Christian teaching insofar as it was based on the belief in a transcendent God and a dualistic, moral world order. "God is dead," but this is only the transcendent God and not the God who is immanent in this world and is identified with the productive forces in nature and man. The teaching of the eternal recurrence expresses Nietzsche's search for totality, unity, and eternality—his longing to transcend the particularity of individual human existence and find a nexus between God, nature, and man. It represents an apotheosis of life, a glorification of the creative principle eternally at work in the productive forces of the cosmos and their eternally returning activity.

Nietzsche and Goethe express the principle of unity not in the abstract, mathematical terms of Spinoza, but in poetic, symbolic form. For both there is no sharp boundary between theory and intuition, between vision and thought. Nietzsche's idea of eternal recurrence assumes the characteristics of a poetic, mystic experience, where "one sees, one does not hear." Goethe's ideas of the "Ur-Pflanze" is a poetic metaphor of his concept of unity.

While the unity of nature and man is stressed by both Goethe and Nietzsche, most interpreters have recognized it only in Goethe's works, where it is clearly evident. Goethe is identified with Schiller's "naïve" artist who is "one with nature."* In interpretations of Nietzsche, however, this unity is either denied or not sufficiently stressed by scholars, who tend to emphasize the subjective element in his philosophy. They interpret his universe as one of human subjectivity in which nature is meaningless until it is given a meaning through man.

Indeed, the unity between nature and man is far more problematic in Nietzsche's than in Goethe's thought. Nietzsche is the "sentimental" artist in whom the harmony and unity that exist instinctively in the naïve artist are fraught with difficulties; but it is a unity for which Nietzsche at all times continues to long and attempts to attain. Without them, neither his teaching of eternal recurrence, nor his conception of the freedom and destiny of man, nor his idea of "amor fati" can be made intelligible. Admittedly, the Nietzschean concept of unity possesses the problematic ambiguity that is characteristic of his philosophy generally, an ambiguity that must be understood in the specifically Nietzschean sense wherein each concept contains its opposite within itself. Nietzsche's concept of unity possesses many elements of Spinoza's pantheism, but it also contains elements of Humean scepticism and Kantian dualism. The union between nature and man, replete with conflicts and doubts, is part of the "primordial contradiction" that Nietzsche sees as the essence of all things.

Elements of dualism are present in Goethe as well, but far less radically or consistently, appearing only in some works and biographical notes. Although Goethe is generally considered to be the naïve artist philosophizing with unconscious naïveté, he is, as Wilhelm von Humboldt acknowl-

---

* Schiller, in *Ueber Naive und Sentimentale Dichtung*, makes a distinction between the "naïve" artist who "is nature" and the "sentimental" artist who has lost this unity and "seeks nature."

edged, often of no less a brooding nature than Schiller, the accepted prototype of the sentimental artist. Goethe himself recognized the disharmony in his soul and often referred to it, particularly in the *Italian Journey*. But it is above all in *Faust*, this most problematic of all his works, where he, like Nietzsche, is torn by questions and doubts: Is the alienation between nature and man solely a modern predicament that could be abolished, or is the duality fundamental? Is a return to pre-Socratic unity and the tragic age possible? Or is the union between nature and man merely a Kantian "idea," an Apollonian illusion and idle dream which, like the union of Faust and Helena, is doomed—as Goethe symbolized in the death of Euphorion? Thus Faust, despairing of the dualism between spirit and nature, cries out: "No road to the unexplored, never to be explored! . . . What pageantry! Yet, mere pageantry! Where shall I endless Nature seize thee?"*

The concept of unity leads to Spinoza's "amor intellectualis dei" (the intellectual love of God), to Goethe's "Naturfroemmigkeit" (nature piety), and Nietzsche's "amor fati" (love of fate). Nietzsche's concept of *amor fati* is primarily of ethical and religious significance and thus will occupy us extensively below, where such a discussion is more useful.

VII

In order to further clarify Nietzsche's concepts of the will to power and the eternal recurrence, it is important to go back to Heraclitus. Nietzsche, erecting his philosophical structure upon a critique of Platonic rationalism and idealism and a rejection of Socrates as the destroyer of tragedy,

---

* Goethe, *Faust*, 15 vols. (Leipzig: Tempel-Verlag), 6:318, 98.

looks farther back to the pre-Socratics, particularly Heraclitus, as his models and precursors.

> All great problems have been posed before Socrates. . . . Kant, Hegel, Schopenhauer, Spinoza! How poor, how one-sided they are! . . . The knowledge of the great Greeks has educated me: Heraclitus, Empedocles, Parmenides, Anaxagoras, Democritus, they are to be venerated, they are richer.[30]

Nietzsche finds in these earliest philosophers of Greece seers and poets as well as thinkers, and is drawn to the mythological and intuitive elements that permeate their thought, even where the first historical efforts toward conceptualization were made. "When I listen to the total sound (*Gesamtklang*) of the older Greek philosophers, I hear sounds which I was accustomed to hear in Greek art and particularly in Greek tragedy."[31]

Heraclitus is the only thinker whom Nietzsche never criticizes in all his various polemics against traditional philosophers. While his other acknowledged early educators, Schopenhauer and Wagner, are abandoned, Heraclitus remains his teacher throughout all his creative periods. It is above all Heraclitus who leads Nietzsche to an overcoming of Schopenhauer's negative, pessimistic philosophy and to his own tragic, Dionysian conception of being. Nietzsche gives full acknowledgment to Heraclitus's greatness:

> Heraclitus, in whose presence I feel warmer and happier than anywhere else. The affirmation of destruction and annihilation which is the essential quality of a Dionysian philosophy, the Yes-saying to contradiction and war, the concept of "becoming"—in all these I recognize that which is closer to me than any other thought.[32]

Heraclitus of Ephesus is essentially Dionysus. Together with the Greek tragedians he is, according to Nietzsche, responsible for deepening the Hellenic mind and bringing about the tragic culture of the early Greeks that became the model for Nietzsche's philosophy.

Three major notions in Heraclitus's work became leitmotifs in Nietzsche's philosophy: life is eternal war, polarity, tension; life is eternal becoming and flux; life is play, "the world of Zeus." These three elements are the basis of Nietzsche's fundamental concepts of the will to power and the eternal recurrence.

Things, for both Heraclitus and Nietzsche, have no existence apart from their continuous interaction, which takes the form of continuous conflict. The will to power manifests itself only against obstacles and is in constant search for that which resists it. But Heraclitus's "fire" and Nietzsche's "will to power" are both positive, creative forces. Heraclitus introduces into Nietzsche's metaphysical conception of the cosmos not only the characteristics of change and war, but also those of balance and law.

> Becoming is justified . . . war is a means to achieve balance. . . . Is the world full of guilt, injustice, contradiction and suffering? Yes, cries Heraclitus, but only for the limited man who does not see the total design; not for the contuitive God; for him all contradiction is harmonized.[33]

There is no scholarly disagreement known to me concerning the Heraclitean influence in Nietzsche's concept of the will to power. But in regard to the doctrine of eternal recurrence some interpreters, among them Baeumler,* have pointed to an alleged opposition between the eternal return

---

* Alfred Baeumler, *Nietzsche als Philosoph und Politiker* (Leipzig: Reclam, 1931).

of the same and the eternally changing Heraclitean river, between being and becoming. However, Nietzsche himself sees no contradiction. He calls becoming a "form of being" ("eine Art des Seins"), and claims that the doctrine of the "eternal recurrence, that is, of the unconditional and infinitely repeated cycle of all things . . . this teaching of Zarathustra could have been taught by Heraclitus."[34]

> Into the mystical night which had obscured Anaximander's problem of becoming, entered Heraclitus of Ephesus and illuminated it with a divine flash of lightning: "Behold becoming," he cries, and no one has ever watched so attentively this eternal motion of the waves and the rhythm of all things.[35]

The Heraclitean river is not only a symbol of change and becoming, but in the sameness and repetition of the motion and the beat of the waves there is a rhythm which, like an Oriental melody, repeats itself again and again. The river symbolizes eternal change and eternal sameness. Becoming and being are one.

The influence of the third Heraclitean element of "play" is of central importance primarily in Nietzsche's aesthetic interpretation of the world, the topic of my last chapter. With Heraclitus, as well as Spinoza and Goethe, Nietzsche arrives at a conception of nature that is free of ends and purposes and creates in the manner of the child and the artist, playfully building and destroying "in innocence." It is a conception of the cosmos that Nietzsche calls "the Innocence of Becoming" ("die Unschuld des Werdens"). The world, for Nietzsche, is an eternal play of dynamic forces, their tension and release, their perishing and coming to be. It is an eternal recurrence of a will to create and destroy, to struggle and to expand.

7
THE ETERNAL RECURRENCE
IN ITS ETHICAL
PERSPECTIVE

From this gateway, moment, a long lane leads backward;
behind it lies eternity.[1]

—Nietzsche

I

The ethical meaning of Nietzsche's eternal recurrence is
here treated apart from the metaphysical for purposes of
clarification, but with the realization that it separates what
belongs essentially together in Nietzsche's unity of thought
in which ethics and metaphysics merge. The world for
Nietzsche means nature and man, united in an inextricably
connected whole whose fundamental principle of the will
to power is at work in both natural and human events. To
sunder this whole is to lose the full impact of his thought.
As pointed out before, this unity is indeed complex and often
contradictory, but to ignore or deny it is to destroy the essence of Nietzsche's problematic mode of thinking.

Interpreters who separate the metaphysical from the ethical perspective for reasons other than those of clarification contend that Nietzsche's idea of eternal recurrence breaks into two irreconcilable doctrines: the idea as an objective fact to be demonstrated by theories of physics, and the idea as a subjective hypothesis to be demonstrated by its ethical consequences. This break into two contradictory parts is unavoidable, given an interpretation of the metaphysical meaning as that of an eternal return of exactly the same identical states, and of the ethical meaning in terms of traditional morality. Among those who see no possible link between the two perspectives of the idea are Hans Vaihinger, Karl Loewith, and Karl Jaspers.

Their ethical interpretation of the idea is centered primarily upon the following passage from the *Nachlass:*

My teaching says: To live thus that you must wish to live again, is the task . . . you will in any case. . . . This is a heavy burden. When you absorb and embody this thought, it will transform you.[2]

This quotation is erroneously interpreted as a "categorical imperative," and thus the teaching of eternal recurrence becomes a regulative idea, a will to eternalization that has no connection with the cosmological aspects of the idea. Man has lost his beliefs and ideals—God is dead. But since man cannot live without goals and ends and moral imperatives, without the hope and promise of a better world, he needs a new hold, a new support, a new illusion to replace the old, discarded ones. In *The Birth of Tragedy* it had been the aesthetic illusion that had made life bearable; now the teaching of eternal recurrence is to provide man with yet another illusion to give content to his actions and put the stamp of eternity upon his life. Eternity is not represented in the cycle of eternal return, but in the goal of the human will to eternalize itself. Nietzsche's teaching becomes a practical postulate, a necessary illusion put in place of old traditional beliefs that had lost their meaning.

Thus, according to Loewith:

> If everything returns . . . then the demand to live "as if" would lose all meaning. The second, the cosmological meaning, creates a fundamental contradiction. . . . If human life is merely a ring within the larger ring of the eternal recurrence of all that is—what meaning would there be in a will to go beyond oneself, to want a European future, to will anything at all? . . . On the basis of its educational character, one must understand Nietzsche's teaching as subjective, as a "fiction," an "As-If" there were an objective occurrence.*

And Jaspers says: "This idea must serve life. As such it is not a metaphysical teaching, a metaphysical conception of being. It cannot be interpreted in logical or scientific terms. A world in which everything returns and can be figured out with mathematical certainty would be senseless."**

Vaihinger stresses the Kantian origin of Nietzsche's idea and calls it "a doctrine of conscious illusion, a heuristic fiction." In *Die Philosophie des Als-Ob* he says: "This Kantian origin of Nietzsche's doctrine has hitherto been completely ignored because Nietzsche had, as was to be expected from his temperament, repeatedly and ferociously attacked Kant, whom he quite misunderstood."*** Like Kant, Vaihinger as-

---

* Karl Loewith, *Nietzsche's Philosophie der ewigen Wiederkunft des Gleichen* (Stuttgart: Kohlhammer, 1956), pp. 91f.

** Karl Jaspers, *Nietzsche* (Berlin: De Gruyter, 1950), pp. 250f.

*** Hans Vaihinger, *Die Philosophie des Als-Ob*, p. 342. Also see: Georg Simmel, *Schopenhauer und Nietzsche*, pp. 253f. Simmel interprets both the teaching of eternal recurrence and the overman as regulative ideas and

serts, Nietzsche recognized that life and science are impossible without imaginary and false conceptions. They both understood the nature of these illusions through and through, but in spite of it they recognized their usefulness and necessity.

The eternal recurrence thus is for Vaihinger, as for Loewith and Jaspers, a "heuristic fiction" that is to be distinguished from a "hypothesis that is linked to what is actually given and therefore certain as an explanatory principle." He points to Nietzsche's early works, particularly *The Birth of Tragedy*, and claims that what is there presented as an aesthetic illusion is later widened into regulative fictions in science and knowledge, and finally in life itself. To prove his theory, he uses Nietzsche's own words: "The lie is more divine than truth." But Vaihinger and Nietzsche speak two different languages here. Nietzsche's "lie" that is more divine than traditional truth is not Vaihinger's illusion. It is the new Dionysian truth, which is problematic, contradictory, open to change, doubt and experimentation, and is derived from a tragic conception of being.

I do agree with the above interpreters that Nietzsche's idea must be understood as an ethical teaching, but disagree that it can be explained within traditional ethics, based on moral imperatives. It is easy enough to see why Nietzsche's aphorism from the *Nachlass* gave rise to misunderstandings, if one fails to read this passage in the spirit of his whole philosophy, which represents a repudiation of a moral conception of life. Not categorical imperatives and obedience

---

"Pruefsteine" for our conduct. And see Oscar Ewald, *Nietzsches Lehre in ihren Grundbegriffen* (Berlin: Hofmann, 1903), pp. 58f. Ewald asserts that the idea of eternal recurrence must be interpreted symbolically and not "realistically or dogmatically. . . . It is an ideal, an ethical demand to live thus that is worthy of being eternalized."

to ethical commands, but the will to power is the mover of human actions.

I further agree that the teaching functions as a regulative idea, but at the same time insist that it is also a constitutive idea. Both are connected in Nietzsche's thought and cannot be separated. Nietzsche's teaching is close to Kant's, as Vaihinger claims. However, it is not Kant as Vaihinger sees him, nor the Kant of the second critique. Kant's Dialectic is not a philosophy of the "as if." His ideas are not heuristic fictions, because they are transcendentally grounded in the very nature of man. They are indeed regulative and provide principles of action, but they do not originate in a source external to man. Instead, they are self-legislative, autonomous laws that express man's inner noumenal self. The "categorical imperative" is not an external command, but man's own moral consciousness. Kant's ideas are not illusions, when employed as principles of action; they become illusions only when falsely applied to the field of knowledge and science.*

Also it is not, as Vaihinger asserts, Kant's second critique that influenced Nietzsche. The *Critique of Practical Reason* —with its separation of man into a noumenal and empirical self, its stress on duty, and its abolition of instincts and impulses from the moral consciousness—is always rejected by Nietzsche, being contrary to his understanding of man. Rather, it is Kant's third critique, the *Critique of Judgment,* which attempts to find a union between the noumenal and the phenomenal in the aesthetic judgment, that influenced Nietzsche profoundly and led, partly through the mediation

---

* Kant, *The Fundamental Principles of the Metaphysics of Morals* (New York: The Liberal Arts Press), p. 57: "That the principle of autonomy is the sole principle of morals can be readily shown by a mere analysis of the conception of morality. For by this analysis we find that its principle must be the categorical imperative, and that this command is neither more nor less than this very autonomy."

of Schiller and Goethe, to his own aesthetic conception of the universe.

II

The interpretation of Nietzsche's idea of eternal recurrence as a categorical imperative and "heuristic" fiction is in total disagreement with Nietzsche's own thought and intention. Clearly Nietzsche's entire philosophy aims at the destruction of a traditional moral interpretation of life. It is precisely that approach which he wants to destroy by his revaluation of values, performed in order to liberate us from the "du sollst" ("thou shalt"), from the goals and ends and ideals of traditional morality. His concepts of the will to power and the eternal recurrence perceive man from a dimension that is not moralistic but aesthetic, obeying not a command of duty, but an inner necessity to form and create. The cycle of eternal return is symbolized by a closed circle. Power is not something outside and beyond it, for the will to power is a will to itself: a will to preserve its power and a will to expand and enhance it. "Power which rests in itself, a law among laws . . . let us beware of adding a goal to the cycle of eternal recurrence. . . . It is a basic law like that of power."[3]

It cannot be denied that the idea of eternal recurrence must be seen as having "formative and transforming" effects upon man: "When you absorb this thought it will transform you." But the question is: Whom does Nietzsche want to transform and "breed"? Is it the "herd" man who needs goals and commandments, who lacks the courage to face life as it is and invents illusions and idols in order to bear it? Is it the "last man," the dwarf who jumps off the shoulder of the climbing Zarathustra and crouches by the wayside? If this had been Nietzsche's intention, the old ideas of heaven and hell would have served his purpose well enough.

Nietzsche calls his teaching a doctrine "strong enough to have the effect of breeding: strengthening the strong, paralyzing and breaking the weak and world weary."[4] And again, "The teaching of the eternal recurrence is a hammer in the hands of the mightiest men."[5] It is not a doctrine for the weak who are broken by any teaching that robs them of the belief in a Beyond and the hope of salvation. It is a doctrine for the "free spirit," the strong, heroic individual. Nietzsche indeed recognizes that the idea is at first a "heavy burden" even for the "higher" individual. Thus he asks:

> How can man bear the eternal return of the same? . . . How if some day a demon were to sneak after you into your loneliest loneliness and say to you: "This life as you now live it, and have lived it, you will have to live once again and innumerable times more; and there will be nothing new in it, but every pain and every joy and every thought and sigh, everything unspeakably small and great must return to you . . . and also this spider and this moonlight between the trees, and also this moment and I myself. The eternal hourglass of existence is turned around ever again . . . and you with it, dust grain of dust!" Would you not throw yourself down and gnash your teeth and curse the demon who spoke thus?[6]

And Nietzsche goes on to say: "I make the great experiment: Who can endure the idea of eternal recurrence? . . . Whoever is destroyed by the pronouncement 'There is no salvation,' shall perish. I want wars in which those who have the courage to life banish the others."[7] In the end, the higher individual "absorbs and embodies this thought"; he becomes part of the circle of eternal recurrence and the totality of all that was and will be. What was at first a heavy burden is now accepted in joyful affirmation and "thus it will transform him."

The higher individual needs no illusions and idols. "Only [the weak,] the decadent need the lie."[8] As has been previously noted, Nietzsche's position in regard to the necessity of illusions is not always clear, particularly in his early works, when he was still under the influence of Schopenhauer and of what he later was to call "weak pessimism." Existence was then still justified in the dream world of Apollo; illusion was the only possible redemption for suffering man and God.

But later, particularly after 1881, Nietzsche's concept of tragedy deepened through the idea of eternal recurrence. Schopenhauer's doctrine is transformed. Zarathustra becomes the teacher of the overman and the eternal recurrence. Tragedy is overcome not by illusion, but by a will to power that grows out of obstacles and conflicts, by a "will to tragedy" which turns weak pessimism into a pessimism of strength, a "pessimism beyond good and evil." Nietzsche now means something entirely different by the aesthetic justification of life. It is no longer the forming of Apollonian images and dream illusions; what it now signifies is a world view that defies any traditional moral interpretation and sees life as essentially creative, in close unity with the productive, ever-recurring activity of nature, which also includes destruction.

The higher individual affirms the eternal return of "all that is greatest and all that is smallest." His will to power is strengthened by struggle and resistance, by the "heavy burden" that destroys the weak. His spirit is tragic and Dionysian: to see the terrible, evil, and ugly in existence, to realize its eternal return, and yet not despair, but continue the everlasting battle for self-overcoming and self-enhancement and the never-ending search for authenticity in life.

Like Dr. Rieux in Camus's *The Plague,* he knows that "the tale he had to tell could not be one of final victory. . . . It could only be the record of what had to be done in the never-ending fight against terror and its relentless onslaughts."* The conquest of the plague is not final. The plague will return and have to be fought again; it will again bring victories of the human spirit and again be followed by its decline.

The Dionysian man who affirms life in its totality "without deduction, exception, and selection," and sees obstacles and conflicts as stimulants and productive elements in the development of the creative personality, is the model for Nietzsche's tragic age. He could, I believe, in many respects also be a model for our own "age of anxiety." He could help us acquire a new focus for redefining and rediscovering a humanity that has become frustrated and twisted by the complexities of our modern technological society, a humanity that despairs at the inconsistencies of life and often abandons the struggle of creative living in the face of inevitable failures.

Perhaps, paradoxically, we could live less painfully with the nearly overwhelming conflicts of life, if—instead of protecting ourselves from them—we would, with Nietzsche, accept them as both inevitable and productive, and value man by "the amount of power and fullness of his will . . . by the amount of resistance, pain, torture he can endure and turn into advantage,"⁹ rather than by the security and material success he can attain.

Erich Fromm, in *Man for Himself,* distinguishes between historical and existential dichotomies. While the former are man-made and can be annulled by human effort, the latter

---

* Albert Camus, *The Plague* (New York: Alfred A. Knopf, 1962), p. 278.

are necessary parts of man's existence and cannot be removed by the human will. "There is only one solution to the problem: to face the truth. . . . Only if [man] recognizes the human situation, the dichotomies inherent in his existence, and his capacity to unfold his powers, will he be able to succeed in his task."* Psychologists today are in full agreement with Nietzsche that the ability to live productively with ambiguities and conflicts, with the existential dichotomies of life, is the sign of a strong and healthy personality, while the weak and sick person will attempt to create deceptive, conflict-free situations in order to survive.

With Nietzsche's Dionysian man we must not see life as a polarity between good on the one side and evil on the other, but must understand it in terms of multiple choices, possibilities, and challenges.

> There are surprises in evil. Suddenly it will turn around and say: you have misunderstood me . . . to your astonishment you pronounce the word: goodness.
> —Kafka, "Wedding Preparation"

Paradoxically, there exists the possibility of what Camus calls an "absurd victory," in which "happiness and the absurd [good and evil] are two sons of the same earth."

> If [Sisyphus's] descent is thus sometimes performed in sorrow, it can also take place in joy. This word is not too much. Again I fancy Sisyphus returning toward his rock, and the sorrow was in the beginning. When the images of earth cling too tightly to memory, when the call of happiness becomes too insistent, it happens that melancholy rises in man's heart: this is the rock's victory, this is the rock itself. The boundless grief

---

* Erich Fromm, *Man for Himself* (New York: Holt, Rinehart and Winston, 1961), pp. 44f.

is too heavy to bear. These are our nights of Gethsemane. But crushing truths perish from being acknowledged. Thus, Oedipus at the outset obeys fate without knowing it. But from the moment he knows, his tragedy begins. Yet at the same moment, blind and desperate, he realizes that the only bond linking him to the world is the cool hand of a girl. Then a tremendous remark rings out: "Despite so many ordeals . . . the nobility of my soul makes me conclude that all is well." Sophocles' Oedipus, like Dostoevsky's Kirilov, thus gives the recipe for the absurd victory. Ancient wisdom confirms modern heroism. *

The idea of eternal recurrence is Camus's "absurd victory." In spite of eternal repetition of "every pain and every joy, every thought and every sigh"—all is well. The idea is "a hammer in the hands of the mightiest men." It serves life not as a moral postulate and heuristic fiction, but as a stimulus for man's will to power. It was not created by man in order to provide him with a goal and necessary illusion— it was created by life itself, whose essence is to grow, to expand, and to overcome. "Life itself created this abysmal thought, it wants to overcome its greatest obstacle."[10]

III

Nietzsche's teaching presents a new ethics whose motto is: "Incipit Tragoedia."[11] It is not a tragedy in the Schopenhauerian but in the Greek sense. Tragedy begins with the "going under" of the hero; but this going under is heroic, and bears within it the means of overcoming. Zarathustra goes under. He is the madman, the tightrope walker, the choking shepherd; but he is also the "convalescent" who accepts the

---

* Albert Camus, *The Myth of Sisyphus* (New York: Random House, 1961), p. 90.

"heavy burden" of the doctrine and becomes the teacher of a "new love." After doubt and despair and sickness, he rises. The circle is no longer the "Drehorgel" of the dwarf and the animals, the senseless, eternal repetition of exactly the same. It is the eternal return of the "Gesamtlage," the pattern and rhythm of life in its rise and fall, in its will to suffer and its will to create. Tragedy ends in a Yes to life, "a Dionysian Yes-saying to the world as it is, without deduction, exception and selection. . . . It is the highest attitude that a philosopher can reach: to stand Dionysiacally toward existence: my formula is *amor fati*."[12]

Amor fati becomes a fundamental concept in Nietzsche's new ethics, and finds its fullest expression in the teaching of the eternal recurrence. It is a concept that can be understood only on the basis of Nietzsche's metaphysical view of the unity of man and nature. Man's fate is inextricably interwoven with the totality of the cosmic fate. The significance and meaningfulness of the human will and its history is found within the nonhuman world, within the necessity of the cosmic whole. In *Homer's Contest* Nietzsche says:

> When one speaks of humanity, there lies behind it the idea that humanity is that which separates and distinguishes mankind from nature. But in reality there is no such separation; the natural qualities and those called specifically "human" are inextricably intertwined together. Man is in his highest and noblest powers entirely nature and bears in himself nature's uncanny dual character.[13]

That Nietzsche's concept of the unity of man and nature is close to Spinoza's pantheistic views has been previously defended. But Nietzsche is also modern man, living in the shadow of Cartesian dualism, Humean scepticism, and Kant's critical philosophy. His numerous seemingly contradictory pronouncements must be understood on the basis of this typically modern duality of thought. Nietzsche's return to a pre-Socratic unity is frustrated by the problematic situation of modern man and the sentimental artist who has lost his unity with nature. But, as above disclosed, Nietzsche never ceased to strive for this unity, for he considered it the basis for his interpretation of man's destiny and freedom.

> The riddle that man faces must be solved within being itself and no other way. Now he begins to investigate how deeply he is immersed in the process of becoming, how deeply he is involved in being itself.[14]

The neglect of Nietzsche's stress on the unity of man and nature has been largely responsible for those interpretations that separate the idea of eternal recurrence into incompatible metaphysical and ethical teachings. Heidegger, however, is one of the few interpreters who acknowledge the unity in Nietzsche's ideas. Neither Heidegger nor Nietzsche makes the traditional distinctions; for each, metaphysics and ethics merge. However, neither the basis of this unity nor the points they emphasize are the same. Above all, Heidegger completely neglects the concept of *amor fati*, in spite of his closeness to the spirit of Zarathustra-Nietzsche. This in part accounts for his often excessively subjective interpretation of Nietzsche on the basis of his own fundamental, and somewhat different, concepts of time, freedom, and the unity of man and nature.

The unity of "Weltsein" and "Menschsein," of "Sein" and "Seienden" is accomplished by both philosophers on different grounds. This difference has been mentioned in connection with their metaphysical doctrines. It is of equal importance to their ethical positions. It must therefore be observed again that Heidegger's unity of nature and man is achieved on the basis of a new ontology, which is grounded in existential phenomena. The foundation for any transcendence into being is for him always existence, *Dasein*. Nature, according to Heidegger as well as Sartre, is a "meaningless mass" that must be given meaning and reality through man by his "care" and "understanding." The subjective element is never completely eliminated. While distinguishing between authentic and inauthentic, ontic and ontological concerns, Heidegger's categories remain existential. The key to his fundamental ontology is found in human existence.

Nietzsche, on the other hand, warns against a humanization of nature, against a reading of human goals and values into what he calls "the innocence of becoming." The doer is not, as for Heidegger, prior to being, creating the "Umwelt" by his decisions, but the reverse is true. Man is part of nature, inextricably interconnected with the totality of the cosmos. Both his fate and his freedom gain meaningfulness only on the basis of his unity with the creative activity of nature. Nietzsche's ultimate aim is to bring man closer to nature, "den Menschen zu vernatuerlichen," in order to reestablish the ancient Greek unity, and "to consider man again as part of nature."[15]

But, true to his problematic nature, here, too, Nietzsche is not free of doubt. He warns against a humanization of nature, but knows that we can never completely avoid the subjective element. He speaks of the unity between nature and man, but he realizes that the duality is fundamental and that nature will never yield all her mysteries. But although the concept of unity is a Kantian idea that transcends human understanding, it nevertheless remains an integral part of the rational being. The Faustian striving for unity will never end, but will always remain alive in the human consciousness.

Nietzsche's deep concern and longing for unity with nature has become a central problem for our time. Man's detachment or alienation from nature in turn is connected with his alienation from himself and others,* with lack of identity and feelings of anxiety. It involves momentous changes in one's entire outlook on life and is one of the most disturbing phenomena of modern Western culture.

Alienation is by no means only a Nietzschean idea and contemporary problem. It has for centuries been the subject of philosophical study: Hegel saw the history of man as the history of man's "Entfremdung" or alienation, and Marx, treating the concept of estrangement in economic terms, introduced it into sociological theories. But our contemporary, technological societies do lead more rapidly than any other to an estrangement from nature and the dilemmas that result from it. Man is in danger of becoming mechanized, routinized, stupefied by technology and mass media —in short, dehumanized. He is alienated, passive, uncommitted, unproductive. No longer able to realize his true nature, he exhibits what Erich Fromm calls the "marketing orientation" whose goal is to become a "salable . . . commodity on a competitive market."** He is a stranger in the world, no longer at home in a nature he wants to control and master rather than feel at one and in harmony with, no longer supported by the integrative function of myth and religion.

---

* The problem of overcoming alienation from society does not arise for Nietzsche, because he stresses individualism and feels that any society—not only nineteenth-century bourgeois, Christian society—is alien and coercive, repressing the creative potentialities of man.
** Erich Fromm, *Man for Himself.*

And here are the trees and I know their gnarled surface; water and I feel its taste. These scents of grass and stars at night, certain evenings when the heart relaxes—how shall I negate this world whose power and strength I feel? Yet all the knowledge on earth will give me nothing to assure me that this world is mine. You describe it to me and you teach me to classify it. You enumerate its laws . . . you take apart its mechanism. . . . And you give me the choice between a description that is sure but that teaches me nothing, and hypotheses that claim to teach me but are not sure. A stranger to myself and to the world. . . . If I were a tree among trees, a cat among cats, this life would have a meaning, or rather this problem could not arise, for I should belong to this world.*

The problems of alienation and identity have produced an age that has been rightfully called "the age of anxiety," an age of confusion, psychological disorientation, and uncertainty in regard to values and norms of conduct. The themes of alienation and anxiety pervade our art and literature; they preoccupy theologians and philosophers as well as psychologists and sociologists. They create the mood that colors the poetry of Yeats, Rilke, and Eliot, and is predominant in the content and style of the works of Kafka, Gide, and Hemingway, to name just a few. The alienated man, whose life seems meaningless and absurd, faces us in the tortured figures of contemporary paintings and sculptures. He is the central hero of our stage, in works like those of Beckett, Brecht, Ionesco, and Genet.

> This stupid world where
> Gadgets are gods, and we go on talking

---

* Camus, *Myth of Sisyphus,* pp. 15, 38.

Many about much, but remain alone,
Alive but alone, belonging—where?—
Unattached as tumbleweeds.

—W. H. Auden, "The Age of Anxiety"

In philosophy, too, particularly in existentialist thought, alienation and anxiety have been stressed as facts of human existence and the most urgent problems of modern man who, having lost the pre-scientific, pre-Cartesian unity with nature, is "thrown" into the world to create his own essential nature, his own freedom and destiny.

ZEUS: Return to Nature, thankless son. Know your sin, abhor it and tear it from you as one tears a rotten, noisome tooth.

ORESTES: You are the king of gods, king of stars, king of the waves of the sea. But you are not the king of man. . . . Yesterday, when I was with Electra, I felt at one with Nature, this Nature of your making. . . . That was the last time, the last I saw my youth. Suddenly, out of the blue, freedom crashed down on me and swept me off my feet. Nature sprang back, my youth went with the wind, and I knew myself alone, utterly alone in the midst of this well-meaning, little universe of yours.

ZEUS: Your vaunted freedom isolates you from the fold; it means exile. Come back to the fold. . . . Come back, I am forgetfulness. . . . I am peace.

ORESTES: I am doomed to have no other law but mine. Nor shall I come back to Nature, the Nature you found good; for I, Zeus, am a man, and you, too, god of gods, abhor mankind.

—Sartre, *The Flies*

IV

Disregarding the fundamental differences in their conception of nature and man's relation to it, Heidegger interprets Nietzsche on the basis of his own philosophy and says in reference to Nietzsche's metaphysical views: "Metaphysics is anthropomorphic . . . the forming and conception of the world in the image of man. . . . This metaphysics makes man, as no other metaphysics before, the unconditional measure of all things."* This passage from Heidegger's book on Nietzsche must be contrasted with a quotation from Nietzsche's own writings:

> The whole conception "man against the world" . . . man as the measure of all things, is recognized as an immense absurdity and rejected by us. . . . We laugh when we find "man and the world" placed next to each other, separated by the sublime presumption of the word "and."[16]

From this fundamental opposition in Heidegger's and Nietzsche's understanding of the relation between man and nature, additional differences result that further contribute to Heidegger's subjectively biased interpretation. Heidegger chooses the concept of time as central for an understanding of Nietzsche's teaching of the eternal recurrence and takes as his central theme the following passage from "On the Vision and the Riddle" in *Zarathustra*:

> "Stop dwarf," I said, "It is I or you! But I am the stronger of the two: you do not know my abysmal thought. That you could not bear!"—But there was a gateway just where we had stopped. "Behold this gateway, dwarf. It has two faces; two paths meet here; no one has yet reached their end. This long lane stretches backward into eternity. And the long lane out there, that, too, is another eternity. They contradict each other . . . and it is here at this gateway that they come to-

---

* Heidegger, *Nietzsche*, 2 vols. (Pfullingen: Neske, 1961), 2:127f.

gether. The name of the gateway is inscribed above: "Moment."
But whoever would follow one of them on and on, further and
further . . . do you believe, dwarf, that these paths contradict
each other eternally?" The dwarf answered: "All that is straight
lies. . . . All truth is crooked; time itself is a circle." And Zarathustra spoke: "From this gateway, Moment, a long lane leads
backward; behind it lies eternity." And he adds: "Are not all
things knotted together so firmly that this moment draws after
it all that is to come?"[17]

It is in the present "Moment" that the concept of eternity
and Nietzsche's doctrine of the eternal recurrence become
comprehensible to Heidegger. But his comprehension is
based on an understanding of the concept of time that is
contrary to Nietzsche's. For both, time is urgent and real,
conceived not in terms of the normal, calculable progression
of minutes and hours, but as something deeper and primordial, as an inescapable presence, the "substance of Being."
For both, the past, present, and future form a dynamic unity.
But Heidegger, in contrast to Nietzsche, stresses the future
and not the past as the fundamental exstasis of existence
and interprets Nietzsche's teaching on that basis. His emphasis is on that part of the above quotation from *Zarathustra* which, if taken only by itself, could indeed justify
his interpretation: "All things are knotted together so firmly
that this moment draws after it all that is to come." However, if the concept of *amor fati* is considered to be of central and primary importance in Nietzsche's thought, then
the emphasis must be on the past, not the future. Another
part of the above quotation is then seen as being of primary
importance: "From this gateway, Moment, a long eternal
lane leads backward: behind us lies eternity."

Thus it can be seen that Nietzsche's eternal recurrence
has been interpreted by Heidegger in terms of the latter's

own concept of authentic temporality. The past and present, time and history, become authentic only by their transcendence; man finds his freedom and meaningfulness only in the projection of *Dasein* into the future. "Higher than actuality is possibility."* To Heidegger, what already was and will return is this present moment with its power to make the past vital and with its possibilities to create the future. What returns is the present moment, which the individual can by resolve and decision transcend, and thereby transform an otherwise insignificant past and present into a meaningful future. Nietzsche's theory of eternal recurrence is thus *vermenschlicht*. Time and eternity become human categories. Freedom and creativity are realized in the human will to transcend; despair and suffering are founded upon human decision and responsibility.

But this is not Zarathustra's "abysmal thought." That which makes Zarathustra shudder is not the decision of the moment, with its terrible freedom and responsibility. It is the consciousness of the future that already was and of the past that will eternally return, with eternal inevitability. Nietzsche's tragedy is of a different dimension from that seen in Heidegger's interpretation. To Heidegger, despair and anguish are existential and can be overcome by man's attitude and decision. Nietzsche's concept of tragedy is, however, deeper and more truly tragic. Its origin is metaphysical and

---

* Heidegger, *Sein und Zeit* (Tuebingen: Niemeyer, 1960). According to Heidegger, the past cannot be truly known by thinking backward. Man can only think forward. This is essential thinking. Heidegger uses the term "andenkendes Denken," which Walter Kaufmann translates as "thinking that recalls." (Walter A. Kaufmann, *Existentialism from Dostoievsky to Sartre*). The basis for this translation is the German word "Andenken," i.e. "memory," "remembrance." But perhaps Heidegger intended to create his own terminology here and wanted to express a mode of thinking that thinks forward. "An," understood as an adverb, has the meaning of "on," "onward."

thus can never be abolished by the human will to transcend. The problems that arise from Nietzsche's conception of time, freedom, and creativity are far more complex than those that result from Heidegger's interpretation of the teaching. Nietzsche and Heidegger both celebrate the moment, but in different senses. The Heideggerian man experiences the fullness of the moment as one in which the past influences, but does not enchain him. His thoughts and will are directed toward the future, undetermined by fate and necessity. He is the creator of that which returns; his creativity involves originality and novelty. The Nietzschean man experiences the moment in a more profoundly tragic sense. It leads him into the abyss, but also into an experience of life and being where the moment becomes the highest exultation of the artist.

V

It is the concept of *amor fati* that provides the basis for Nietzsche's conception of freedom and creativity and is also the means by which the negative element of the teaching is overcome. "My new road to a 'Yes' . . . a philosophy which does not negate any more. It wants to achieve the opposite . . . to say Yes to the world as it is: my formula for it is *amor fati*."[18] Through *amor fati* man accomplishes an identification with the processes of nature and with the past that returns again and again.

> [He] assimilates, incorporates the past, however foreign, turn-ing it, so to speak, into blood. The deeper the roots of man's inner nature, the more of the past it will appropriate or dom-inate; and the mightiest, most formidable nature would be known by a strong, historical sense.[19]

It is here, in the identification with nature, that Nietzsche performs the important transitions not only from the "thou shalt" to the "I will," but also from the "I will" to the "I am." The first stage involves the criticism and destruction of Christian values and moral imperatives. "We free spirits feel the glory of a new dawn at the news of the death of the old God—the seas are open once more."[20] "Morality is destroyed . . . what remains is the 'I will.' "[21] But the step to the "I will" already contains the second transition to the "I am," for Nietzsche's "I will" is not identical with Heidegger's; it is not primarily a willing toward the future, but a will to identify with the past and make it one's own, "to set free the past and transform the 'it was' into a 'thus I willed it.' "[22] The step from the "it was" to the "thus I willed it" is achieved on the basis of man's unity with the fatality of the cosmos. There is no antinomy between will and fate. The "I will" is also the "I am."

> This is my last wisdom: I want that which I must. . . . I want nothing else than this eternally returning world that is not foreign to me, but is at once my "Ego" and my "Fatum." I want myself eternally again as a ring within the larger ring of the world.[23]

The passage from the *Nachlass*, quoted before, gains a new clarity. "To live thus that you must wish to live again, is the task . . . you will in any case." The two parts of this quotation are no longer in contradiction.

"Ego Fatum." There is no more antithesis between "Weltsein" and "Menschsein." "I myself belong to the causes of the eternal recurrence. . . . The knot of causes returns in which I am entwined—I return eternally to the same life, with all that is greatest and with all that is smallest."[24] The last step to the "I am" is not achieved on basis of intellectual understanding; it has the qualities of mystery and poetry. It is Plato's "Eros," Goethe's "Eternal Feminine," Dante's "Love." It is man's eternal longing for wholeness and unity, which Nietzsche expresses in *Zarathustra*:

> And this is all that I create and strive for, that I may compose and transform into one what is fragment and riddle and dreadful accident—and how could I bear to be a man, if man were not also creator and solver of riddles and redeemer of accidents?[25]

"*Ego Fatum.* . . . The fatality of man cannot be detached from the fatality of all that was and will be . . . one is a piece of fatum, one belongs to the whole."[26] The question that faces the Nietzschean man is how he can find freedom within the fatality of all that was and will be, within a world that possesses "no order, but necessity." Nietzsche denies "free will" in the traditional sense and calls it "a contemptible trick devised by theologians in order to make mankind 'responsible' in their sense."[27] His concept of freedom is also contrary to Schopenhauer's negation of the will to live and the Kantian notion of freedom, which is based on transcendence into the noumenal realm of moral consciousness. It is also not identical with Heidegger's "free resolve."

In *The Gay Science* Nietzsche says: "The total character of the world is chaos, not in the sense of a missing necessity, but of a missing order."[28] Nietzsche's world lacks the order of either a mechanistic or a teleological universe, but it does not lack necessity. However, it is not the necessity of a causally connected system, that "deep-seated illusion which was first manifested in Socrates, that unshakable belief that thought, guided by the principle of causality, could reach the very depth of being."[29]

> [It is not a necessity] to act thus and thus in obedience to a

law or law-giver, whereas apart from the law it would be free
to act otherwise. But precisely that inability to act otherwise
might spring from being itself which did not behave in such
and such a way in response to a law, but because it was
constituted in such and such a way . . . it is neither free nor
unfree, but merely thus and thus.[30]

"Necessity is fatum." It is not the necessity of a law that
is external to us or beyond us, but the necessity to act "thus
and thus" in accordance with the fatality of being itself
and the eternal return of all that is. This necessity is not
felt as coercion or anguish ("Necessity not as distress, as a
painful constraint and coercion"[31]), but as a manifestation of
the inner forces of being and life. "Highest fatalism, yet
identical with creativity."[32]

Freedom to Nietzsche is thus achieved through man's
identification with the cosmic whole, whereby an otherwise
strange fate is transformed into one's own. It is "a fundamental mistake to separate man and fate as two different
things. . . . In truth every man is himself a part of cosmic
fate. You yourself, you poor fearful one, are the unconquer-
able Moira, you are benediction and damnation, and also
the chain in which even the strongest is bound."[33] The
essence of Nietzsche's notion of freedom is most fully expressed in the concept of *amor fati*: "Not only to endure
necessity, but to love it."[34]

Zarathustra, the godless one, has found a new faith: "cir-
culus vitiosus deus." He has found a new love: "I want to
love that which is necessary. *Amor fati* be my last love."[35]
At last Zarathustra has grasped and "absorbed" the new idea,
which was at first a "heavy burden." "He is no longer shepherd, no longer man—he is transformed, surrounded by light
. . . he laughs. Never yet on earth did man laugh as he
laughs."[36] Zarathustra has become one with all things; he

does not negate any more. In Dionysian rapture he beholds the play of the cosmic forces, "der Dinge eigenen Tanz," in their eternally returning pattern of destruction and creation. "Such a free spirit stands with joyful and confident fatalism amid the All, in the belief that only the particular and singular is to be condemned; that in the totality of being everything is redeemed and affirmed."[37]

In the teaching of the eternal recurrence Nietzsche creates a new ethics that is free of moral imperatives, guilt, responsibility, and resentment, and wants to regain "the innocence of becoming." It is an ethics that abolishes the need for transcendence and redemption, and affirms this life without reduction and curtailment. It protests against defeat and negation and affirms "struggle, pain, destruction as necessary because of the abundance of forms surging constantly into life, because of the enormous fecundity of the world will; we feel the furious prodding of this pain in the same moment in which we become one with the immense lust for life."[38]

In Nietzsche's new ethics "the unconscious activity of nature breaks out in the consciousness of man."* The creative individual does not aim toward that which is good and useful and pleasant, but toward an inner fitness, which expresses the very essence of things. He does not act in obedience to moral laws and imperatives, but out of the fullness and abundance of his creative powers.

Nietzsche's ethics celebrates the heroic will of the individual who erects upon the altar of the dead transcendent God the new divinity, man, and becomes the prophet of a new "meaning of the earth." It glorifies the will to power and its eternally active dynamic forces: the will to destroy and create, the will to go under and overcome—in eternal recurrence.

* Kant, *Critique of Judgment*.

PART III

The Innocence of Becoming

The world is becoming and perishing, creation and destruction, without any moral content, in eternal innocence.

Nietzsche, Philosophy in the Tragic Age of the Greeks *(X, 41)*

8

THE AESTHETIC
INTERPRETATION OF BEING

Nietzsche's tragic, Dionysian world view develops from his conception of nihilism and his destruction of traditional values. It is expressed in the teachings of the eternal recurrence and the revaluation of values, and culminates in his later writings in the conception of being he calls "die Unschuld des Werdens," the innocence of becoming. Here Nietzsche expresses his unified world view wherein ethics, metaphysics, and religion merge in an aesthetic interpretation of all being: a view in which life and culture are not conceived as moral but as aesthetic phenomena.[1]

"Die Unschuld des Werdens" is the innocence of the child that shatters and rebuilds in playful, guileless joy. It is the Heraclitean "fire" that rises and falls, that consumes and cleanses. It is the freedom and purity of nature that creates and destroys without goals and purposes in the eternal rhythm of the cycle of life. It is the "great silence of art" in which Nietzsche's tragic view is most fully expressed.

In this aesthetic interpretation of the universe the Heraclitean concept of "play" assumes an important role. Nature and art create in a playful manner, "building and destroying in innocence," disinterested in practical, utilitarian ends, unconcerned with the traditional concepts of good and evil.

> Heraclitus has no reason to prove—as Leibnitz did—that this world is the best of all possible worlds; it suffices that it is the beautiful, innocent play of the Aeon. . . . And just as the child and the artist play, plays the eternally active fire—it builds and destroys in innocence.[2]

In the "innocence of becoming" Nietzsche wants to create a conception of being that transcends moral distinctions and is free of all imperatives, all guilt and responsibility, all bitterness and *ressentiment*. In a world where "God is dead" there are no cosmic purposes and ends to which we are responsible. No one can be blamed or punished for things being as they are and acting "thus and thus."

> We others . . . whose antagonists are the apostles of revenge and *ressentiment* . . . who want to regain the innocence of becoming, are the missionaries of a purer thought: that no one has given man his qualities . . . no one bears guilt. . . . We are the results of an eternal design, will, wish. . . . The whole cannot be judged, measured, compared, or even negated . . . because there is nothing else but the whole. . . . This is the innocence of all being. . . . Only the innocence of becoming gives the greatest courage and freedom, it frees absolute necessity from ends.[3]

But while the innocence of becoming is free of guilt and responsibility, it is not free of strife and conflict and Dionysian pathos. Its essence is tragic—not a tragedy of guilt and punishment, of sin and atonement, but the tragedy of the creative activity that includes destruction; not a tragedy of tearful lament and a will to escape, but a heroic Yes to life and the fatality of all that is, a "will to be the eternal joy of becoming itself, a joy that includes a delight in destruction. . . . In order to experience the eternal delight of creation, in order for the will to live to be eternally affirmed, there must also be the eternal pain of giving birth [*die Qual der Gebaererin*]."[4]

The innocence of becoming is the unity and inseparability of things we call opposites and contradictions: the unity of being and becoming, of good and evil, of freedom and necessity, of nature and man. It is the purity of nature, untouched and unspoiled by human values and goals. In a letter to von Gersdorff, Nietzsche writes:

The storm broke violently in gale and fury; I experienced a feeling of enormous stimulation. . . . What is man to me and his excited willing, his "thou shalt," "thou shalt not." How different the lightning, the storm and hail: free forces without morals. How glad, how strong they are; pure willing without the obscuring activity of the intellect.[5]

9
THE SILENCE OF ART

Thus the aesthetic individual looks at the world. He shares the creative experience of the artist and recognizes that there is law in the strife of the manifold and that the artist stands both contemplatively above as well as creating within the work of art. He sees how necessity and play, opposition and harmony, must be present together in the creation of a work of art.[1]

—Nietzsche

I

The innocence of becoming, free of traditional values and goals, is the "silence of art"—a silence and calmness that is, paradoxically, dynamic: full of tension and polarity, yet possessing form and balance; full of frenzy and passions that destroy and attack, yet also form and transform. In the aesthetic experience we reach the highest intensification of our emotional life while, at the same time, experiencing a sense of repose.

In the silence of art, life and art merge. What we ex-

perience in art is not a single or simple emotion, but the
dynamic process of life itself in its continuous oscillation
between opposite poles, between chaos and form, destruction and creation, joy and despair. The formative powers of
the creative man are like the generative forces of nature,
both struggling and overcoming, both "building and destroying in innocence."

> One must understand the basic artistic phenomenon which is
> called "life"—the productive force which builds under the
> most difficult conditions.[2]

> Art owes its continuous evolution to the Apollonian-Dionysian
> duality, just as the propagation of the species depends on the
> duality of the sexes, their constant conflicts and periodic acts
> of reconciliation.[3]

Nietzsche's artist-creator takes the chaotic matter that is
full of tension and Dionysian excess and shapes it into an
artistic unity within diversity. He does not use norms or
final causes or ends, as does Plato's demiurge in the *Timaeus*,
but he creates out of the fullness and richness of his opposing
powers. He is "the artist god who realizes himself fully in
building as well as in destroying, in good as in evil; who,
in creating, rids himself of the tensions of his overflowing
fullness and the suffering of his inner contradictions."[4]

Nietzsche's concepts of art are aesthetic only on the surface; in their essential qualities they are metaphysical.
Heidegger is correct in saying: "When we arrive at the sum-
mit of Nietzsche's aesthetics, we have no more aesthetics."[*]
Art for Nietzsche is fundamentally not an expression of

---

[*] Heidegger, *Nietzsche*, 2 vols. (Pfullingen: Neske, 1961), 1:86f.

culture, but it is what Heidegger calls "eine Gestaltung des Willens zur Macht," a manifestation of the will to power. And since the will to power is the essence of being itself, art becomes "die Gestaltung des Seienden im Ganzen," a manifestation of being as a whole. With the reversal of Platonism, metaphysics no longer involves transcending into supersensuous realms, but instead deals with the categories of becoming and the senses. Art becomes the expression of being itself, no longer grasped by abstractions and pure reason, but by what we sense and feel. "The phenomenon of the artist is the most pellucid—through it the basic principles of power and nature are most clearly seen."[5] "Art and not morality is the true metaphysical activity of man."[6]

"The world is a work of art." Nature is seen as an aesthetic phenomenon, a Kantian creation of art that possesses "purposiveness without purpose," that is free and pure, and "acts not out of poverty and distress, but out of the fullness of its potentialities and an artistic urge."[7] But no longer does a work of art represent an illusory dream world in which no contradiction and opposition exist. No longer is art a means by which suffering is redeemed in the contemplation of beautiful images. Now art is under the sponsorship of the god Dionysus, who represents an interpenetration of two opposing forces; who rejoices in pain and suffering, realizing that they are the necessary preconditions of all creation. Now art is the manifestation of the creativeness of life and possesses the same fundamental duality. Art does not represent illusions, but truth. In the aesthetic experience of Dionysian *Rausch*, the artist tears asunder the veil of Maya and beholds the very sources of reality. He beholds a truth that does not merely describe and explain, that does not only order the world into the uniformity of general laws—but a truth that is deeper and more profound, that deals with the multiplicity and diversity of intuitions and a "sympathetic vision of things."*

In the aesthetic experience, man celebrates his reunion with nature: "Nature itself, long alienated, hostile and subjugated, celebrates again the reconciliation with her prodigal son, man."[8] Art, now identified with the fundamental life principle of the will to power, is affirmation and benediction.

> Dionysian art wants to convince us of the eternal delight of existence. . . . Now struggle, pain, and destruction . . . are seen as necessary. . . . In spite of terror and pity we rejoice in living not as individuals but as part of the life force with whose procreative lust we have become one.[9]

The creative activity in art and nature is compared by Nietzsche to the activity of play. But by "play" Nietzsche does not mean games of illusion and simulated images, or the forming of pleasurable feelings and associations. Instead, as noted above, play represents an activity that does not aim at any practical utilitarian needs and ends, being unconcerned with good and evil, truth and falsity. It involves creativity in the playful manner of the child and of the eternally active Heraclitean fire, "building and destroying in innocence." Nietzche's play theory of art, while diverging in many respects, has elements in common with Schiller's as well as Darwin's and Spencer's theories. He would agree with Schiller's view that "man only plays when, in the full meaning of the word, he is man, and he is only completely

---

* Nietzsche's conception of art has many elements in common with contemporary aesthetic theories, particularly with Bergson's "aesthetic intuition" and the "sympathetic vision" of De Witt H. Parker (*The Principles of Aesthetics*).

man when he plays."* But, unlike Nietzsche, Schiller did not consider play a general organic activity, but a specifically human one which led to a freedom that, influenced by Kant's idealism, existed only in the "intelligible" and not the phenomenal world. In this respect the points of contact are stronger between Nietzsche's views and Darwin's and Spencer's biological and naturalistic theories, wherein play and beauty are regarded as general natural phenomena.

II

Nietzsche's conception of art, expressing a new Dionysian conception of being, "die Gestaltung des Seienden im Ganzen," is based on categories that arise out of his revaluation of values and are therefore contrary to the traditional concepts of the true, the good, and the beautiful. These new Dionysian values belong to an entirely new dimension of thought and require a new terminology. We wish here again that Nietzsche had "had the courage to create [his] own language, in keeping with the hazards and the novelty"[10] of his ideas, instead of using terms "borrowed" from the vocabulary of traditional philosophers. The notion of "Dionysian value" represents a "category confusion." If a phenomenon has value, then it is not Dionysian, and if it is Dionysian, then it has no value.

I would like to use a term introduced by Albert Hofstadter into the field of aesthetics, and replace "value" with "validity" as the essential characteristic of Nietzsche's philosophy in which the concepts of metaphysics, ethics, and art are fused into a new vital unity. Hofstadter clarifies the differ-

---

* Friedrich Schiller, *On the Aesthetic Education of Man in a Series of Letters* (New York: Ungar Publishing Co., 1954), Letter XV.

ence between value and validity through their linguistic associations:

> Both value and validity stem from the Latin *valere*, to be strong, healthy, powerful, effective . . . valid and validity are in continuity with this semantic tradition. . . . Value, on the other hand, is connected with *valere* by mediation of the French *valoir*. . . . A thing is valuable because it has value, and its value is a property in virtue of which it is useful, desirable, good. . . . Thus, whereas the emphasis in the concept of validity is on the combination of rightness and power in the object, the emphasis in the concept of value is on the presence in the object of something good, useful, desirable or estimable.*

The essence of Nietzsche's "Unschuld des Werdens," of his metaphysics, ethics, and art, is a power that is outside the sphere of "the good, the useful, desirable or estimable," and cannot be properly expressed through the category of value. It is a power that is not directed toward ends and purposes and functional usefulness, but aims instead at an inner "fitness and rightness" that expresses the very essence of things —a rightness that is based on an inner necessity that is very different from compulsion.[11] This power possesses the validity of nature and of "the artist who sees a law in becoming and play in necessity,"[12] "where nothing happens for the sake of anything—which is the same as to say perhaps that everything happens for the sake of everything."**

Nietzsche's fundamental power possesses a vitalistic validity. It is full of dialectical, opposing forces, full of tension and struggle, but it achieves form and balance within a dynamic unity. The superabundance and ecstasy of the

---

* Albert Hofstadter, "Validity versus Value," *The Journal of Philosophy* 59 (October 11, 1962): 608ff.

** Ibid., p. 616.

Dionysian is harmonized in the unification with the Apollonian. This basic principle possesses validity of form, a beauty that is free of purpose and intent to please, that is neither good nor useful nor desirable, but expresses an inner power and necessity "where even the ugly is redeemed" and made meaningful in the fatality of the whole.[13] Nietzsche's creative power reveals itself both in the *Rausch* of the artist and in the productive forces of nature. Both create not for the sake of external purposes, but out of the fullness and necessity of their own being. The world becomes an aesthetic phenomenon, a free and purposeless working from within. Man becomes the creator-god who in his productive activity experiences a oneness with being itself. "In art a certain absoluteness of existence is in fact arrived at by man."[*] In sum, Nietzsche's fundamental principle of power, at work in life and art, is not related to criteria of value judgments; it is not concerned with the good or true or beautiful in the traditional meaning of those terms. It does not possess value, but a vital, essential, and inner validity.

III

"The silence of art" is, for Nietzsche, primarily expressed in Greek art, and most fully in Greek tragedy. This silence is based upon a concept of the tragic wherein true serenity must grow out of conflict and pain, where affirmation is the result of an overcoming of negation and pessimism, and where silence expresses the highest feeling of victory and power.[14] Nietzsche's understanding of serenity and silence in Greek art is rooted in three of his already-discussed ideas: *Rausch,* strong pessimism, and Dionysus.

Nietzsche introduces entirely new concepts into the under-

---

[*] Ibid., p. 606.

standing of the Greek genius, and our debt to him for his profound new insights must be acknowledged. Calling Nietzsche "the most profound scholar of antiquity," Jacob Burckhardt was the first to recognize his immense contribution to the interpretation of Greek art and culture.* As argued before, Nietzsche's interpretation completely disagreed with the views of the German classicists, including Goethe, Schiller, Lessing, and Herder, who followed the leadership of Winckelmann. But while differing in their fundamental aspects of interpretation, Nietzsche did share with the classicists a belief in the supremacy of Greek culture. He longed with Goethe and Faust for a reunion with Helena, the symbol of Greek beauty and harmony. He felt with them an affinity to the Greeks that was so close as to recall Plato's myth, related by Aristophanes in the *Symposium,* of the severed halves who long to meet and be reunited again.

However, the reasons that Nietzsche and the classicists advance for their common belief in the superiority of Greek culture and the need for its revival are completely opposed. The qualities that they stress as essentially Greek are not the same. While for Nietzsche the fundamental characteristics of Greek art, as of all great art, are *Rausch,* strong pessimism, and Dionysus, for Winckelmann and his followers they are *Unbezeichnung,* optimism, and Apollo.

A work of art possesses "Unbezeichnung" if it does not exhibit any emotion and passion or suggest any suffering and conflict. Just as "beauty is like the clear water from the spring which is the healthier the less taste it has,"** art is the greater the more it possesses balance and symmetry, "noble simplicity and serenity." Greek art, according to

---

* Jacob Burckhardt, *Griechische Kulturgeschichte* (Berlin: Spemann, 1898).

** J. J. Winckelmann, *Geschichte der Kunst des Altertums,* 4 vols. (Heidelberg: G. Weiss, 1882), 4:137.

Winckelmann, does not want to imitate nature, but give an idealized version of it. It wants to represent the generic and universal, eliminating the particular and individual. It longs with Diotima to rise beyond the particularity of sensible objects to the Idea of Beauty, to rise above the suffering and limited life of the individual to the contemplative life of the gods.

For Nietzsche, the basic aesthetic phenomenon is not *Unbezeichnung*, but *Rausch*. The initial stage of artistic creation is not serene contemplation, or passivity, or harmony, but a state of frenzy and intoxication in which we are brought close to the primitive intensity of ancient religious rites. In this state of ecstasy and Dionysian dithyramb, the artists lifts the veil of dreams and fair illusions and perceives the terrors of existence. He tears the mask from the serene, sublime Olympian and sees the terrible behind the beautiful, pain and suffering behind serenity and noble simplicity. But *Rausch* is a power that also forms and overcomes. Out of terror and pain it creates a beauty and serenity that are no longer *unbezeichnet*, but rich and dynamic as are nature and life.

Along with the classicists' view of Greek culture as complacent and serene goes their interpretation of the Greek spirit as optimistic and gay. Hellenism was conceived as being an idealized form of humanity whose spirit was rational, clear, harmonious, and joyous, living "in a moderate climate that gives birth to a joyous disposition; where games and festivals abound, where clouds and heavy mists rarely prevail and nature acts in a serene and gladsome atmosphere."* But to Nietzsche, true gaiety and serenity can be achieved only after a baptism of fire. The beauty of

---

* Ibid., 4:1; Walter Pater, *The Renaissance* (Portland: T. B. Mosher, 1912), p. 201: "Our modern culture may have more color, the medieval spirit greater heat and profundity, but Hellenism is pre-eminent for light."

ancient Greece was an outcome of suffering and pain; the greatness of its spirit was the result of profound inner strife and opposition. "What suffering must this race have endured in order to accomplish such beauty."[15]

Nietzsche rejects Winckelmann's and Goethe's vision of the Greeks as a race of beautiful children. The unique value of their culture was not based upon a polytheism that was gay and joyous, upon Dorian worship that was rational and measured, but upon a religion that was dark and mysterious, worshiping older chthonian divinities who possessed elements of the daemonic. Without knowledge of despair and terror, without impulses that were cruel and savage, the Greek spirit, says Nietzsche, could never have developed the depth and totality that make it so incomparably great. Their humanity was not a product of an instinctive naïve unity but grew out of a tragic ground wherein obstacles had to be overcome and savage instincts had to be governed and redirected.

The driving force behind Hellenic culture was contest, the striving to surpass and overcome. And in this contest it is precisely those characteristics that are accounted as cruel and savage which can prove to be fruitful and provide the fertile soil "which can yet turn every desert into luxurious farm land."[16]

The Greeks, the most humane men of ancient times, have a trait of cruelty, a tigerish lust to annihilate—a trait that is also very distinct in that grotesquely enlarged mirror image of the Hellenes, Alexander the Great.[17]

"Man in his highest and noblest powers is entirely nature and bears in him nature's uncanny dual character."[18] What seems like repose and sublimity is the outcome of conflict and frenzy; what seems like gaiety and optimism is the result

of an overcoming of pessimism, and a victory over violent
and destructive forces within us.

> Examine the lives of the best and most fruitful men and
> peoples, and ask yourselves whether a tree, if it is to grow
> proudly into the sky, can do without bad weather and storms:
> whether unkindness and opposition from without, whether
> some sort of hatred, envy, obstinacy, mistrust, severity, greed
> and violence do not belong to the favorable circumstances
> without which a great increase even in virtue is hardly pos-
> sible.[19]

Greek art is thus not *unbezeichnet,* nor is Greek culture
gay and optimistic as the classicists had claimed, but they
are tragic and pessimistic. However, it is not the weak pessimism of romanticism or of the Schopenhauerian teaching.
To Nietzsche weak pessimism is overcome in Greek art and
culture and turned into a pessimism of strength.

> The deep meaning of the tragic artist lies in this: that he
> affirms the economy of the whole which justifies the horrible,
> evil, problematic. . . . Art becomes the only effective force
> against the will to negate life, as anti-Christian, anti-Buddhis-
> tic, anti-nihilistic par excellence.[20]

And thus Nietzsche concludes that the German classicists
failed to understand the Greek spirit. "They did not succeed
in breaking through the enchanted gate which leads to the
magic mountain of Hellenism; they did not advance further
in their courageous struggle than the longing glance which
Goethe's Iphigenie casts from the barbaric Taurus to her
homeland across the seas."[21]

Winckelmann's Greece of "noble simplicity and serene
greatness" had its base in an Olympian realm where Apollo

reigned. The gods bore the countenance of Winckelmann's cold, marble figures which lacked expression, the signs of sorrow, suffering, pain. The air was still and motionless and nothing disturbed the serene activity of pure contemplation. But just as once the priesthood of Apollo had brought the Thracian deity back into the temple of Delphi and had merged his orgiastic abandon with the measured beauty of their native gods, so now Nietzsche brings Dionysus back into the Greek world that the classicists had created. With this bold stroke he razed Winckelmann's Olympus to the ground and destroyed its happy harmony. We hear cries of pain and primitive fear in the deep stillness; we see terror in the mask of the beautiful. Classical beauty is no longer static and lifeless; its sunny, optimistic mood is darkened by the agonies of life; its clarity and rationality become obscured, but also deepened, by the elements of doubt and irrationality. The idealized forms are replaced by the actual, living individual as he suffers and questions and probes into the problems and paradoxes of existence. Only thus, claims Nietzsche, could the Greeks have produced a culture and art that are tragic.

IV

Dionysus, the patron of the heroic individual and the symbol of tragic wisdom, becomes the central phenomenon for the understanding of the Greek genius. "As long as we have no answer to the question 'what is Dionysian?' the problem of the Greeks remains completely unknown and unimaginable."[22] But now Dionysus is no longer only the symbol of chaos and destruction; he is also the god of spring and production. Dionysian frenzy is not only a principle of decay and destructive passions, but it is an orgiastic power, a kind of Platonic madness that possesses the elements of creativity. Dionysus represents, as Plutarch observed, "the whole wet element" in nature—blood, semen, sap, wine, and all the life-giving juices. He is in fact a synthesis of both chaos and form, of orgiastic impulses and visionary states—at one with the life of nature and its eternal cycle of birth and death, of destruction and creation.

Nietzsche's *Gesamtlage,* the total pattern and basic rhythm of life and nature that return again and again in eternal recurrence, is akin to the ritual pattern of ancient Dionysian rites. While tragedy grew out of the Dithyramb sung in honor of the god Dionysus, the rites of Dionysus, in turn, grew out of the prehistoric ritual of the Year-Daemon—a theory developed by Gilbert Murray and other English scholars and now widely accepted. The story of the god who annually dies and is reborn in the spring, the story of his suffering and death and the rejoicing that accompanied his rebirth with its assurance of fertility, is the story of all life and its annual, ever-recurring triumph of birth over death, of light over darkness, of fertility over decay.

The entry of Dionysus into the Greek scene and his fusion with Apollo did not destroy the superiority of Greek culture and the majesty of Doric art. Without Dionysian depth, Apollonian beauty would be lifeless and expressionless, and could not evoke an aesthetic response in us. Without Dionysian questioning and probing, the Apollonian world would reflect a shallow, unearned optimism, a misinterpretation of life that leaves the inescapable paradoxes and conflicts out of it. The force of Apollo must be counterbalanced by the force of Dionysus. This fundamental duality, its constant opposition and its constant reconciliation, is for Nietzsche the essence of life and of every great work of art. Great art and culture have at all times arisen from the interpenetration of two opposing forces. "Now come with me to the tragedy and let us sacrifice in the temple of both gods."[23]

Nietzsche's introduction of the concept of Dionysus into the understanding of the Greeks was an act of genius. It shows his extraordinary ability to penetrate deeply into the human soul and understand the complexities of human psychology. Thomas Mann calls him a "born psychologist," the greatest critic and psychologist in the history of thought.[*] And Freud names Nietzsche as his precursor, thereby recognizing his immense contribution to the development of modern psychology.[**] It is Nietzsche, the precursor of modern psychology, who, through his reinterpretation of antiquity, succeeded in bringing ancient Greece closer to our own psychoanalytical age—an age which might have turned from the classical picture of sterile placidity, had it not discovered through Nietzsche a Greece whose agonies and problems are close to our own. Indeed, it can be argued that it was Nietzsche's reinterpretation of the Greek spirit that contributed to Freud's fascination with the figures of Greek myth and tragedy. Narcissus, Medusa, Oedipus, embodying some of Freud's major psychoanalytical concepts, are seen through Nietzsche's revelations concerning the long unseen power and depth of the Greek understanding of man.

It has been questioned whether Nietzsche was in fact the first to introduce this new interpretation of Greek culture, which diverges radically from the classical view. But it cannot be denied that he was indeed the first to develop the new tragic concept fully and comprehensibly, to provide it with a philosophical basis and—above all—to give it a positive interpretation. Among those who, prior to Nietzsche, ex-

---

[*] Thomas Mann, *Neue Studien* (Stockholm: Bermann Fischer, 1948).
[**] Ernest Jones, *The Life and Work of S. Freud*, 3 vols. (New York: Basic Books, 1953–57).

pressed disagreement with the classical interpretation were Friedrich Schlegel, Schelling, Kleist, Heine, Hoelderlin and Novalis.* But while they did discern a tragic undercurrent in the Greek character and poetry, they, on the whole, did not really break with Winckelmann's gospel of Greek serenity and quiet sublimity, and still were far removed from the Nietzschean Dionysian principle.

The scholar who comes closest to Nietzsche's interpretation of the Greeks is Jacob Burckhardt. In his *Greek History of Culture* he says:

> The Greeks were unhappier than is usually believed. . . . What they created and suffered, they created and suffered freely and differently from other nations. . . . That is why they are considered to be a people of genius, with all the faults and suffering that belong to genius.**

Heidegger, among others, claims that it was Burckhardt who was the first to interpret Greek culture as Dionysian and that he, in fact, influenced Nietzsche who, in 1872, heard Burckhardt lecture on this theme in Basel.*** However this may be, the fact remains that Burckhardt's ideas by no means attained the depth and force of the concept Dionysus that Nietzsche's insights possess. Burckhardt's Greeks are not yet Nietzsche's heroic titans who overcome the dark, sinister side

---

* Friedrich Schlegel, *Werke* (Wien: Konegen, 1882), 1:40: "In him (Sophocles) was unified the divine drunkenness of Dionysus, the deep inventiveness of Athena, and the gentle contemplativeness of Apollo"; Heinrich Kleist, *Penthesilea*; Heinrich Heine, *Die Goetter Griechenlands*; Goethe, *Faust* II, "Die klassische Walpurgisnacht." Goethe in this scene shows an awareness of the mysterious aspects of Hellenism; but, on the whole, I believe that Nietzsche is right when he claims that Goethe did not understand the Greeks (*Goetzendaemmerung,* VIII, 172).

** Jacob Burckhardt, *Griechische Kulturgeschichte,* p. 11.

*** Heidegger, *Nietzsche,* 1:123f.

of existence and accept life in its totality. His Greek tragedy
is not yet a joyous hymn to life. Charles Andler points to
this and says:

> For Burckhardt there is no mythology that is more sinister
> in its sadness than the Greek. Nietzsche would not have con-
> tested Burchhardt's contribution to the interpretation of the
> Hellenic temperament by his fortunate and new induction
> which he derived from the myths, from Orphic poetry and
> from the most ancient monuments of Greek civilization. But
> for Nietzsche the unique superiority of the Greeks is con-
> tained in the fact that they knew how to accept a world in
> which savage and destructive passions reign. They knew how
> to create a strong and joyful victory within a life of struggle
> and death.*

Nietzsche himself claims that he "was the first who took
seriously this wonderful phenomenon which bears the name
Dionysus, and contributed to the understanding of this older,
abundant and overflowing Hellenic instinct."[24]

V

As previously discussed, the key to Nietzsche's understanding of Greek art and culture and of the Dionysian
phenomenon is Greek tragedy, while the classicists see their
Apollonian ideal realized in Greek plastic art. For Winckelmann and his followers it is the Laocoön group, the Apollo
of Belvedere, the Venus of Medici that most fully represent
the "grand style of classic restraint and tranquil grandeur,"
and are the visible forms of the concepts of unity, simplicity,

---

* Charles Andler, *Nietzsche, sa Vie et sa Pensée,* 6 vols. (Paris: Bossard, 1920), 1:289f.

and universality. For Nietzsche, it is the tragedies of Aeschylus and Sophocles that are the highest manifestations of the Greek spirit and the tragic age he wants to revive.

The main themes and concepts of Greek tragedy have been introduced in the first section and elaborated upon throughout this study, since they are of primary importance not only in Nietzsche's ideas about Greek tragedy, art, and culture, but in his entire philosophy and world view. It is precisely because Greek tragedy expresses so fully the basic principles of Nietzsche's teaching that he was drawn to study it. Thus, whether we want to examine his aesthetics, his metaphysics, or his views on the problems of knowledge, religion, or ethics, it is always these central themes, contained in Greek tragedy, that we have to return to in order to understand him. These themes, summed up briefly, are all centered in what he calls the tragic view.

The tragic view, whose fundamental demands are realized in Greek tragedy, represents the highest apotheosis of life, affirming it in its totality and recognizing not only the inevitability, but also the productive power of its negative elements, of evil, terror, and pain. The negative pessimistic foundation of tragedy and life is not denied or glossed over by deceptions and illusions, but is, by the heroic will of the tragic hero, turned into a pessimism of strength through a process that Nietzsche calls overcoming.

Dionysus, the central phenomenon of Nietzsche's tragic view, is at once the patron of Greek tragedy and the basic principle of art and life. He is not only the symbol of primal chaos, of savage urges and orgiastic frenzy that threaten to destroy all forms, but also of fertility, measure, and control. In fact, "Dionysus cannot live without Apollo . . . [just as] Apollo cannot live without Dionysus." Pure form is inert without the life-giving energy of elemental striving forces;

pure energy is dissipated and chaotic without the organizing power of forms. But in spite of synthesis and periodic acts of reconciliation, the initial opposition between the two creative forces cannot be abolished, if the artistic and cultural ideal and true tragic greatness—as Nietzsche sees them—are to be achieved.

The tragic view sees art, exemplified in Greek tragedy, as akin to life. Both the artistic and natural forces create in the same manner, in the same tragic rhythm where dialectical powers are constantly at work in eternal recurrence—creating and destroying without purposes and goals in eternal innocence.

Apollonian-Dionysian—two states in which art itself appears as the power of nature in man.[25]

Poetry does not lie outside the world as a fantastic invention of poetic vision, but it wants to be the unadorned expression of truth itself.[26]

As with the concept of Dionysus, Nietzsche's position in regard to art undergoes changes and development. In his later thought, he departs from his educator Schopenhauer and the latter's aesthetic teaching, and arrives at conclusions that are opposed to his earlier ones—conclusions that also abolish the inconsistencies contained in his early works. Thus, in *The Birth of Tragedy*, he speaks of a justification and redemption of suffering through Apollonian illusions and dreams. "The primal Oneness, ever suffering and contradictory, needs beautiful visions and delightful illusions in order to redeem itself."[27] But in the very same work he also says:

Dionysian art wants to convince us of the eternal delight of existence. . . . We recognize that everything that is generated must be prepared to face painful dissolution. We are forced to gaze into the horrors of individual existence—and yet we should not be paralyzed with fear. . . . Now we see struggle, pain, destruction of appearances as necessary, because of the abundance of forms surging constantly into life, because of the enormous fecundity of the world will; we feel the furious prodding of this pain in the same moment in which we become one with the immense lust for life and are aware in Dionysian delight of the eternity and indestructibility of that lust.[28]

It is important to again point out the inconsistencies that are contained in *The Birth of Tragedy*, because this book was "overrated" and misunderstood not only in Nietzsche's time, but also in our own. We must agree with Nietzsche that "in order to do justice to *The Birth of Tragedy*, we should forget a few things."[29] We wonder with him why "just what was mistaken in this book had influence and fascination . . . [and why] that which was fundamentally valuable in it was overlooked."[30] The essential principles, worked out comprehensively in later writings, are already here in this early book: The world is justified and redeemed in "the abundance of forms surging constantly into life . . . [in] the immense lust for life and . . . in [the] Dionysian delight of the eternity and indestructibility of that lust."

Its lack of consistency would tempt one, in agreement with Nietzsche, to call *The Birth of Tragedy* "a first book in the worst sense of the term,"[31] were it not for the richness, brilliance, and originality of its ideas that make it possible to overlook its faults; but, while acknowledging its fascination, we must guard against any interpretation of Nietzsche's philosophy on the basis of this book alone. A unity and consistency of Nietzsche's basic philosophical conceptions is possible only when his break with Schopenhauer is complete

—which was not yet the case during the period of *The Birth of Tragedy*. Only then does the meaning of art as a metaphysical activity become clear and consistent with the fundamental concepts of his tragic philosophy.

Now art is not a fair illusion, a "metaphysical supplement" to primal terror and pain; but in its creative activity expresses the essence of being itself. Now pain and suffering are not negated and in need of redemption, but are affirmed as positive powers and necessary stimulants to life and art. The function of tragedy is no longer to provide a veil of deception in order to cover up the evil, pain, and dissonance of life; it is not a means to cure us of Dionysian dithyrambic madness through the enchantment of the Delphic god. The function of tragedy is the union of Apollo and Dionysus and the overcoming of pessimism in the truly tragic sense by turning weak pessimism into a pessimism of strength. Pain and joy, abyss and height, dissonance and harmony, Dionysus and Apollo are one.

> The psychology of tragedy is not to get rid of terror and pity . . . thus it was misunderstood by Aristotle . . . but, beyond terror and pity, to be the eternal joy of becoming itself . . . that joy which also includes the joy of destruction.[32]

In the experience of tragedy we celebrate the union of nature and man, of Dionysus and Apollo. "At last, by a wondrous, metaphysical act of the Hellenic 'will', the pair accepted marriage and thus begot Attic tragedy, which exhibits the salient features of both parents."[33]

> The chariot of Dionysus is bedecked with flowers and garlands; panthers and tigers stride beneath his yoke. . . . Not only does the bond between man and man come to be forged once more by the magic of the Dionysian rite, but nature itself . . . rises again to celebrate the reconciliation with her prodigal son, man.[34]

10
NIETZSCHE'S DIONYSIAN FAITH

I beseech you, my brothers, remain faithful to the earth and do not believe in those who speak of otherworldly hopes.[1]

—Nietzsche

I

The "Innocence of Becoming" represents in its anti-moralistic, aesthetic interpretation of life a new faith beyond good and evil. "God is dead," but this is only the moral, transcendent God. The question from the *Gay Science*, "whither is God?", is now answered in a new Dionysian religion. "You call it the self-destruction of God; it is merely an excoriation. He merely discarded his moral character. And you will see him soon again beyond good and evil."[2]

With the "death of God" and the devaluation of the "highest values" the moral world order is destroyed, creating thereby a "space of freedom" in which man regains the "innocence of existence" and a tragic meaning of life. Nietzsche's polemic against the Platonic-Christian tradition has mainly one central objective: to abolish the transcendent realm which devaluates life on earth to mere appearance, considering it only a path and transition toward a future sacred existence. But what is sacred in Nietzsche's new religion is this life. In spite of suffering and pain it is holy and possesses many of the same qualities long attributed to a divine Beyond. The creative principle is no longer transcendent, but immanent in this world, in the unity of man, nature, and God.

Nietzsche's religious views have much in common with those of Goethe; and both, in turn, are influenced by Spinoza's pantheistic principles of which the principles of unity and anti-teleology were discussed in a previous section. But, additionally, Goethe and Nietzsche share many ideas on religion that are not found in Spinoza. Again I use Spinoza and Goethe to help clarify Nietzsche's thought. As previously argued, Nietzsche's excessive language and aphoristic style, his passion and tendency to exaggerate, often obscure the true meaning of his teaching. By relating his ideas to those of Spinoza and Goethe, I hope to tone down the shrillness of Nietzsche's voice and make us listen where we might otherwise refuse.

My comparison of Nietzsche's and Goethe's religious views is based primarily on Goethe's *Faust*, and is undertaken in the awareness that it does not present a complete analysis of Goethe's thought. Its complexity and richness go far beyond the scope of this discussion, for Goethe's creative genius does not find full realization and expression in *Faust* alone. His other works are related to *Faust* as complementary opposites and manifold modes of existence. However, *Faust*, more than any other drama by Goethe, helped to liberate us from the Gothic and sterile age that Nietzsche called the age of decadence, and led to the inauguration of the age of genius. It created in the figure of Faust the prototype of the man of action whose will to live grew out of a tragic ground.

My interpretation of Goethe's *Faust* as tragic in the Nietz-schean sense is contrary to the position of those Goethe interpreters who, with Gottfried Keller, remained, on the whole, unaware of Goethe's problematic nature and saw in him mainly the contemplative, epic, and nontragic poet.* But other scholars have challenged these interpretations, seeing the dialectical and daemonic elements in Goethe. Thus we find the following in Charles Andler's six-volume study of Nietzsche's thought:

> All the ideas that occupied Nietzsche . . . are they not already realized in Goethe's spirit? Apollonian and Dionysian, philology and poetry, science and art, all these syntheses which constituted culture for Nietzsche, are they not anticipated in Goethe?**

Nietzsche himself failed to see the tragic elements in *Faust* or in such works as *Satyros* and *Prometheus*. He did not recognize how far removed the "Walpurgisnacht" in *Faust II* is from Winckelmann's spirit of "quiet grandeur." In spite of his sometimes ecstatic admiration, his attitude, on the whole, lacked understanding of Goethe's problematic nature, and the two souls that lived in Goethe's breast: the "naïve" poet of *Werther, Tasso, Egmont* and *Iphigenie,* which are figures that belong to the harmonious state of Paradise before the Fall, and the "sentimental" poet of *Faust,* who has eaten the apple and lost the Paradise. Paradoxically, Nietzsche did not recognize in Goethe those qual-

---

* Walter Muschg, "Goethes Glaube an das Daemonische," *Deutsche Vierteljahrschrift fuer Literaturwissenschaft und Geistesgeschichte* (July 1958). Muschg quotes Gottfried Keller and Richard Wilhelm, who found in Goethe the repose and peace of old Chinese wisdom and compare him to Lao-tse.

** Charles Andler, *Nietzsche, sa Vie et sa Pensée,* 6 vols. (Paris: Bossard, 1920), 1:26.

ities which were closest to his own, seeing only the contemplative man in the grand style, the embodiment of harmony and measure. This is the more surprising since it represents a contradiction to his own concept of measure and greatness, which, according to him, can arise only from the tragic ground of conflict and suffering. How could Goethe, without the problematic and daemonic, become for Nietzsche "the last German for whom I have reverence . . . the man baptized with the name of Dionysus?"[3]

In spite of the fact that Nietzsche calls Schopenhauer his educator, it is Goethe whose influence continued from early youth to maturity. It was the reading of Goethe's works during his childhood and student years that helped shape the youthful mind and made the first impressions that were to last during Nietzsche's entire life. He never ceases to quote Goethe and even when, as during his Schopenhauer period, he criticizes Goethe most severely, he is closer to him than he himself admitted or even realized. I fully agree with Charles Andler, who names Goethe as one of Nietzsche's precursors, and with Hermann A. Korff, who calls him a "Goethe-pupil."[*] But he is a Goethe pupil only in the Nietzschean sense. Nietzsche, like Goethe, firmly rejected veneration without critique. Lessing had pointed out that a miserable poet should not be criticized at all; that a mediocre one ought to be treated mildly and indulgently, but that a great genius should be subject to the most rigorous and most merciless criticism. "The man who remains a pupil requites his teacher but ill. And why would you not pluck at my wreath?"[4]

Nietzsche's strongest criticism is directed toward the *Faust* drama. Thus he says: "The Goethean man here avoids

---

[*] Hermann August Korff, *Die Lebensideen Goethes* (Leipzig: J. J. Weber, 1925).

the Rousseauean man, because he hates everything violent and powerful, every leap—that is every deed; and thus the world-liberator Faust is in the end only a world-traveller."[5] "The Faust idea . . . should this really be the greatest German 'tragic idea'? . . . By means of a trick played on the devil in the decisive moment . . . he brings 'the good man with the dark urges' at the right time into heaven."[6] It is hard to understand why Nietzsche interpreted Faust as a Christian drama of sin and expiation. Perhaps it was his bitter disappointment in Wagner and his passionate denial of Parsifal that led to a false identification of Parsifal and Faust and thereby to an interpretation of *Faust*'s ending as a Christian "Himmelfahrt" (a journey into heaven), a tragedy without a tragic end.

It is equally unclear why he identified Faust with the intellectual man of the Enlightenment who destroyed the unity of thought and being, of intellect and nature. Actually, the weary scholar and practitioner of black magic represents Goethe's rejection of the optimism of the Enlightenment and its emphasis on intellect and reason. The frictions in Faust's soul grow out of his despair over the futility of the power of rationalism and the longing for a "naïve" unity with nature. His bold attempt to wrest the inner secrets from the cosmos, his reaching for the richness and fullness of life in spite of its eternal suffering, are of a Dionysian spirit and possess the elements of tragedy.

We wonder why Nietzsche with his deep psychological understanding lacked insight into Goethe's Faustian dilemmas and did not recognize them as his own. It is in the *Faust* drama that we find Goethe's "Diwan" soul and the Dionysian soul of Zarathustra, a soul that wanders and errs and in suffering and torment reaches for the stars above. It is the soul that dies and is born in an eternal cycle of destruction and creation.

Und so lang' du das nicht hast,
Dieses: Stirb und Werde!
Bist du nur ein trueber Gast
Auf der dunklen Erde.

And until you have possessed
Dying and Rebirth
You are but a sullen guest
On the gloomy earth.

—Goethe, *West-Oestlicher Diwan*,
"Selige Sehnsucht"

II

Nietzsche's and Goethe's views of a unified world, as influenced by Spinoza's teaching, oppose the Judaeo-Christian
tradition with its fundamental dualism, its transcendent God
who exists in a supernatural Beyond. Their God is immanent
in the natural world. He is not a person, or a will or an
intellect, but he is the totality of all things. "God is the immanent and not the transient cause of all things."* As noted
before, because of temperamental and cultural differences
this mutual repudiation of traditional Judaeo-Christian
theology is expressed in different ways. Spinoza uses an abstract, mathematical style while Nietzsche's polemic is violent and aggressive. Goethe's criticism of orthodox Christianity preserves, in most instances, a calm balance, a
"standing beside" (*ein daneben Stehen*). In a letter to Lavater he says: "I am not an anti-Christian (*Widerchrist*), an
un-Christian (*Unchrist*), but yet a decided non-Christian
(*Nichtchrist*)."**

---

* Spinoza, *Ethics*, pt. 1, Prop. XVIII.
** Letter to Lavater, July 29, 1782, in *Goethes Briefe*, 8 vols. (Berlin:
O. Elsner, 1902–5).

But in his *Venetian Epigrams* we find a different, more aggressive mood, which is closer to the polemical intensity of Nietzsche's *Antichrist*. It is here that Goethe expresses his pagan antipathy to the "cross," which Nietzsche refers to in the *Twilight of the Idols:* "Goethe, the last German for whom I have reverence . . . also we understand each other in regard to the 'cross.' "[7] However, both respect Jesus as a person and distinguish his teaching from its interpretations by his disciples. Thus Nietzsche says in the *Antichrist:* "Actually there was only one Christian and he died on the cross."[8] And Goethe, in a conversation with Eckermann, speaks of the greatness which emanated from the person of Jesus and the profound reverence he felt for him.[*]

Goethe's and Nietzsche's unified world view leads to a position essentially pantheistic in character. This position, influenced by Spinoza, stresses two essential ideas: God and the world are not related as cause and effect, creator and creature, but are identical in substance; and, secondly, the creative principle is immanent in the world. Spinoza's God, eternal, infinite, self-created substance, is the immanent and not the transcendent cause of things, wherein the effect is not in substance other than the cause, but, on the contrary, reveals the nature of the cause. God is both *natura naturans,* in whose nature all things are attributes and modes, and *natura naturata,* in which this nature expresses itself in space and time. The world is not created *ex nihilo* by divine will and design; the world is God. Goethe writes to his friend F. H. Jacobi:

> You think in terms of supreme reality, but this is the basis of Spinoza's system on which everything rests, the source from which everything flows. He does not prove the existence of

---

[*] Eckermann, *Gespraeche mit Goethe,* March 11, 1832.

God. Existence is God. And if others on this account brand him Atheus, I should like to label and praise him as Theissimus, indeed Christianissimus.*

Although I have pointed to similarities among Spinoza's, Goethe's, and Nietzsche's pantheism, I have by no means intended to equate Spinoza's pantheism with that of either Nietzsche or Goethe. Indeed, there exist many significant differences in their respective pantheistic philosophies, the most fundamental being the manner in which their identification of God and the world, of creator and creature, is undertaken. Following Hegel, who referred to Spinoza's philosophy as "Akosmismus," the term "acosmic pantheism" can be justifiably applied to Spinoza's doctrine, while the term "humanistic pantheism" would be consistent with Goethe's and Nietzsche's views.

In Spinoza's acosmic pantheism there is a tendency to consider the world of space and time as subordinate to divine substance, and ultimately submerged in the all-engulfing One. God, or substance, is central, and everything else, being an attribute or mode, has no genuinely independent existence and importance, but is only an aspect and product of divine action, a moment in the self-expression and self-fulfillment of the Absolute. "Whatever is, is in God and nothing can either be or be conceived without God."** While Spinoza does not deny the reality of the universe of particular, individual things, their true essence is conceived only *sub specie aeternitatis,* in relation to divine substance, and not in isolation and independence from it. The concrete world in which we exist is accorded secondary significance. In Goethe's and Nietzsche's "humanistic panthe-

---

* Letter to F. H. Jacobi, June 9, 1785, in *Goethes Briefe.*
** Spinoza, *Ethics,* pt. 1, Prop. XV.

ism," on the other hand, the divinity is somehow lowered into the world. It is nature, with man as its highest achievement, whose importance and infinite significance is stressed. Neither Nietzsche's and Goethe's humanistic pantheism nor Spinoza's acosmic pantheism is free of ambiguities and antinomies. The relation between God and the world is by no means clear in Spinoza's teaching. Not only immanence, but also transcendence; not only naturalistic and materialistic, but also supernatural and idealistic elements are present in Spinoza's system. Indeed, he is both the follower of the dynamic pantheism of the Renaissance and its joyful rediscovery of nature and, simultaneously, is influenced by the neo-Platonic theory of emanation and its hierarchical order of descending levels of reality. Thus God is conceived as simple, self-identical, perfect, absolute reality, transcending all relations and determinations; or alternately as the necessary ground and all-inclusive totality of the moving changing world of modes—His eternal, immutable nature being expressed by the rich diversity of the concrete and particularized temporal world. Further, the human mind and the material world are, on the one hand, taken to be, in their essential nature, attributes of God, existing *sub specie aeternitatis in Deo,* and partaking of His infinite, eternal, indivisible nature; but they are also other than this nature by virtue of their finite, modal expression in the temporal world of sensible experience. In short, the relation between substance and mode, God and the world, is not one of genuine reciprocity, wherein each term is definable in terms of the other; rather, the relation is asymmetrical, whereby one of the terms remains absolute and *sui generis.*

Ambiguities are also present in Goethe's and Nietzsche's thought. In spite of its humanistic character, their pantheism is not free of elements of transcendence. While violently attacking Platonic-Christian transcendent metaphysics, Nietzsche remains deeply rooted in its tradition. And in spite of the fact that, by a reversal of Platonism, he creates a new metaphysics of change and becoming, a longing to shatter the *principium individuationis* and penetrate behind phenomena is never absent in the complexity of Nietzsche's thought. He abolishes the Kantian distinction between the noumenal and phenomenal, and denies the existence of the "thing in itself" as a metaphysical foundation, and yet he continues to refer to the "Ur-Eine," the mystical ground and "womb of being." And Goethe, too, longs with Faust to enter the "realm of mothers" and "see what binds the world together in its innermost essence." He never abandons his belief in an eternal order above the phenomenal world, but it is a realm "to be revered in silence" and not to be entered, not to be known.

However, despite elements of transcendence, to both Goethe and Nietzsche it is not to the supernatural order, but "this world to which we must remain true"; this world of change and contradiction and tragic involvement. Their philosophies are philosophies of life, wherein the understanding of man and his place in the universe are of primary concern. In Goethe's and Nietzsche's pantheism, man is central; but it is man as part of nature. The creative powers in nature and in man are identified; and it is this element of creativity, immanent in both nature and man, which possesses the attributes of the divine.

III

Nietzsche's humanistic pantheism has been called atheistic by Henri Lubac and Max Scheler, among others. Scheler refers to it as a "postulatory atheism of earnestness and responsibility," and Lubac as "an atheistic humanism."* The latter names, in addition to Nietzsche, Feuerbach, and Nicolai Hartmann as adherents of this atheistic humanism and quotes Feuerbach: "The question of the existence or nonexistence of God is the question of the nonexistence or existence of man."** If it is an atheism, it is, however, not one in the usual sense. Nietzsche himself calls it an "honest atheism" (*redlicher Atheismus*) and relates it to the innocence of becoming.

> The rise of the Christian God has created the strongest feelings of guilt. . . . The prospect is not to be denied that the complete and definite victory of atheism may release mankind from this feeling. . . . Atheism and a kind of second innocence belong together.[9]

This new kind of atheism does not deny the existence of God because it is unprovable and incomprehensible, but otherwise deemed desirable and even indispensable. It wills the destruction of God so that man may live. Indeed, Nietzsche's higher man rejoices at the proclamation of the death of God and experiences a feeling of liberation. "We philosophers and 'free spirits' feel at the pronouncement of the death of God the rays of a new dawn. . . . At last the horizon appears free again."[10] But it is alone the Christian, transcendent, moral God, whose worship depreciates this life and destroys man's creative impulses, who has fallen, and not the God who is immanent in the productive powers of nature and man, the God "beyond good and evil." "That which differentiates us is not that we find no God, either in history or

---

* Max Scheler, *Philosophische Weltanschauung* (Bonn: Fr. Cohen, 1929); Henri Lubac, *Le Drame de l'Humanisme Athée* (Paris: Editions Spes, 1945).

** Ibid., p. 27.

in nature or behind nature . . . but that we feel that what had been revered as god is not god-like."[11]

The new divinity that is erected upon the altar of the dead God is man.* The proclamation "God is dead" is not only a statement of fact; it is also a decision. It is the expression of the heroic will of the individual to abolish the false values of a transcendent faith and its concepts of sin and guilt in order to achieve a revaluation of values in the innocence of becoming. Man's greatness and worth are no longer based upon his relation to a transcendent God. His reason, freedom, and immortality are no longer attributes of divine origin, imparted by God to his creatures; but they grow out of his own creative powers. "We have murdered God. . . . Perhaps man will rise higher and higher when once he ceases to flow into a God."[12]

Nietzsche, as perhaps no other philosophical thinker before him, brings man into the center of his thought and thereby creates what Berdyaev refers to as a "new religious anthropology."

In Nietzsche, humanism conquers not from above through grace, but from beneath through man's own powers—and this is the great achievement of Nietzsche. Nietzsche is the forerunner of a new religious anthropology. Through Nietzsche the new humanity moves out of godless humanism to divine humanism. . . . Nietzsche is . . . a prophet of the religious renaissance of the West. Zarathustra's hatred for the last man who has invented happiness is a holy hatred. . . . Zarathustra preached creativity rather than happiness—he called man toward the mountain top rather than to the bliss on the plain. . . .

---

* Jung finds this phenomenon occurring in those rare individuals whom he calls truly "modern men." In the dreams of such individuals "there is . . . no submission or reconciliation to a deity. The place of the deity seems to be taken by the wholeness of man." (C. G. Jung, *Psychology and Religion* [New Haven: Yale University Press, 1938], p. 99).

Nietzsche senses the creative calling of man. . . . He curses
the good and the happy because they hate those who create.
We should share Nietzsche's torment; it is religious through
and through.*

Man, the center of Nietzsche's new religion, is neither the
Christian man nor the man of the Enlightenment; guided
neither by divine grace nor by the natural laws of reason.
He is modern man, torn and problematic, searching for
meaning and content in life, and for a faith that does not
deny the "creative calling of man."

In Nietzsche's "honest atheism," where the traditional God
is dead and belief in the whole system of values and meanings one had lived by is lost, man is abandoned to himself
and faces nothingness. This void drives the mediocre man
into resignation, weak pessimism, and nihilism, but for the
higher individual this void is felt both as a loss and as a
liberation. The concept of nothingness and nonbeing gains,
by an act of will, content and meaning. It is no longer
Democritus's empty space or a mere contrast to Platonic
essences of true being; nor is it a means for an ontological
interpretation of evil. Nothingness is a new positive, affirmative concept, and is ontologically as fundamental as being.
"The paradox of every radical negativity is that it must affirm
itself in order to be able to negate itself. . . . No actual negation can be without an implicit affirmation."* *

The act of accepting the nothingness and the meaninglessness of a godless world is in itself a meaningful act. It is an
act of courage, honesty, and integrity, which expresses an
unconditional will to truth and the courage to face a world

---

* Nicholas Berdyaev, *The Meaning of the Creative Act* (New York:
Collier, 1962), p. 82.
* * Paul Tillich, *The Courage to Be* (New Haven: Yale University Press,
1952), p. 176.

without God—without refuge or promise or divine grace. In the abyss of nothingness Nietzsche's "free spirit" creates a new freedom and sovereignty of man, a new religion that has its roots in the human will, the will to create and to reestablish man's unique place in the cosmos, which, he felt, was lost with the rise of Christianity.

Nietzsche's concept of nothingness has influenced twentieth-century existentialists, especially Heidegger and Sartre who have put nothingness (*Das Nichts, le néant*) in the center of their ontological thought. Most elements of contemporary existentialist thought are already here in Nietzsche's concept: the experience of absurdity and despair, the experience of being "thrown" into a world that lacks *a priori* essences, and established values and norms. But Nietzsche's dialectic, like that of Hegel, makes negation a positive, dynamic power in nature and history. Nonbeing is part of being, eternally present and eternally overcome in the process of life. Despair is not only a negative emotion but it possesses the elements of overcoming, the courage to create one's own values and meaning of life—a courage that Paul Tillich calls "the courage of despair": "The courage to take upon oneself the loneliness of such creativity and the horror of such visions is an outstanding expression of the courage to be as oneself."[*]

This courage of despair is found in contemporary art, in literature, and in philosophy. In spite of the claims of those critics who see our age as unheroic, and our literature, art, and existentialist philosophy as negative and nihilistic, I believe that all great art and systems of thought, no matter how radically negative and pessimistic they may appear, must, paradoxically, contain elements of affirmation. The

---

[*] Ibid., p. 143.

spirit of despair and anxiety is not one of apathy, resignation, and absolute negativity, but one of tragedy, which wants to create and overcome. It is a call not from above, but from the depth of the abyss and the anguish of our inner consciousness to face the absurdity of the human condition, the desert and "wasteland" around us, and transform it into a "fruitful farmland"—into a new tragic religion that affirms the totality of life "with all that is greatest and all that is smallest" and deems it holy.

Existentialism, that is the great art, literature, and philosophy of the twentieth century, reveal the courage to face things as they are and to express the anxiety of meaninglessness. It is a creative courage which appears in the creative expressions of despair. Sartre calls one of his most powerful plays *No Exit*, a classical formula for the situation of despair. But he himself has an exit: he can say "no exit," thus taking the situation of meaninglessness upon himself. T. S. Eliot called his first great poem "The Wasteland." He described the decomposition of civilization, the lack of conviction and direction, the poverty and hysteria of the modern consciousness. But it is the beautifully cultivated garden of a great poem which describes the meaninglessness of the Wasteland and expresses the courage of despair.*

"The essence of man is existence." This is true for Nietzsche as it is for Sartre. Not God or *a priori* principles and absolute norms, not the laws and ideas of reason constitute man's essential nature; what he is is that which he makes of himself by his acts and creativity. The above sentence is also true of Goethe's Faustian man who, in despair at finding the ultimate meaning of life, turns away from revealed truths and learned books and the black arts of magic.

---

* Ibid., p. 143f.

He turns to actual existence as he wanders with Mephistopheles through its depth and heights, its suffering and
glory.

Nietzsche's "honest atheism" is anti-Christian; "but anti-
Christian is by no means anti-religious."[13] In *Beyond Good
and Evil* he says: "I love the great despisers because they
are the great reverers."[14] Nietzsche's "atheism" represents a
passionate and tortured search for a meaningful religion. His
uncompromising honesty led him to reject orthodox Christianity and official forms of theism which, he felt, negated
life and destroyed man's instincts and creativity, his will
to power.

I beseech you, my brothers, remain faithful to the earth and
do not believe in those who speak of otherworldly hopes.[15]

Christian faith is a sacrifice, a sacrifice of all freedom, all pride
and self-assurance of the mind: it is servitude, self-mockery
and self-mutilation.[16]

But behind Nietzsche's violent polemic against organized
religions is a longing and yearning of a religious spirit, and
it was of such force that it perhaps destroyed him. In an early
poem, "To the Unknown God," written at the age of twenty,
he calls himself God-possessed.

I must know thee, Unknown One,
Thou who searchest out the depths of my soul
And blowest like a storm through my life.
Thou art inconceivable and yet my kinsman!
I must know thee and even serve thee.

The unknown God to whom Nietzsche paid homage in his

youth possessed him throughout his life. We find him again
in *Zarathustra*.

> No! Do come back
> With all thy tortures!
> To the last of all that are lonely,
> Oh, come back!
> All my tear-streams run
> Their course to thee:
> All my heart's final flame
> Flares up for thee!
> Oh, Come back,
> My unknown God! My pain! My last-happiness![17]

IV

The fundamental difference between Spinoza's acosmic
pantheism, with its central emphasis on God, and Goethe's
and Nietzsche's humanistic pantheism, with its emphasis on
man, inevitably leads to further disparities in their religious
views. These are contained primarily in the following characteristics, which are neglected by Spinoza but stressed by
Goethe and Nietzsche: the emphases on polarity and strife,
on the individual, and on the aesthetic aspects of the
universe.

The religious experience of the Faustian Dionysian man
does not take place in a sphere of quiet contemplation, but
within the struggles and tensions of the heroic will to overcome. Nietzsche's will to power and Goethe's eternally striving will become the fundamental principles of their humanistic pantheism. Theirs is a religious experience that is
far removed from Schopenhauer's negative salvation and
from the Christian "cross," as Nietzsche and Goethe under-

stand it. Instead, it has its foundation in a tragic view that culminates in an affirmation of life and a glorification of the totality of all being, where the devil himself is present in heaven, and the horrible and evil are accepted as necessary and holy.

"Reverence for God is the reverence for the interconnectedness of all things."[18] Perhaps a passage from Buber's *Eclipse of God* should be added to the above quotation from the *Nachlass* to express the essence of this new religion: "Faith is not a feeling in the soul of man, but an entrance into the whole reality without reduction and curtailment."* The new Dionysian faith grows out of man's eternal need to enter into a unity with nature. It is Zarathustra's attempt to lift the veil of illusion and behold the "womb of being." It is Faust's entrance into the "realm of mothers," to see "what binds the world together in its innermost essence." There is at first despair at the impossibility of penetrating into reality itself. "Into the innermost essence of nature, oh, you philistine, no created being may enter."** There is at first the horror of the Faustian man, as he gazes into the ground of being and cries out at the sight of the *Erdgeist*: "Woe, I cannot endure you!"*** But in despair and terror Zarathustra and Faust find their new faith: To say Yes to life with its good and evil; to affirm destruction and chaos as part of the eternal cycle of living and dying and of the everlasting change that pervades all nature. "For even in the shortest moment, in the smallest atom of his life, he faces something sacred that will infinitely outweigh all struggle and anguish. . . . That is the meaning of the tragic disposition."[19] And

---

* Martin Buber, *The Eclipse of God* (New York: Harper, 1957), p. 3.
** Goethe, *Spruchweisheit*, "Der Physiker," in *Gesammelte Werke*, 15 vols. (Leipzig: Tempel-Verlag), 3:21.
*** Ibid., *Faust* (Leipzig: Tempel-Verlag), 6:99.

again, "Prayer must be transformed into benediction."[20]

Nietzsche's and Goethe's creative principle, immanent in nature and man, is a basic formative law of life that contains both the negative and affirmative, both struggle and overcoming. This fundamental principle is for Nietzsche the will to power, and for Goethe the principle of polarity and enhancement. The divine force does not dwell in the peaceful holiness of a Beyond, but is encountered in what Nietzsche calls the Dionysian and Goethe the daemonic. Both concepts are close to the religious tradition of antiquity and contrary to the Christian interpretation of the daemonic. Christianity brought the conception of good and evil into the daemonic and destroyed its creative power, whereas in the tradition of antiquity daemons are demigods who are connected with man in a mysterious way. They are forces of nature, strange and dark, like the older chthonic deities and the fate of Moira. They contain not only the elements of contradiction and strife, but also those of productivity and creation.

These principles are symbolized by Goethe in the figure of Mephistopheles, in whose negative character there is something paradoxically positive; he is part of that force "which forever wills evil and forever creates good." They are symbolized by Nietzsche in the god Dionysus, the Thracian deity who invaded the classic Olympus with his bands of satyrs, merging bacchanalian orgiasm with the serene harmony of the native gods, and finally representing a synthesis of both frenzy and form, of destruction and creation. The great individual, the creator of culture, is for Goethe and Nietzsche always guided by daemonic forces: "The higher a man is, the more he is under the influence of the daemonic."[*]

---

[*] Eckermann, *Gespraeche mit Goethe,* March 24, 1829.

He is Prometheus, man raised to titanic proportions who "in his heroic striving toward universality and in his attempt to transcend the limits of individuation and become one with all being, experiences in himself the primordial contradiction of all things."[21]

Goethe's and Nietzsche's God is found in the world in which we live, in a world that is full of burning contradictions. God and the devil, heaven and hell, good and evil are joined together in the eternal play of opposing forces. The devil is found among the heavenly figures in the Faustian scene of the "Prologue to Heaven." Here Mephistopheles is on equal footing with the archangels and converses with God. This scene calls to mind a passage in *Ecce Homo*, in which Nietzsche says: "It was God himself who, at the end of his great work, coiled himself up in the form of a serpent at the foot of the tree of knowledge. It was thus that he recovered from being a God. He had made everything too beautiful . . . the devil is simply God's moment of idleness on that seventh day."[22]

V

A further difference from Spinoza's "Akosmismus" is the greater importance of the principle of individuality in both Goethe's and Nietzsche's pantheistic views. Although this element is not absent in Spinoza's philosophy, there is a tendency for the significance of the finite individual to disappear in the infinite All-One. It is Leibniz's monadology which supplements for Nietzsche and Goethe the Spinozistic teaching and preserves the principle of individuality within the larger unity of the cosmic whole. Each monad is an independent unity which is active in accordance with its own innate nature, but, at the same time, represents a creative mirror of the universe. Thus a harmony is established between the qualities of unity and individuality, which are central in Goethe's and Nietzsche's thought but insufficiently stressed by Spinoza. Goethe expressed this in a letter to Jacobi: "Divine nature . . . I only recognize it in *rebus singulares;* no other but Spinoza himself can encourage their deeper contemplation, although all particular things seem to disappear before his eyes."*

Goethe and Nietzsche glorify the heroic individual. In his creative spirit they see a manifestation of divine nature; in his affirmation of the totality of life they hear the language of religion. He is creator and lawgiver, who breaks the old tables and sets his own standards. He is Prometheus, who defies the gods and, conscious of his own powers, cries out: "They are mine, and mine is their use!" And yet, at the same time, the great individual is, as Jaspers expressed it, "ein Widerschein des Ganzen des Seins," a manifestation of the totality of being.** He transcends the narrow limits of individuation and searches for a unity with the universal. In this attempt he is torn by the antithesis between man and his divinities, between nature and spirit; but he nonetheless experiences "an obscure sense of mutual dependency . . . and joins forces with his gods. . . . In Dionysian rapture and mystical self-abrogation . . . his unity with the essence of the universe is revealed to him."[23]

Nietzsche refers to the heroic individual as the higher man or the free spirit, and only seldom does he use the word *Uebermensch* (overman, superman). Again, as was the case with the previously mentioned concepts of *The Birth of Tragedy,* it is what was misunderstood in the *Uebermensch*

---

* Letter to Jacobi, June 9, 1785, in *Goethes Briefe.*
** Karl Jaspers, *Die Grossen Philosophen,* 2 vols. (Muenchen: Piper & Co., 1959).

idea that had fascination and gained wide attention and notoriety. But Nietzsche's overman is not something extra-human or trans-human, as has been claimed; neither is he the blond beast, the man of savage cruelty and unsublimated raw nature in whose uncontrolled will everything is permitted.

When Nietzsche says in *Zarathustra* "I teach you the over-man; man is something that should be overcome,"[24] he does not mean that the overman should transcend humanity, but rather that he should become truly human. "When the soul begins again to mount, it comes not to something alien, but to its very self."* What must be overcome is the "last man," the "herd man" who is complacent and resigned, uncommitted and uninspired; who is one of the multitude in the market place, unable to understand the deeper meaning of Zarathustra's message; who is the dwarf, the symbol of mediocrity, and the inner plague that returns again and again to pull us down from the mountain heights and its pure and "innocent" air. Above all, the last man is part of all of us—and even of Zarathustra—returning again and again to face us in our eternal struggle of self-overcoming and our eternal search for our true self.

What is often overlooked is Nietzsche's deep faith in man, in his creative energies and potentialities. "What I hope in man is that he is an overture and a going under. And in you, too, there is much that lets me love and hope." Our true self, according to Nietzsche, is greatly above what we ordinarily take it to be:

As long as you see the stars high above you, you do not gaze as one who has insight.[25]

---

* Plotinus, *Enneads,* VI, ix, 11.

Your true self is immeasurably high above you or at least above that which you understand as your I.[26]

Overcoming is therefore for Nietzsche primarily self-overcoming and self-realization: the overcoming of fears and cowardice, of despair and anguish by transforming these negative passions, which threaten to take possession of us, into active powers. The will to power is not power over others, but power over ourselves—the sublimation of our instincts and our passions.

The essential characteristic of Nietzsche's overman, and indeed the center of his whole philosophy, is creativity. And it is this creative aspect in man as well as in nature around him which constitutes the divine element. Virtue is not obedience to external commands, or self-denial, or suppression of individuality. It is the realization of our essential nature by the release and unfolding of our creative powers. Virtue is excellence in the Platonic and Aristotelian sense, "the activity by which the potentialities peculiar to man are realized." It is the power to order our life, giving it form and authenticity, and making it into a work of art.

Nietzsche's overman has been compared to Aristotle's "great-souled" man* who gives of himself not out of duty or kindness, but out of the fullness and superabundance of his own powers.

The one goes to his neighbor because he seeks himself, and the other because he would fain lose himself.[27]

[The higher man] . . . has true kindness, nobility, greatness of soul which does not give in order to take, which does not

---

* Walter Kaufmann, *Nietzsche* (Princeton: Princeton University Press, 1950), p. 335.

want to excel by being kind; "lavishness" as a type of true kindness; abundance of personality as a presupposition.[28]

The distinguished man, too, helps the unhappy, not from compassion, but from an internal pressure that has been built up by an excess of power. . . . In the foreground is the feeling of fullness, the consciousness of riches, which would like to give and lavish.[29]

The overman has also been compared to Emerson's "Oversoul," in which we find the totality of being.

Within man is the soul of the whole; the wise silence; the universal beauty, to which every part and particle is equally related; the eternal One. And this deep power in which we exist and whose beatitude is all accessible to us, is not only self-sufficing and perfect in every hour, but the act of seeing and the thing seen, the seer and the spectacle, the subject and the object, are one. We see the world piece by piece, as the sun, the moon, the animal, the tree; but the whole, of which these are the shining parts, is the soul.*

Nietzsche's overman is Goethe's Faust, particularly the Faust of the second part of the drama. The essential characteristic that they share is their titanically striving will, expressed in Nietzsche's will to power and symbolized by Goethe in the "Eternal Feminine." Whereas in Marlowe's version of *Faust* Doctor Faustus seeks power over popes and emperors, Goethe internalized Faust's quest. His striving is close to Nietzsche's concept of self-overcoming—a search for totality, for the fullness and ever-creative activity of life, and for a meaning that transcends the ordinary

---

* Ralph Waldo Emerson, "The Oversoul," in *Essays* (New York: Crowell, 1951), p. 190.

standards of good and evil. The productive, ever-striving human will is, to both, the essence of man's greatness and the manifestation of the immanence of the creative principle—of the unity of God, nature, and man. We find the leitmotif of *Faust* and the essence of life and man, as presented here by Goethe, at the beginning and at the end of the drama.

> Am Anfang war die Tat.
> In the beginning was the deed.

> Wer immer strebend sich bemueht, den koennen wir erloesen.
> Whoever strives with all his heart, for him there is redemption.*

And Nietzsche says in *Zarathustra*:

> Not whence you come shall hence constitute your honor, but whither you are going; your will, and your foot which has a will to go over yourself—these shall constitute your honor.[30]

Nietzsche's and Goethe's divine element is found in the soul of the Dionysian-Faustian man, in his eternal will to suffer and strive, to grow and create.

Nietzsche himself never recognized the close affinity between Faust and Dionysus, but it is Goethe, the man—not the poet—who is for him the personification of the Dionysian.

> Goethe . . . a grand attempt to overcome the eighteenth century through a return to nature, through a going-up to the naturalness of the Renaissance, a kind of self-overcoming on

---

* Goethe, *Faust* (Leipzig: Tempel-Verlag), 6:124, 525.

the part of that century. . . . He did not sever himself from life, he placed himself within it . . . and took as much as possible upon himself, above himself, within himself. What he aspired to was totality; he strove against the separation of reason, sensibility, emotion, will . . . ; he disciplined himself to a whole, he created himself. . . . Goethe conceived as a strong, highly cultured human being who, keeping himself in check and having reverence for himself, dares to allow himself the whole compass and wealth of naturalness, who is strong enough for his freedom; a man of tolerance, not out of weakness but out of strength, because he knows how to employ to his advantage what would destroy an average nature. . . . A spirit thus emancipated stands in the midst of the universe with a joyful and trusting fatalism, in the faith that only what is separate and individual may be rejected, that in the totality everything is redeemed and affirmed—he no longer denies. . . . But such a faith is the highest of all possible faiths: I have baptized it with the name Dionysus.[31]

The misinterpretation of Nietzsche's overman as the savage "blond beast," a Cesare Borgia, is partly the fault of Nietzsche himself because of his often unfortunate choice of terms and his exaggerated, excessive language. But what, in fact, does Nietzsche mean when in *Ecce Homo* he says: "rather a Cesare Borgia . . . than a Parsifal"? This sentence does not express a justification of cruelty, savagery, and uncontrolled passions, or admiration for Cesare Borgia. What it does say is that there is more hope for the overman and the development of man's creative powers in a Cesare Borgia, whose instincts, while not yet ordered and sublimated, are not extirpated, as Nietzsche believes they are in Parsifal. Evil, for Nietzsche as for Goethe, is a positive power. The passions and primitive instincts of a Cesare Borgia can be made to act as dynamic forces, as obstacles to be overcome, as necessary "movers" in the development of the will to power. But in Parsifal Nietzsche sees a man of weakness, whose instincts and urges were extirpated, not sublimated, destroying the fertile soil of inner chaos and conflict. "I estimate power of a will according to how much resistance, pain and torture it endures and knows how to transform to its advantage."[32]

To extirpate passions, as Nietzsche accuses Christian morality of doing, is to remove the source of energy and strength, the stimulant that gives ground for hope. Not extirpation of instincts, but sublimation, control, and discipline of passions lead to the creation of the overman and his will to power, which is not brute force or social domination, but a power to enhance, organize, and integrate, and thereby achieve self-overcoming.* In *Homer's Contest* Nietzsche writes:

> Those capacities which are dreadful and accounted inhuman are, indeed, perhaps the fruitful soil out of which alone all humanity in impulse, act and deed can grow.[33]

And, further, in *The Twilight of the Idols*, he says:

> All passions have a phase when they drag down their victims with the weight of folly—and later, very much later, a phase when they wed the spirit, when they spiritualize themselves. Formerly one made war on passion itself on account of the folly inherent in it: one conspired for its extermination—all the old moral monsters are unanimous that "il faut tuer les

---

* Like Freud, Nietzsche recognized that extirpation of passions—a process later called "repression" by Freud—merely removes passions from consciousness, but does not annihilate them. Like Freud, he sees the dangers that result from this repression. Thus the highly repressed herd man can become a far greater danger than one who acts out his passions, since these accumulated energies will explode and turn nightmares into reality.

passions." The most famous formula for doing this is contained in the New Testament, in the Sermon on the Mount . . . [where] it is said, with reference to sexuality, "if thine eye offend thee, pluck it out"; fortunately, Christians do not follow this prescription. To exterminate the passions and desires merely in order to do away with their folly and its unpleasant consequences—this itself seems to us today merely an acute form of folly. . . . The church combats the passions with excision in every sense of the word: its "cure" is castration. It never asks: "How can one spiritualize, beautify, deify a desire?" —it has at all times laid the emphasis of its discipline on extirpation. But to attack the passions at their roots means to attack life at its roots.[34]

However, we must admit that to understand the overman in all his aspects—or at least the transitional stage (*Zwischenstadium*) that leads to his development—requires a leap over the traditional "ethical stage"; not a leap into the Kierkegaardian religious stage, but to a morality that denies all conventions and is a morality "beyond good and evil," where . . . "what is evil and senseless and ugly seems as it were permissible, as it seems permissible in nature, because of an excess of procreating, restoring powers which can yet turn every desert into luxurious farmland."[35]

It is thus that Faust in his unlimited drive for action destroys the idyllic existence of Philemon and Baucis in order to fulfill his vision and build a free land for a free people. It is thus that Nietzsche says:

A man who strives for great things regards everyone whom he meets on his way as either a means or a delay or an obstacle—or as a temporary bed to rest on. The highly developed goodness toward his fellow men, which is characteristic of him, is not possible until he has reached his height and dominion.[36]

It is hard to make this leap with Nietzsche-Zarathustra, or even with the Faust of the second part of the drama; but we must understand that what Nietzsche strives for is not the stage of transition but the overman, "a man of tolerance not out of weakness, but out of strength . . . a man who helps the unhappy . . . from an excess of power . . . who has a will to go over and beyond himself." The road to the overman and self-overcoming is a road of dangers and risks and leads all those who take it through an abyss.

> In climbing upward the depth grows deeper and becomes an abyss.[37]

> I say unto you: one must have chaos in oneself in order to give birth to a dancing star.[38]

Thomas Mann expresses this duality when he says in *Death in Venice*:

> And has not form two aspects? Is it not moral and immoral at once: moral in so far as it is the expression and result of discipline, immoral—yes, actually hostile to morality—in that of its very essence it is indifferent to good and evil, and deliberately concerned to make the moral world stoop beneath its proud and undivided sceptre?[*]

VII

The essence of the Faustian, Dionysian creative individual and of Nietzsche's and Goethe's humanistic pantheism has its foundation not in morality but in aesthetics. Both men stress the essential connection between religion and art.

---

[*] Thomas Mann, *Death in Venice* (New York: Alfred A. Knopf), p. 13.

Nietzsche speaks of a "Jenseits der Kunst" and says: "Religion is love above yourself—a work of art is the image of such a love."

The entrance into reality, into the unity of God, nature, and man is through the aesthetic experience. The creative individual and artist become microcosmic participants in the productive processes of the macrocosm. They become one with the very forces of nature and the creative principle immanent in them.

> Nature speaks to us through Dionysian art and its tragic symbolism . . . "Be like me, the original mother, who under constant change and appearances, is eternally creating, eternally giving birth and finding joy and satisfaction". . . . In spite of pity and terror, we are happy in having life, not as individuals, but as part of a life force with whose procreative lust we have become one.[39]

Like those of art, the forces of nature work without purposes and ends, without moral imperatives; they create freely according to their own living pattern and laws. It is an idea that inspired men like Leonardo da Vinci, Bruno, Shaftesbury, and Schelling. It is an idea stressed by Kant when, in the *Critique of Judgment*, he pointed out that in the creative individual the unconscious activity of nature breaks out into the consciousness of man.

This identification, this deep unity with the fundamental life forces, achieved in the aesthetic experience, possesses the elements of religion. Goethe states in a conversation with Eckermann: "God did not retire to rest after the well known six days of creation. He is constantly active as on the first.* He is active in a Mozart, a Raphael, a Shakespeare. Every

---

* Eckermann, *Gespraeche mit Goethe*, March 11, 1832.

creative individual serves God without a church and without a dogma. He serves him out of the abundance and richness of life. In the *Italian Journey,* describing his impressions in front of a Raphael and a Titian, Goethe says: "All that is capricious, all that is fanciful, collapses. Here is serenity, here is God." Nietzsche, speaking of a "Jenseits der Kunst," points out that the great artists of all times have been creators of religious and metaphysical ideas.[40] Dante's *Divina Commedia,* Michelangelo's frescoes, the Gothic cathedrals—they all have a metaphysical and religious significance. They are not merely representative of fragmentary aspects of life or merely expressive of momentary feelings, but reveal a deep unity and continuity, life as a whole, which includes the transitory and the eternal, the finite and the infinite.

> And it is the eternally One that reveals itself in the manifold.
> —Goethe, *Faust*

> Beauty is the Infinite finitely presented.
> —Schelling, *Philosophy of Art*

> Art is the overcoming of the transitory. Something remains of the fool's play, the death dance of human life, something lasting: works of art. They form a silent empire of images and relics beyond the fleeting moment—almost succeeding in making the transitory eternal.
> —Hermann Hesse, *Narcissus and Goldmund*

Nietzsche's and Goethe's God realizes himself in the creative activity of nature and man, which "weaves the living garment of the deity." He is the artist-creator who shapes the fundamental chaos into a unity of artistic balance and form.

> He is the supreme artist who realizes his joy and glory in creation and destruction, in good and evil, and who in creating frees himself from his painful internal contradictions and the fullness of his powers.[41]

And Goethe says to Eckermann:

> Let people serve Him who gives to the beast his fodder and to man his meat and drink. But I worship Him who has infused into the world such power of production that, when only a millionth part of it comes out into life, the world swarms with creatures to such a degree that war, pestilence, fire and water cannot prevail against them. That is my God.*

The fullest expression of Nietzsche's tragic faith is found in the teaching of the eternal recurrence. James Gutmann calls the idea of eternal recurrence a religious and mystical experience.** Nietzsche himself speaks of it as a revelation where "one sees . . . one does not seek; one takes, one does not ask who gives; a thought suddenly flashes up like lightning, it comes with necessity, without faltering."[42] The eternal recurrence is an expression of Nietzsche's belief in the eternity and unity of God, nature, and man; it is a pantheistic benediction of all existence. It is the "religion of all religions."

VIII

Nietzsche's, Goethe's, and Spinoza's pantheistic philoso-

---

* Ibid., February 20, 1831.
** James Gutmann, "The Tremendous Moment of Nietzsche's Vision," *The Journal of Philosophy,* no. 25 (December 1954).

phies, sharing many views and differing in others, lead to additional significant points of comparison. Their mutually shared conception of the universe as a unified whole, in which God, nature, and man are inextricably interwoven, leads to Spinoza's "amor intellectualis dei," Goethe's "Naturfroemmigkeit," and Nietzsche's "amor fati." While these concepts are by no means identical, they have many elements in common. To those already discussed—unity, immanence, and anti-teleology—primarily two others must be added: determinism and freedom. The universe is conceived by the three thinkers as an organically connected whole in which nothing is contingent, where every event is but a link within the whole and follows from its nature with eternal necessity: "In rerum natura nullum contingens."* Goethe's deterministic views, influenced by Spinoza, are evident in his early as well as in his later works; but there is a significant distinction between his early creative period, wherein the individual and his specific destiny is central, and the later period when—in a position closer to Nietzsche's—the fate of the individual is projected upon a cosmic scale, and seen *sub specie aeternitatis* as part of the cosmic forces that "work according to eternal, necessary, and in this sense, divine laws in such a way that even the divinity itself cannot change them."**

Nietzsche expresses his deterministic position primarily in his teaching of the eternal recurrence, in which everything is held to return again and again in the eternal and necessary recurrence of the same. "The fatality of man cannot be detached from the fatality of all that was and will be . . . one is necessary, a piece of fatum; one belongs to the whole. . . ."[43]

---

* Spinoza, *Ethics*, pt. 1, Prop. XXIX.
** Goethe, *Saemtliche Werke*, 131 vols., 4 secs. (Weimar: Hermann Boehlau, 1870–1918), sec. 1, 29:12.

I myself belong to the causes of the eternal recurrence. . . .
The knot of causes returns in which I am entwined. . . . I return eternally to the same life, with all that is greatest and
with all that is smallest.[44]

But determinism and freedom are not conceived as
mutually exclusive concepts in opposition to each other by
either Spinoza, Goethe, or Nietzsche. While they deny freedom in its traditional sense as identified with free will, they
affirm freedom in the sense of self-determination, a freedom
that is realized within the totality of the cosmos and the
necessity of all that is. By an identification with the cosmic
forces and their necessary laws, man's otherwise alien fate
is transformed into his own. The laws of nature are not
external to him, nor are they beyond him; rather, they are
within him. To act in accordance with them is to act not
with compulsion and coercion, but from the inner necessity
of one's own nature. Spinoza's "God or nature," as an all-
inclusive and self-creating unity, is the eternal cause of
itself and all there is. Its self-creative activity, in accordance
with the necessary laws of its own being, is conceived as
self-determined and free. "That thing is said to be free which
exists by mere necessity of its own nature and is determined
in its actions by itself alone."* Not as isolated, single, im-
potent beings in the modal world, as conceived by limited
understanding, does man achieve his freedom, but as part
of God's eternal, creative power, as apprehended by *scientia
intuitiva,* and fully realized in the intellectual love of God.

To the Spinozistic elements of determinism and unity is
added the concept of "amor fati" in Nietzsche's interpretation of freedom. While here, too, Spinoza's influence is not
entirely absent, significant dissimilarities do exist between
Nietzsche's concept of love of fate and Spinoza's intellectual

---

* Spinoza, *Ethics,* pt. 1, Def. VII.

love of God, dissimilarities that result from previously noted differences inherent in an acosmic pantheism, and the distinctly different, humanistic pantheism of Nietzsche. The crucial point for both, however, is similar: the affirmative spirit has the ability "not only to endure necessity, but also to love it."[45]

> This is my last wisdom, I want that which I must. . . . I want to love that which is necessary. *Amor fati* be my last love.[46]

> Such a spirit who has become free stands amid the cosmos with a joyous and trusting fatalism, in the faith that only the particular is loathsome, and that in the whole all is redeemed and affirmed . . . he does not negate any more. Such a faith is the highest of all possible faiths. I have baptized it with the name of Dionysus.[47]

The two concepts that perhaps express most fully Nietzsche's idea of freedom and his "joyous, trusting fatalism" are the eternal recurrence and the innocence of becoming. The teaching of the eternal recurrence is claimed as the "highest formula of affirmation that can ever be reached. . . ."[48] It is the formula of the free, creative individual who desires nothing beyond this eternally returning world, for it is not foreign to him; rather, it is at once his "ego" and his "fatum." The concept of the innocence of becoming expresses the freedom and purity of nature, which, unspoiled by human values and goals, by moral imperatives and guilt, by fears and responsibility, freely destroys and creates from the inner necessity of its own fullness and superabundance. Nietzsche's conception of the universe, as above discussed, is indeed essentially aesthetic: "Highest fatalism, yet identical with creativity."[49]

Like Nietzsche's, Goethe's conception of freedom cannot be understood without the Spinozistic element of unity, the nexus and interconnectedness of God, nature, and man. In his early writings, this unity is not yet achieved, so that an antinomy exists between fate and freedom, between human and divine will. The heroic, titanic individual acts in defiance of his gods and creates in accordance with his own image, as expressed by the bold words of Goethe's *Prometheus*: "Here I sit, kneading men in my image, a race like myself, made to suffer, weep, laugh and delight, and forget all about you, as I have forgotten."* But in his later works, Goethe speaks of a "victorious fatalism," a "love of fate" that is quite similar to Spinoza's loving affirmation and Nietzsche's *amor fati*. The creative individual is now conscious of his oneness with the divine forces that are immanent in nature; he finds his freedom and meaningfulness as a microcosmic participant in the macrocosmic activity of nature and its eternal, necessary, divine laws. It is by means of this union that the individual becomes whole, undivided, harmonious, and free.

IX

Spinoza has been called an atheist, Goethe calls himself "a decided non-Christian," and Nietzsche calls himself an "Antichrist." But, as Nietzsche remarks in *Beyond Good and Evil*: "Anti-Christian is by no means anti-religious,"[50] and the "great despisers" may in fact represent the "great reverers."[51] As already stated, their "atheism" consists mainly in their repudiation of the dualistic separation of God and nature. It does not express a negation of all faiths, but rather reveals the tragic predicament of modern man, who

---

* Goethe, *Prometheus* (Leipzig: Tempel-Verlag), 1:273.

has lost his belief in a transcendent, anthropomorphic God but has not freed himself from the power of this faith. Spinoza expresses this power and his longing for a new relation with the divine behind a mask of abstract, mathematical terms. Faust cries out in despair in the Easter scene of *Faust I*: "The message I hear indeed, but what is missing is faith."* And Nietzsche's cry of distress, "Whither is God?", is, in spite of its blasphemous tone, the voice of the true "de profundis" of modern man. Jaspers contends that only superficial readers, blinded by Nietzsche's aggressive extremism, see in him nothing but hostility to all things religious and Christian, even though only Christianity as a dogma and substantive faith was alien to him.**

Spinoza's, Goethe's and Nietzsche's God is encountered by an entrance into the totality of being without deduction and exception, where good and evil, the ugly and the beautiful, the limited and unlimited dwell side by side; "where even the ugly and horrible are redeemed and made meaningful in the fatality of the whole."⁵² "Also the most unnatural is nature; also the coarsest philistinism has something of nature's genius. Whoever does not see her everywhere, does not see her at all."*** And Spinoza calls good and evil, beauty and deformity, order and disorder mere prejudices and fictions, modes in which the human imagination is affected in different ways; they have no existence in nature, which sets no ends before itself.****

The nexus of God, nature, and man is for all three thinkers not a purely abstract theoretical relation, understandable by the intellect alone, but proceeds from the totality of man

---

* Ibid., *Faust* (Leipzig: Tempel-Verlag), 6:108.
** Karl Jaspers, *Nietzsche and Christianity* (Chicago: Henry Regnery, 1961), p. 7f.
*** Goethe (Weimar ed.), sec. 2, 11:6.
**** Spinoza, *Ethics*, pt. 1, Appendix.

and touches the very depth of the human personality. As in all religious experience, there is an element of mystery in this new relation to the divine. Pascal's "eternal silence of the infinite spaces" is present in Spinoza's God, whose infinite attributes, beyond comprehension by human reason, are accessible only to an intuitive insight. The mysteries of religion are symbolized by Goethe in his "realm of mothers," where "naught will you see in that vast void afar, nor hear your footstep when it's pressed, nor find firm ground where you can rest."* They are present in Nietzsche's "most silent hour in which one hears, one does not seek," the hour in which he conceived the teaching of the eternal recurrence, "the religion of all religions."[53]

It is a relation that all three thinkers characterize as love. Goethe speaks of the piety of nature, and in his "Nature Fragment" he says:

> Nature . . . her crown is love. Only through love can we approach her . . . she isolates everything in order to connect everything . . . she is benign . . . she is wise and silent, . . . I praise her in all her works.**

Nietzsche bases his new Dionysian faith upon his concept of *amor fati*.

> It is a Dionysian Yea-saying to the world as it is, without deduction, exception and selection . . . it is the highest attitude that a philosopher can reach; to stand Dionysiacally toward existence: my formula for this is *amor fati*.[54]

Nietzsche's love of fate and Goethe's love of nature arise out of a relation that is lived, experienced, and suffered. Their

---

* Goethe, *Faust* (Leipzig: Tempel-Verlag), 6:415.
** Ibid. (Weimar ed.), sec. 2, 11:6.

religious experience takes place not in quiet contemplation and detachment but within the sphere of the daemonic and Dionysian, within the living reality of struggle, tension, negation, and despair.

Spinoza's "amor intellectualis dei," on the other hand, is generally held to be a radical abstraction, a love that is transpersonal, exalted above all strife and opposition, and resulting in a state of perfect peace. The emphasis is on the term *intellectual,* which is interpreted as a state of pure contemplation, an "actus purus." But perhaps what Spinoza intended to emphasize by the use of the attribute *intellectual* was not so much purity and abstractness, but his objection to the Judaeo-Christian conception of an anthropomorphic, personal God. Thus he stresses his own relation to God as impersonal and "disinterested" in the Kantian sense, free from purpose and yet not free of feeling—albeit, admittedly, a feeling of a semi-rational character—what Kant called *Geistesgefuehl.* While it must be conceded, with Hegel, that Spinoza's relation to God does not contain negation and opposition, and certainly far less does it contain Goethe's daemonic and Nietzsche's Dionysian elements, it nevertheless is not conceived as cold and detached, but as a relation of love. This love, like Goethe's and Nietzsche's concepts, is essentially understood as a desire and drive to connect and relate and unify, and thus express the fundamental essence of the universe.

Spinoza's *amor intellectualis dei,* while differing in many respects, moves close to Goethe's nature piety (*Naturfroem-migkeit*) and Nietzsche's *amor fati* in their similar expression of a new faith that is based primarily on a deep sense of unity among God, nature, and man. It is in this cosmic unity that all three thinkers find the meaning of life, the essence of man, and a new living relation to God. Thus

Goethe writes to Riemer: "To have a positive religion is not necessary. To be in harmony with oneself and the whole is what counts."* Spinoza says in *Ethics*: "If we desire to act in accordance with our own nature, in possession of the idea of God, I refer to it as religion."** And Nietzsche expresses his Dionysian faith of cosmic unity in the *Nachlass*: "Reverence for God is reverence for the interconnectedness of all things."[55]

X

Nietzsche's new tragic faith rejects the concepts and values of Christianity, but it does not abolish the problem of salvation. Redemption is not only the leitmotif of Wagner and the central theme of Christianity; it also represents an important problem in Nietzsche's as well as in Goethe's thought. However, the tragic philosopher demands that redemption be found in this world and not in a world beyond, within tragedy and suffering and not beyond it. Redemption is symbolized by Goethe in *Faust's* final scene of the ascent to heaven. It is expressed by Nietzsche in the unified concept of the will to power and the eternal recurrence.

However, it is precisely because of this last scene that Nietzsche attacks the *Faust* drama and fails to understand its Dionysian spirit. He could never forgive Goethe for bringing the erring titan into heaven, a heaven which he interprets as Christian. He does not recognize that the unchristian Goethe of the *Venetian Epigrams* remains a pagan and merely uses the Catholic heaven of the last scene in *Faust* as a symbol for his concept of unity. Christian symbolism is employed by Goethe in the interest of poetic effect.

---

* Letter to Riemer, December 1824, in *Goethes Briefe*.
** Spinoza, *Ethics*, pt. 4, Demonstration to Prop. XXXVII.

This is expressed in a conversation with Eckermann in which Goethe is quoted as saying:

> You must admit that the conclusion where the redeemed soul is carried up, was difficult to manage; and amid such supersensual, scarcely conceivable matters, I might have lost myself in the void, if I had not, by means of sharply drawn figures and images from the Christian church, given my poetical design a desirable form and substance.*

Nietzsche is not alone in this interpretation; it is shared by those Goethe scholars who understand the last scene of *Faust* literally as an acceptance of the sinning, erring titan into a Christian heaven by a benevolent, all-forgiving God. Indeed, it is easy to see the reasons for this interpretation. We find Faust in a Catholic heaven, surrounded by choirs of angels and Blessed Boys, by Mater Gloriosa, Pater Profundus, and Pater Seraphicus. It is a heaven so full of holy spirits and aromatic incense that Thomas Mann is correct in calling it an operatic setting.** However, *Faust*, in my opinion, is not a Christian drama of guilt and expiation or a morality play of crime and punishment. It is a true tragedy, as Goethe called it, a tragedy in the great tradition of Aeschylus and Sophocles, a tragedy in the spirit of Dionysus. Perhaps one can explain the difficulties of interpretation on the basis of the ambiguity of the drama itself.***

---

* Eckermann, *Gespraeche mit Goethe,* June 1831.

** Thomas Mann, *Last Essays* (New York: Alfred A. Knopf, 1959), p. 128.

*** Goethe himself recognized the difficulty of defining the extraordinary dimensions of his drama by a single set of criteria and said in a conversation with Eckermann, May 6, 1827: "They come and ask me what idea I meant to embody in my *Faust;* as if I knew myself and could inform them. It would have been a fine thing indeed, if I had strung so rich, varied, and highly diversified a life as I have brought to view in *Faust* upon the slender thread of one pervading idea."

It is the same ambiguity that we find in Nietzsche's thought and in all great art and philosophy in terms of the unresolvable paradoxes of life.

The central theme of *Faust* and the essence of life and man, as presented here by Goethe, are expressed in the following passage: "Whoever strives with all his heart, for him there is salvation." These words from the last scene correspond to those at the beginning of the drama: "In the beginning was the deed." Faust is saved, but it is not a Christian salvation by the grace of God. It is a truly tragic redemption in man's eternal will to live and suffer, to strive and create. It is a redemption within the drama of existence, within self-degradation and deception, corruption and cruelty. It is a salvation within tragedy, not from tragedy. It is here that the tragic will of life finds its deepest meaning: life is not redeemed in the peace and harmony of heaven but in the strength and force of the individual's willing. Nietzsche expresses this idea in *Zarathustra*:

> How deeply one can suffer almost determines the order of rank.
> Not whence you come shall hence constitute your honor, but whither you are going. Your will, and your foot, which has a will to go over and beyond yourself—that shall constitute your new honor.
> The will is a creator. . . . Will—that is the name of the liberator and joy-giver. . . . To recreate all "it was" into "thus I willed it"—that alone should I call redemption.
> —Nietzsche, *Thus Spake Zarathustra*

Nietzsche's will to power and Goethe's striving will are presented by both thinkers *sub specie aeternitatis*. For both, it is man's eternally striving, creative will in which they find the bases for their concepts of eternity, immortality, and unity. This is clearly evident in Nietzsche's teaching of the eternal recurrence and the will to power, which represent a repudiation of the transcendent Beyond and a transference of its divine attributes to the earthly realm and man's heroic will.

> And do you know what "the world" is to me . . . this world: a monster of energy without beginning, without end . . . a sea of forces flowing and rushing together, eternally changing, eternally flooding back, with tremendous years of recurrence . . . blessing itself as that which must return eternally, as a becoming that knows no satiety, no disgust, no weariness: this is my Dionysian world of the eternally self-creating, the eternally self-destroying, this mystery world of the twofold voluptuous delight. . . . This world is the will to power—and nothing besides! And you yourselves are also this will to power—and nothing besides![56]

> Have you ever said Yes to a single joy? O my friends, then you said Yes too to all woe. All things are entangled, ensnared, enamored; if ever you wanted one thing twice, if ever you said "You please me, happiness! Abide, Moment!" then you wanted all back. All anew, all eternally, all entangled, ensnared, enamored—oh, then you loved the world. Eternal ones, love it eternally and evermore; and to woe, too, you say: go, but return! For all joy wants—eternity.[57]

> And this is all my creating and striving, that I create and carry together into One what is fragment and riddle and dreadful accident. And how could I bear to be a man if man were not also a creator and guesser of riddles and redeemer of accidents?[58]

However, in regard to Goethe, the Christian symbolism

of the last scene in heaven again has obscured the issues, and has led to an interpretation of his concepts of eternity, immortality, and unity on the basis of traditional Christianity and its dualistic world order. But Goethe himself says: "Man has a right to the belief in immortality. But if the philosopher tries to deduce the immortality of the soul from a legend, that is very weak and inefficient. To me the eternal existence of my soul is proved by my idea of activity."*

Immortality, for Goethe, arises out of the concept of the unlimited activity of the human will. Faust's soul is not immortalized in a Christian heaven, but in the supreme expansion of his creative life. When he enters heaven, he does not enter a new sphere, but only an extension of the old realm of the problematic. He brings with him his smallness and his greatness, his frustrations and his joys. Thus the "Blessed Boys" welcome him as their teacher and guide. "We were early removed from the choirs of life; but he has learned—he can teach us."** The movement of life expands beyond the great divide and is eternally the same. The forces that organize and govern the individual merge with the cosmic forces and their eternal rhythm of destruction and creation. Death, like all destruction, is but a necessary part of the cosmic process of becoming a "device of nature for creating abundant life."***

While the *Faust* drama starts in heaven and ends in heaven, Goethe does not intend to symbolize in this circle the Christian concept of an all-directing providence. The circle represents the pantheistic view that Goethe shares with Nietzsche, the view of a unified universe where God,

---

* Eckermann, *Gespraeche mit Goethe,* February 2, 1829.
** Goethe, *Faust* (Leipzig: Tempel-Verlag), 6:530.
*** Ibid., "Hymn to Nature."

nature, man, and the devil are inextricably interwoven in the cosmic drama and the creative powers of man are identified with the productive forces of the cosmos.

Significantly, in the last scene of the *Faust* drama the God of the "Prologue" is not present. Instead, we find Gretchen and Helena, united with the Mater Gloriosa in the heavenly sphere. The "Eternal Feminine" (*das ewig Weibliche*) becomes the supreme symbol of holiness, representing man's striving will—eternal, holy, and divine.

Goethe's Eternal Feminine, symbolizing unlimited activity, and Nietzsche's will to power, eternally creating and eternally recurring, are closely related. They are Goethe's and Nietzsche's fullest expression of their dynamic dialectical philosophies and their pantheistic faith. The meaning of life is found not in the peace of heaven, but in the strength and indestructible force of the human will. Redemption is achieved in the Dionysian soul of Zarathustra and in the "Diwan" soul of Goethe; in the heroic, tragic will to suffer and create, to die and become.

> Und so lang' du das nicht hast,
> Dieses: Stirb und Werde!
> Bist du nur ein trueber Gast
> Auf der dunklen Erde.
> > —Goethe, *West-Oestlicher Diwan*,
> > "Selige Sehnsucht."

Life looked back and around thoughtfully and said softly: "O Zarathustra, you are not faithful enough to me. You do not love me nearly so much as you say; I know you are thinking of leaving me soon. There is an old heavy, heavy growl-bell that growls at night all the way up to your cave; when you

hear this bell strike the hour at midnight, then you think
between one and twelve—you think, O Zarathustra, I know it,
how you want to leave me soon."
"Yes," I answered hesitantly, "but you also know—" and I
whispered something into her ear, right through her tangled,
yellow, foolish tresses.
"You know that, O Zarathustra? Nobody knows that."
And we looked at each other and gazed at the green meadow
over which the cool evening was running just then, and we
wept together. But then life was dearer to me than all my
wisdom ever was.
Thus spoke Zarathustra.
                    —Nietzsche, *Zarathustra,* The Other Dancing Song

Like Goethe, Nietzsche glorifies the creative principle
within nature and man. Creativity is the essence of the will
to power and the deepest meaning of the tragic culture,
which Nietzsche sees as "the only hope for the future of
mankind."

In doubt and despair, Nietzsche's philosophy leads to
the vision of an age in which the individual shall again—
as in the Renaissance—emerge and become the bearer of
culture. No longer finding his identity only as a member
of a group; no longer dominated by the depersonalizing
forces of mass society, he will be free to achieve the full
realization of his true self, which "lies high above you or
at least above that which you understand as your I." He
will sin and err, but he will not commit the crucial sin—
that of unproductivity.

Nietzsche's vision of the future is based on views that
arise from an aesthetic, nonsocial approach and are shared
by such critics as Ortega y Gasset and T. S. Eliot, among
others. Like them, he sees the "tyranny of the multitude" as

a threat to "high culture"—a tyranny that crushes beneath it everything that is different and individual and brings about the standardization of tastes and finally the destruction of the creative power of the individual.

> Man as a member of a mass is no longer his isolated self. The individual is merged in the mass, to become something other than he is when he stands alone. On the other hand, in the mass the individual becomes an isolated atom whose individual craving to exist has been sacrificed, since the fiction of a general equality prevails.*

Nietzsche saw with sharp insight the deepest roots of the dehumanizing tendencies of our technological mass society. With passionate concern he searched for a way out of this modern dilemma, and found it in the depth of the human personality and his creative, self-affirming will to power. But again we must bear in mind that the power that Nietzsche's creative individual possesses does not aim at domination over others, but over himself—a power which, like Spinoza's *conatus* and Goethe's Eternal Feminine, strives toward self-improvement and self-realization.

> He who is spiritually rich and independent is also the most powerful man in any case. . . . I have found power where people do not look for it, in simple and obliging men without the least inclination to domineer—and conversely the inclination to domineer has often appeared to me an inner sign of weakness: they fear their slavish soul and cast a king's mantle about it.[59]

Nietzsche's creative individual may indeed become an

---

* Karl Jaspers, *Man in the Modern Age* (Garden City, N.Y.: Doubleday & Co., 1951), p. 39.

inspiration for our age, and help restore the integrity of creative life, which is threatened by the dangers of automation. William James expresses the same idea when he says:

> In picking out from history our heroes and communing with their kindred spirits,—in imagining as strongly as possible what differences their individualities brought about in this world . . . each one of us may best fortify and inspire what creative energy may lie in his soul.*

And Nietzsche writes in *Schopenhauer as Educator*:

> Only he who rests his hope on a great man receives his first initiation into culture.[60]

The tragic vision, as presented by Nietzsche, offers no facile solutions. It "grants us no peace, torments us ceaselessly, hunts us out of every retreat and forbids us all concealment."** But within tragedy, absurdity, and struggle, Nietzsche finds the "exit and hole" out of negation and despair. He finds it in a Dionysian celebration of life and in his faith in the potential of man: his integrity, his courage, and his will to create.

> Nun feiern wir, vereinten Siegs gewiss,
> Das Fest der Feste:
> Freund Zarathustra kam, der Gast der Gaeste!
> Nun lacht die Welt, der grause Vorhang riss,
> Die Hochzeit kam fuer Licht und Finsternis.

---

* William James, quoted in Eric Bentley, *A Century of Hero Worship* (Boston: Beacon Press, 1957), p. 237.
** Karl Jaspers, *Nietzsche and Christianity* (Chicago: Henry Regnery Co., 1961), p. 105.

Now, certain of united victory,
We celebrate the feast of feasts:
Friend Zarathustra has come, the guest of guests!
Now the world is full of laughter, the gruesome curtain
is rent,
The wedding day has come for light and darkness.[61]

NOTES

KEY TO ABBREVIATIONS EMPLOYED IN NOTE SECTION

273

Die Goetzendaemmerung	The Twilight of the		
	Idols	1889	GD
Der Antichrist	Antichrist	1888	AC
Ecce Homo	Ecce Homo	1889	EH
Nietzsche Contra Wagner	Nietzsche Contra Wagner	1889	NCW
Nachlass	Unpublished Notes		NL

All references are to volume and page numbers (Roman and Arabic numbers respectively) of the *Grossoktav-Ausgabe*:

1st edition: 15 vols. (Leipzig: Naumann, 1895–1901).
2nd edition: 19 vols. (Leipzig: Alfred Kroener Verlag, 1901–13).

Both editions of the *Grossoktav-Ausgabe* were used for reference, since most libraries do not possess a complete set of either, but provide a mixture of both. There is a slight disparity in page numbers in the two editions. Vols. I–VIII of both editions contain Nietzsche's finished works. Vols. IX–XV of the first edition and vols. IX–XVI of the second edition contain notes and fragments, the so-called *Nachlass*. In the second edition the *Nachlass* was revised; only vols. XIII and XIV remained the same, while vols. IX, X, XI and XII were extensively changed and vol. XV was rearranged into 2 vols., namely, XV and XVI. The new volume XV contains *Ecce Homo*, which was not included in the first edition. Vols. XVII–XIX, containing the *Philologica*, were added in the second edition.

KEY TO THE *GROSSOKTAV-AUSGABE* (1ST AND 2D EDITIONS) OF NIETZSCHE'S COLLECTED WORKS:

Vol. I: *Die Geburt der Tragoedie* (The Birth of Tragedy), pp. 1–177.
                   Unzeitgemaesse Betrachtungen (Untimely Meditations):
                   I. *David Strauss*, pp. 178–277.
                   II. *Vom Nutzen und Nachteil der Historie fuer das Leben* (Of the Use and Disadvantage of History for Life), pp. 278–384.
                   III. *Schopenhauer als Erzieher* (Schopenhauer as Educator), pp. 385–494.
                   IV. *Richard Wagner in Bayreuth*, pp. 495–591.
Vol. II: *Menschliches-Allzumenschliches*, I (Human, All-too-Human).

Vol. III:	*Menschliches-Allzumenschliches*, II.
Vol. IV:	*Morgenroethe* (Dawn).
Vol. V:	*Die Froehliche Wissenschaft* (Gay Science).
Vol. VI:	*Zarathustra*.
Vol. VII:	*Jenseits von Gut und Boese* (Beyond Good and Evil), pp. 2–275. *Zur Genealogie der Moral* (Toward a Genealogy of Morals), pp. 276–485.
Vol. VIII:	*Der Fall Wagner* (The Case Wagner), pp. 1–58. *Goetzen-Daemmerung* (Twilight of the Idols), pp. 59–182 *Nietzsche Contra Wagner*, pp. 183–212. *Antichrist*, pp. 213–332. *Dichtungen* (Poems), pp. 333–79.
Vols. IX–XV:	1st ed.: *Nachlass*.
Vols. IX–XVI:	2d ed.: *Nachlass* (vol. XV: *Ecce Homo*, pp. 1–131; *Der Wille zur Macht*, I [Will to Power], pp. 132–469; vol. XVI: *Der Wille zur Macht, II*).
Vols. XVII–XIX:	2d ed.: *Philologica*

PREFACE

1. Letter to Georg Brandes, August 1, 1888. In *Friedrich Nietzsches Gesammelte Briefe*, 5 vols. (Leipzig: Insel-Verlag, 1908).
2. NL, XIII, 57.
3. GM, VII, 289.
4. Letter to Erwin Rohde, March 2, 1868.
5. Letter to Peter Gast, December 22, 1888.

PART I: DIONYSUS

1. The Tragic World View

1. UIV, I, 523
2. EH, XV, 2
3. GD, VIII, 173
4. GT, I, 153
5. Ibid., 111
6. Ibid., 108, 56
7. Ibid., 4
8. Ibid., 8
9. Letter to Franz Overbeck, July 1885
10. EH, XV, 65
11. NL, XVI, 387
12. EH, XV, 61
13. GT, I, 33
14. Ibid., 143
15. Ibid., 29
16. Z, VI, 229
17. Ibid., 21
18. Ibid., 234
19. UIII, I, 392

20. Ibid., 429
21. EH, XV, 5
22. GT, I, 100
23. Ibid., 11
24. FW, V, 325f
25. NL, XVI, 391
26. GT, I, 2; FW, V, 327
27. Z, VI, 226
28. GD, VIII, 173
29. Z, VI, 226
30. NCW, VIII, 193
31. GD, VIII, 173
32. NCW, VIII, 193
33. NL, XVI, 391

34. Z, VI
35. NCW, VIII, 194
36. GT, I, 121, 124
37. Ibid., 117, 169
38. Ibid., 89
39. Ibid., 7
40. Ibid., 156f
41. EH, XV, 64
42. GT, I, 35
43. Ibid., 39
44. Ibid., 116f
45. Ibid., 111
46. Ibid., 68
47. Ibid., 24f

2. Nihilism

1. NL, XV, 145
2. Ibid., 141, 137
3. EH, XV, 80
4. Letter to Erwin Rohde,
   May 23, 1887
5. NL, XV, 145f
   FW, V, 163f
   GM, VII, 399f
6. NL, XV, 145
7. FW, V, 163
8. NL, IX, 128f
9. Ibid., XV, 440
10. GM, VII, 399
11. NL, XV, 151
12. Ibid.
13. FW, VIII, 82
14. NL, XV, 160
15. Z, VI, 169
16. J, VII, 11
17. NL, XVI, 84
18. Ibid., XV, 156
19. Ibid., XVI, 73; XV, 211
20. Ibid., XV, 212
21. Ibid., 159
22. Ibid., XVI, 85

23. FW, V, 147
24. Ibid., 214f
25. Ibid., 163
26. Ibid., 164
27. NL, XV, 156
28. Ibid., 166
29. FW, V, 272
30. GD, VIII, 83
31. AC, VIII, 281
32. NL, XV, 241
33. FW, V, 217
34. NL, XVI, 85
35. Ibid., 402
36. FW, V, 164
37. NL, XV, 137
38. Ibid., 138
39. Ibid., 223
40. AC, VIII, 219
    NL, XV, 204
41. UII, I, 294
42. AC, VIII, 219
43. UII, I, 308
44. Ibid., 294
45. NL, XII, 252

3. *The Problem of Truth*

1. MAM, III, 22
2. NL, XVI, 56
3. Ibid., 365
4. Ibid., XII, 84
5. MAM, III, 22
6. NL, XV, 441
7. Ibid., XI, 35
8. Ibid., XV, 439
9. FW, V, 275
10. NL, XII, 24
11. J, VII, 12
12. Ibid., 55
13. NL, XII, 24
14. Ibid., XIII, 35
15. J, VII, 12
16. Ibid.
17. NL, XII, 49
18. Ibid., XVI, 56
19. Z, VI, 488
20. MAM, II, 32
21. NL, XVI, 27
22. Ibid., 97
23. Ibid., 29
24. UI, I, 216
25. GT, I, 128
26. GD, VIII, 81
27. NL, XVI, 40
28. GD, VIII, 77
29. NL, XVI, 68
30. J, VII, 12
31. Fr. *Nietzsche's Gesammelte*
    Briefe, II, 394; III, 142, 176
32. Ibid., II, 178
33. FW, V, 252
34. NL, X, 141
35. J, VII, 56
36. NL, XI, 200
37. Ibid., XV, 419
38. J, VII, 160
39. Ibid., 18
40. Ibid., 161f
41. NL, XVI, 96
42. Ibid., XII, 410
43. Ibid., XVI, 12
44. FW, V, 38
45. NL, XV, 439f
46. J, VII, 187
47. NL, XV, 3
48. Ibid., X, 200
49. Ibid., XVI, 56
50. Ibid., XII, 49
51. Z, VI, 153f
52. EH, XV, 100
53. MR, IV, 297
54. NL, XVI, 253
55. Z, VI, 169
56. GT, I, 105
57. J, VII, 274
58. Z, VI, 168
59. NL, IX, 198
60. MR, IV, 7f
61. J, VII, 273f

PART II: ETERNAL RECURRENCE

4. *The Doctrine's Importance*

1. NL, XIII, 264
2. Ibid., XV, 182
3. EH, XV, 85
4. NL, XII, 415
5. EH, XV, 86
6. FW, V, 265ff;
    Z, VI, 231f, 238f, 334f, 469f
7. EH, XV, 85

8. Ibid.
9. Z, VI, 400
10. EH, XV, 65

11. UII, I, 298
12. Z, VI, 217

5. The Scientific Basis of Nietzsche's Theory of Eternal Recurrence

1. NL, XII, 51
2. Ibid., XV, 182
3. Nietzsche's Briefwechsel mit F. Overbeck (Leipzig: Insel-Verlag, 1916), p. 153
4. Ibid., p. 252
5. NL, XII, 51f
6. Ibid., XVI, 397
7. Ibid., 398
8. Ibid., 101
9. Ibid., 104f
10. Ibid., 400
11. Ibid., XIII, 80
12. Ibid., XVI, 106
13. Die Briefe Peter Gast's an Fr. Nietzsche, 2 vols. (Muenchen: Verlag der Nietzsche-Gesellschaft, 1914–34), I, 163f
14. NL, XVI, 13
15. Ibid., 398
16. Ibid., 154, 110; XII, 148
17. Z, VI, 318
18. NL, XVI, 387
19. Ibid., XII, 58
20. Ibid., XVI, 115
21. Ibid.

6. The Eternal Recurrence in its Metaphysical Perspective

1. NL, XVI, 17
2. Ibid., 104
3. Ibid., 152, 17
4. Ibid., 77
5. Ibid., IX, 309
6. Ibid., XVI, 67
7. Ibid., XV, 486
8. Ibid., XVI, 40
9. J, VII, 28f
10. NL, XVI, 133, 156
11. GT, I, 11
12. NL, XIII, 236
13. FW, V, 285
14. GD, VIII, 128f
15. NL, XVI, 148
16. GD, VIII, 128
17. NL, XVI, 120
18. AC, VIII, 219
19. NL,
20. GD, VIII, 101
21. NL, XII, 60
22. Ibid., XVI, 115
23. Ibid., XIII, 337
24. Ibid., XII, 217
25. Letter to F. Overbeck, July 30, 1881
26. NL, XII, 156
27. J, VII, 14
28. NL, XVI, 153
29. Ibid., XIV, 353
30. Ibid., XIII, 337f
31. Ibid., XI, 118
32. Ibid., XII, 239
33. Ibid., X, 31, 40
34. EH, XV, 65
35. NL, X, 30

7. The Eternal Recurrence in its Ethical Perspective

1. Z, VI, 231
2. NL, XII, 64
3. GD, VIII, 126;
   NL, XII, 60
4. NL, XVI, 279
5. Ibid., 321
6. FW, V, 265
7. NL, XII, 409
8. EH, XV, 64
9. NL, XV, 416
10. Ibid., XII, 369
11. FW, V, 266
12. NL, XVI, 383
13. HW
14. UIII, I, 431
15. NL, XI, 250
16. FW, V, 279
17. Z, VI, 231f
18. NL, XVI, 383
19. UII, I, 287

20. FW, V, 272
21. NL, XIII, 363
22. EH, XV, 100
23. Dionysus-Dithyramben, 20;
    VIII, 383
24. Z, VI, 322
25. Ibid., 206
26. GD, VIII, 100
27. Ibid., 99
28. FW, V, 149
29. GT, I, 105
30. NL, XVI, 109f
31. J, VII, 165
32. NL, XVI, 301
33. MAM, III, 235
34. FW, V, 272
35. NL, XII, 141
36. Z, VI, 234
37. GD, VIII, 163
38. GT, I, 117

PART III: THE INNOCENCE OF BECOMING

8. Aesthetic Interpretation of Being

1. UI, I, 183
2. PTG, X, 42
3. NL, XVI, 202, 222

4. GD, VIII, 173
5. Letter to v. Gersdorff,
   April 7, 1866

9. The Silence of Art

1. PTG, X, 41
2. NL, XVI, 386
3. GT, I, 19
4. Ibid., 8
5. NL, XVI, 225
6. GT, I, 8
7. NL, XIV, 332
8. GT, I, 24
9. Ibid., 117

10. Ibid., 11
11. NL, XIII, 13
12. PTG, X, 40
13. FW, V, 209
14. UIII, I, 225
15. GT, I, 172
16. NCW, VIII, 194
17. H, IX, 273
18. Ibid.

19. FW, V, 57
20. NL, XVI, 270, 272
21. GT, I, 143
22. Ibid., 6
23. Ibid., 172
24. GD, VIII, 170
25. NL, XIV, 369
26. GT, I, 58

27. Ibid., 117
28. Ibid.
29. EH, XV, 61
30. Ibid.
31. GT, I, 2
32. EH, XV, 64
33. GT, I, 19
34. Ibid., 24

10. Nietzsche's Dionysian Faith

1. Z, VI, 13
2. NL, XII, 329
3. GD, VIII, 163f
4. EH, XV, 5
5. UIII, I, 426
6. MAM, III, 264
7. GD, VIII, 165
8. AC, VIII, 265
9. GM, VII, 388
10. FW, V, 272
11. AC, VIII, 281
12. FW, V, 217
13. J, VII, 178
14. Z, VI, 16
15. Ibid., 13
16. J, VII, 70
17. Z, VI, 367
18. NL, XII, 327
19. UIV, I, 523
20. NL, XIV, 276
21. GT, I, 71
22. EH, XV
23. GT, I, 69, 24
24. Z, VI, 13
25. Ibid.
26. UIII, I
27. Z, VI
28. NL, XVI, 326
29. J, VII
30. Z, VI, 297
31. GD, VIII, 162f

32. NL, XV, 416
33. H, IX, 273
34. GD, VIII, 84
35. NCW, VIII, 193f
36. J, VII
37. Z, VI
38. Ibid.
39. GT, I, 16
40. MAM, II, 200f
41. GT, I, 8
42. EH, XV, 90
43. GD, VIII, 100
44. Z, VI, 322
45. FW, V, 272
46. NL, XII, 141
47. GD, VIII, 163
48. EH, XV, 90
49. NL, XIV, 301
50. J, VII, 78
51. Z, VI, 16
52. FW, V, 219
53. NL, XII, 415
54. Ibid., XVI, 383
55. Ibid., XII, 327
56. NL, XVI, 401f
57. Z, VI, 469
58. Ibid., 206
59. NL, XI, 388, 251
60. UIII, I, 403
61. J, VII, 279

SELECT BIBLIOGRAPHY

A. NIETZSCHE'S WORKS

I. German Editions

Nietzsches Werke. Grossoktavausgabe. 1st ed.: 15 vols. Leipzig; Naumann, 1895–1901. 2d ed.: 19 vols. Leipzig: Alfred Kroener Verlag, 1901–1903.

Gesammelte Werke. Kleinoktavausgabe. 16 vols. Leipzig: Alfred Kroener Verlag, 1899–1912.

Gesammelte Werke. Musarionausgabe. 23 vols. Muenchen: Musarion-Verlag, 1920–1929.

Gesammelte Werke. Taschenausgabe. 11 vols. Stuttgart: Alfred Kroener Verlag, 1906–1913.

Werke in Drei Baenden. hrsg. von Karl Schlechta. 3 vols. Muenchen: Carl Hauser Verlag, 1960.

Werke. Kritische Gesamtausgabe. hrsg. von Giorgio Colli und Mazzino Montinari. Berlin: Walter De Gruyter & Co. (This edition has not yet been completed. 30 vols. are planned.)

Nietzsche, Friedrich. *Also sprach Zarathustra.* Leipzig: Alfred Kroener Verlag, 1918.

——. *Die Philosophie im tragischen Zeitalter der Griechen.* Muenchen: M. Titelkupfer, 1968.

——. *Die Unschuld des Werdens, Der Nachlass.* Ausgewaehlt

von Alfred Baeumler. 2 vols. Leipzig: Alfred Kroener Verlag, 1931.

II. English Translation

The Complete Works of Friedrich Nietzsche. Edited by Oscar Levy. 18 vols. London and New York: MacMillan, 1903–1913.

Nietzsche: An Anthology of his Works. Edited and translated, with an introduction by Otto Manthey-Zorn. New York: Washington Square Press, 1964.

The Philosophy of Nietzsche. New York: The Modern Library, 1954.

The Portable Nietzsche. Selected and translated by Walter A. Kaufmann. New York: Viking Press, 1954.

Nietzsche, Friedrich. The Antichrist. Translated, with an introduction by H. C. Mencken. New York: A. A. Knopf, 1923.

———. Beyond Good and Evil. Translated, with an introduction by Marianne Cowan. Chicago: Henry Regnery, 1955.

———. The Birth of Tragedy and The Genealogy of Morals. Translated, with an introduction by Francis Golffing. Garden City, N.Y.: Doubleday, 1956.

———. Joyful Wisdom. With an introduction by Kurt F. Reinhardt; translated by Thomas Common. New York: F. Ungar Pub. Co., 1960.

———. On the Genealogy of Morals. Translated by W. A. Kaufmann and R. J. Hollingdale. Ecce Homo. Translated by W. A. Kaufmann. New York: Vintage Books, 1967.

———. Philosophy in the Tragic Age of the Greeks. Translated, with an introduction by Marianne Cowan. Chicago: Henry Regnery, 1962.

———. Schopenhauer as Educator. Translated by James W. Hillesheim and Malcolm B. Simpson. Introduction by Eliseo Vivas. Chicago: Henry Regnery, 1965.

————. *Thus Spake Zarathustra.* Translated, and with an introduction by R. J. Hollingdale. Penguin Classics, 1961.

————. *The Use and Abuse of History.* Translated by Adrian Collins, with an introduction by Julius Kraft. Indianapolis: Bobbs-Merrill, 1957.

————. *The Will to Power.* Translated by W. A. Kaufmann and R. J. Hollingdale. New York: Random House, 1967.

B. NIETZSCHE'S LETTERS

Gesammelte Briefe. 5 vols. Leipzig: Insel-Verlag, 1902–1909.

Briefe. Ausgewaehlt und herausgegeben von Richard Oehler. Leipzig: Insel-Verlag, 1917.

Nietzsche Briefwechsel mit Franz Overbeck. Edited by C. A. Bernoulli and Richard Oehler. Leipzig: Insel-Verlag, 1916.

Die Briefe Peter Gasts an Friedrich Nietzsche. 2 vols. Muenchen: Verlag der Nietzsche-Gesellschaft, 1923–1924.

Selected Letters of Friedrich Nietzsche. Edited by Oscar Levy. Garden City, N.Y.: Doubleday, 1921.

Selected Letters by Friedrich Nietzsche. Edited and translated by Christopher Middleton. Chicago: University of Chicago Press, 1969.

Friedrich Nietzsche, Unpublished Letters. Edited and translated by Kurt F. Leidecker. New York: Philosophical Library, 1959.

Nietzsche: A Self-Portrait from his Letters. Edited and translated by Peter Fuss and Henry Shapiro. Cambridge, Mass.: Harvard University Press, 1971.

C. NIETZSCHE LITERATURE

Andler, Charles. *Nietzsche, sa Vie et sa Pensée.* 6 vols. Paris: Bossard, 1920.

Andreas-Salomé, Lou. *Friedrich Nietzsche in seinen Werken.* Wien: Konegen, 1894.

Baeumler, Alfred. *Nietzsche, der Philosoph und Politiker.* Leipzig: Reclam, 1931.

Bentley, Eric R. *A Century of Hero-Worship.* Philadelphia and New York: Lippincott, 1944.

Bertram, Ernst. *Nietzsche:: Versuch einer Mythologie.* Berlin: Bondi, 1918.

Bindschedler, Maria. *Nietzsche und die poetische Luege.* Basel: Verlag fuer Recht und Gesellschaft, 1954.

Biser, Eugen. *'Gott ist tot'. Nietzsches Destruktion des christlichen Bewusstseins.* Muenchen: Koesel-Verlag, 1962.

Blackham, Harold. *Six Existentialist Thinkers: Kierkegaard, Jaspers, Nietzsche, Marcel, Sartre, Heidegger.* London: Harper Torchbooks, 1959.

Brandes, Georg. *Friedrich Nietzsche.* Translated by Chater. London: Heinemann, 1914.

Brinton, Crane. *Nietzsche.* Cambridge: Harvard University Press, 1941.

Chaix-Ruy, Jules. *The Superman from Nietzsche to Teilhard de Chardin.* Translated by Marina Smyth-Kok. London: University of Notre Dame Press, 1968.

Danto, Arthur C. *Nietzsche as Philosopher.* New York: The MacMillan Co., 1965.

Deussen, Paul. *Erinnerungen an Friedrich Nietzsche.* Leipzig: Brockhaus, 1901.

Egli, Marcel J. J. *Ueberwindung des Nihilismus.* Zuerich: 1952.

Ewald, Oscar. *Nietzsches Lehre in ihren Grundbegriffen.* Berlin: Hofmann, 1903.

Fink, Eugen. *Nietzsches Philosophie.* Stuttgart: W. Kohlhammer Verlag, 1968.

Foerster-Nietzsche, Elizabeth. *Das Leben Friedrich Nietzsches.* 2 vols. Leipzig: Naumann, 1895–1904.

Gautier, Jules de. *De Kant à Nietzsche*. Paris: Mercure de France, 1930.

——. *Nietzsche, Les maitres de la pensée antichrétienne*. Paris: Editions du Siècle, 1926.

Giesz, Ludwig. *Nietzsches Existenzialismus und Wille zur Macht*. Stuttgart: Deutsche Verlagsanstalt, 1950.

Gutmann, James. "The Tremendous Moment of Nietzsche's Vision." *The Journal of Philosophy*, no. 25 (December 1954).

Havenstein, Martin. *Nietzsche als Erzieher*. Berlin: Mittler, 1922.

Heidegger, Martin. *Nietzsche*. 2 vols. Pfullingen: Neske, 1961.

——. "Nietzsches Wort 'Gott ist tot,' " in *Holzwege*. Frankfurt a. M.: Klostermann, 1957.

Hina, Horst. *Nietzsche und Marx bei Malraux*. Tuebingen: Niemeyer, 1970.

Jaspers, Karl. *Nietzsche*. Berlin: De Gruyter, 1950.

——. *Nietzsche and Christianity*. Chicago: Henry Regnery Co., 1961.

——. *Nietzsche und das Christentum*. Hameln: F. Seifert, 1946.

Joel, Karl. *Nietzsche und die Romantik*. Leipzig: Diederichs, 1905.

Kaufmann, Walter A. *Nietzsche: Philosopher, Psychologist, Antichrist*. Princeton: Princeton University Press, 1950.

Klages, Ludwig. *Die Psychologischen Errungenschaften Nietzsches*. Bonn: H. Bouvier, 1958.

Knight, A. H. J. *Some Aspects of the Life and Work of Nietzsche*. Cambridge: Harvard University Press, 1933.

Lavrin, Janko. *Nietzsche, A Biographical Introduction*. London: Studio Vista, 1971.

Lea, F. A. *The Tragic Philosopher. A Study of Nietzsche*. New York: Philosophical Library, 1957.

Loewith, Karl. *Kierkegaard und Nietzsche oder Philosophie und*

Theologische Ueberwindung des Nihilismus. Frankfurt a. M.: Klostermann, 1933.

———. *Nietzsches Philosophie der ewigen Wiederkunft des Gleichen.* Stuttgart: Kohlhammer, 1956.

———. *Von Hegel bis Nietzsche.* Zuerich und New York: Europa, 1941.

Mann, Thomas. "Nietzsche's Philosophy in the Light of Recent History," in *Last Essays.* New York: Alfred A. Knopf, 1959.

Mittasch, Alvin. *Friedrich Nietzsche als Naturphilosoph.* Stuttgart: Alfred Kroener Verlag, 1952.

Morgan, George Allen. *What Nietzsche Means.* Cambridge: Harvard University Press, 1943.

Oehler, Richard. *Nietzsche und die Vor-Sokratiker.* Leipzig: Duerr, 1904.

Podach, E. F. *The Madness of Nietzsche.* Translated by F. A. Voight. London and New York: Putnam, 1931.

———. *Ein Blick in die Notizbuecher Nietzsches.* Heidelberg: Wolfgang Rothe Verlag, 1963.

———. *Friedrich Nietzsches Werke des Zusammenbruchs.* Heidelberg: Wolfgang Rothe Verlag, 1930.

Salin, Edgar. *Jacob Burckhardt und Nietzsche.* Basel: Verlag der Universitaetsbibliothek, 1938.

Sandvoss, E. *Sokrates und Nietzsche.* Leiden: E. J. Brill, 1966.

———. *Hitler und Nietzsche.* Goettingen: Musterschmidt-Verlag, 1969.

Schestow, Leo. *Dostojewski und Nietzsche, Philosophie der Tragoedie.* Translated by R. von Walter. Koeln: Marcan, 1924.

———. *Tolstoi und Nietzsche.* Translated by N. Strasser. Koeln: Marcan-Block, 1923.

Schlechta, Karl. *Der junge Nietzsche und das klassische Altertum.* Mainz: F. Kupferberg, 1948.

————. *Der Fall Nietzsche.* Muenchen: Carl Hauser Verlag, 1959.

————. *Nietzsches grosser Mittag.* Frankfurt a. M.: V. Klostermann, 1954.

Simmel, Georg. *Schopenhauer und Nietzsche.* Leipzig: Duncker & Humblot, 1907.

Stambaugh, Joan. *Untersuchungen zum Problem der Zeit bei Nietzsche.* Den Haag: Martinus Nijhoff, 1959.

Vaihinger, Hans. *Nietzsche als Philosoph.* Berlin: Reuther and Reichard, 1902.

Wolff, Hans M. *Friedrich Nietzsche. Der Weg zum Nichts.* Bern: Francke Verlag, 1956.

Zweig, Stefan. *Der Kampf mit dem Daemon: Hoelderlin, Kleist, Nietzsche.* Leipzig: Insel-Verlag, 1925.

D. OTHER WORKS CITED

Aristotle. *Nichomachean Ethics,* in *The Basic Works of Aristotle.* New York: Random House, 1941.

————. *Politics,* in *The Basic Works of Aristotle.* New York: Random House, 1941.

Beckett, Samuel. *Waiting for Godot.* New York: Grove Press, 1954.

Bentley, Eric. *A Century of Hero Worship.* Boston: Beacon Press, 1957.

Berdyaev, Nicholas. *The Meaning of the Creative Act.* New York: Collier, 1962.

Buber, Martin. *The Eclipse of God.* New York: Harper, 1957.

Burckhardt, Jacob. *Griechische Kulturgeschichte.* Berlin: Spemann, 1898.

Capek, Milic. "The Theory of Eternal Recurrence in Modern Philosophy of Science with Special Reference to C. S.

Peirce," in *Journal of Philosophy* 57, no. 9.

Camus, Albert. *The Plague.* New York: Alfred A. Knopf, 1962.

———. *The Myth of Sisyphus.* New York: Random House, 1961.

Dilthey, Wilhelm. "Erfahrung und Denken," in *Gesammelte Schriften.* 12 vols. Leipzig: B. G. Teubner, 1921.

Eckermann, J. P. *Gespraeche mit Goethe.* Stuttgart: Cotta, n.d.

Emerson, Ralph Waldo. *Essays.* New York: Crowell, 1951.

Freud, Sigmund. *The Complete Psychological Works of Sigmund Freud.* London: Hogarth Press, 1953.

Fromm, Eric. *Man for Himself.* New York: Holt, Rinehart and Winston, 1961.

Goethe. *Saemtliche Werke.* 131 vols. 4 secs. Weimar: Hermann Boehlau, 1870–1918.

———. *Saemtliche Werke.* 40 vols. Stuttgart: Cotta, 1840.

———. *Saemtliche Werke.* 15 vols. Leipzig: Tempel-Verlag.

Goethes Briefe. 8 vols. Berlin: O. Elsner, 1902–1905.

Hegel, G. W. F. *The Philosophy of History.* New York: Willey Book Co., 1944.

———. *The Phenomenology of Mind.* New York: The MacMillan Company.

———. *Glaube und Wissen. Gesammelte Werke.* 4 vols. Berlin: Duncker & Humblot, 1832.

Heidegger, Martin. *Sein und Zeit.* Tuebingen: Niemeyer, 1960.

———. *Was ist Metaphysics.* Frankfurt a. M.: Klostermann, 1955.

Hofstadter, Albert. "Validity versus Value." *The Journal of Philosophy* 59: 21.

Jacobi, Friedrich Heinrich. *Sendschreiben an Fichte.* Hamburg: Fr. Perthes, 1799.

Jaspers, Karl. *Man in the Modern Age.* Garden City, N.Y.: Doubleday & Co.

———. *Die Grossen Philosophen*. 2 vols. Muenchen: Piper & Co., 1959.

Jones, Ernest. *The Life and Work of S. Freud*. 3 vols. New York: Basic Books, 1953–1957.

Jung, C. J. *Psychology and Religion*. New Haven: Yale University Press, 1938.

Kant, Immanuel. *The Fundamental Principles of the Metaphysics of Morals*. New York: The Liberal Arts Press, 1954.

———. *Critique of Judgment*. New York: Hafner Publishing Co., 1951.

Kaufmann, Walter A. *Existentialism from Dostoevsky to Sartre*. New York: Meridian Books, 1957.

Korff, Hermann August. *Die Lebensideen Goethes*. Leipzig: J. J. Weber, 1925.

Lubac, Henri. *Le Drame de l'Humanisme Athée*. Paris: Edition Spes, 1945.

Mann, Thomas. *Neue Studien*. Stockholm: Bermann Fischer, 1948.

———. *Death in Venice*. New York: Alfred A. Knopf.

Muschg, Walter. "Goethes Glaube an das Daemonische." *Deutsche Vierteljahrschrift fuer Literaturwissenschaft und Geistesgeschichte* (July 1958).

Pater, Walter. *The Renaissance*. Portland: T. B. Mosher, 1912.

Plotinus. *Enneads*. New York: Appleton-Century-Crofts.

Reichenbach, Hans. *The Direction of Time*. Berkeley: University of California Press, 1956.

Sartre, Jean Paul. *No Exit* (bound with) *The Flies*. Translated by Stuart Gilbert, New York: Alfred A. Knopf, Inc., 1947.

Scheler, Max. *Philosophische Weltanschauung*. Bonn: Fr. Cohen, 1929.

———. "Zur Idee des Menschen." *Die Wissenschaft und die Gesellschaft*. Leipzig: Der Neue Geist, 1926.

Schiller, Friedrich. *On the Aesthetic Education of Man in a Series of Letters.* New York: Frederick Ungar Publishing Co.

———. "Ueber Naive und Sentimentale Dichtung." *Philosophische Schriften. Schillers Werke.* 10 vols. Leipzig: Bibliographisches Institut.

Schlegel, Friedrich. *Werke.* Wien: Konegen, 1882.

Schopenhauer, Arthur. *The World as Will and Idea.* New York: Doubleday & Co., 1961.

Spinoza, Benedict. *Ethics.* New York: Hafner Publishing Co., 1955.

Tillich, Paul. *The Courage to Be.* New Haven: Yale University Press, 1952.

Vaihinger, Hans. *The Philosophy of the As-If.* New York: Harcourt-Brace, 1929.

———. *Die Philosophie des Als-Ob.* Leipzig: Meiner, 1911.

Whitehead, A. N. *Science and the Modern World.* New York: MacMillan, 1941.

Winckelmann, J. J. *Geschichte der Kunst und des Altertums.* 4 vols. Heidelberg: G. Weiss, 1882.

INDEX

Pfeffer, Rose.
Nietzsche:
disciple of
Dionysus.

DATE DUE